P9-CRU-875

MULTICULTURAL EDUCATION SERIES

James A. Banks, *Series Editor*

(continued)

Is Everyone Really Equal?

An Introduction
to Key Concepts
in Social Justice Education

SECOND EDITION

Özlem Sensoy and Robin DiAngelo

TEACHERS COLLEGE PRESS

TEACHERS COLLEGE | COLUMBIA UNIVERSITY

NEW YORK AND LONDON

Published by Teachers College Press, 1234 Amsterdam Avenue, New York, NY 10027

Copyright © 2017 by Teachers College, Columbia University

Cover design by Katherine Streeter.

All rights reserved. No part of this publication may be reproduced or transmitted in any form or by any means, electronic or mechanical, including photocopy, or any information storage and retrieval system, without permission from the publisher. For reprint permission and other subsidiary rights requests, please contact Teachers College Press, Rights Dept.: tcpressrights@tc.columbia.edu

Library of Congress Cataloging-in-Publication Data is available at loc.gov

ISBN 978-0-8077-5861-8 (paper)
ISBN 978-0-8077-7617-9 (ebook)

Printed on acid-free paper
Manufactured in the United States of America

24 23 22 21 20 19 18 17   7 6 5 4 3 2 1

To all those whose shoulders we stand on and lean on—
may ours be as steady for the next generation.

Contents

Series Foreword

Since publication of the first edition of this visionary, practical, and engaging book, a number of events around the world have stimulated the rise of xenophobia, institutionalized racism, and the quest for social cohesion and nationalism (Banks, 2017). These events include the migration of Syrian and other refugees to European nations and the xenophobic responses they evoked as well as the populist revolts that resulted in the 2016 passage of the Brexit referendum in England to leave the European Union (Erlanger, 2017). The election of Donald Trump as President of the United States in 2016 and the popularity of Marine Le Pen in France and other right-wing politicians in European nations are also manifestations of the resurgence of neoliberalism and the pushback on social justice in nations around the world. The election and rising popularity of conservative politicians have led to an increase in reported Anti-Semitic and Islamophobic attacks in the United States and other nations. Reported attacks and threats on Jewish centers increased significantly after Trump won the presidential election in 2016 (Haberman & Chokshi, 2017). Reported harassment and attacks on Muslims in the United States increased after Trump issued an executive order on January 27, 2017 that banned immigrants from seven predominantly Muslim nations (Chokshi & Fandos 2017; Shear & Cooper, 2017).

Martin Luther King Jr. said, "The arc of the moral universe is long, but it bends toward justice" (King, 1965). The chilling and pernicious events described above do not necessarily invalidate the belief that the quest for social justice is long and "bends toward justice." However, they exemplify the major thesis of Arthur W. Schlesinger Jr.'s (1986) illuminating book, *The Cycles of American History*, in which he argues that during the past two centuries of American history periods of social justice and idealism have rotated with periods of pragmatism and conservative backlash. The election of Donald Trump as president of the United States after Barack Obama engineered the passage of progressive legislation related to health care and the environment during his 8-year occupancy of the White House epitomizes Schlesinger's thesis. The dismal and toxic "cycle" of American history that was initiated by the Trump administration and the White nationalism that it sanctioned (Painter, 2016) underscores how much we need the second edition of this informative and helpful book. Teachers, like other Americans and Canadians, will be influenced by the disconcerting and dispiriting racial climate in the United

States and in many other nations today. These developments require multicultural and progressive teacher educators to work more diligently to promote social justice and equality today than was perhaps the case when the first edition of this book was published.

This trenchant and timely book is written to help both preservice and practicing teachers attain the knowledge, attitudes, and skills needed to work effectively with students from diverse groups, including mainstream groups. A major assumption of this book is that teachers need to develop a critical social justice perspective in order to understand the complex issues related to race, gender, class, and exceptionality in the United States and Canada and to teach in ways that will promote social justice and equality.

One of the most challenging tasks that those of us who teach multicultural education courses to teacher education students experience is resistance to the knowledge and skills that we teach. This resistance has deep roots in the communities in which most teacher education students are socialized as well as in the mainstream knowledge that becomes institutionalized within the academic community and the popular culture that most students have not questioned until they enroll in a multicultural education or diversity course. Sensoy and DiAngelo—who have rich and successful experiences teaching difficult concepts to teacher education students—thoughtfully anticipate student resistance to many of the concepts discussed in this adept and skillfully conceptualized book. They respectfully and incisively convey to readers the important difference between opinion and informed knowledge. They also convincingly describe why informed and reflective knowledge is essential for effective teaching in diverse schools and classrooms. The authors also provide vivid and compelling examples, thought experiments, and anecdotes to help their readers master challenging and complex concepts related to diversity, social justice, and equity.

Sensoy and DiAngelo draw upon their years of experience working with predominantly White teachers and their deep knowledge of diversity issues to construct explicit definitions of complicated concepts such as racism, sexism, classism, ableism, and internalized oppression. Another important feature of this book is the wide range of issues and groups with which it deals, including race, gender, exceptionality, and social class. The authors also present an informative discussion of intersectionality and how the various concepts related to diversity interrelate in complex and dynamic ways that create institutionalized and intractable forms of marginalization.

This well-written and practical book will help practicing educators deal effectively with the growing ethnic, cultural, and linguistic diversity within U.S. society and schools. Although students in the United States are becoming increasingly diverse, most of the nation's teachers are White, female, and monolingual. Race and institutionalized racism are significant factors that influence and mediate the interactions of students and teachers from different ethnic, language, and social-class groups (G. R. Howard, 2016; T. C. Howard, 2010; Leonardo, 2013). The growing income gap between adults (Stiglitz, 2012)—as well as between youth that are described by Putnam (2015) in *Our Kids: The American Dream in Crisis*—is another significant reason why it is important to help teachers understand how race, ethnicity, gender, and class influence classroom interactions and student learning and to comprehend the ways in which these variables affect student aspirations and academic engagement (Suárez-Orozco, Pimentel, & Martin, 2009).

American classrooms are experiencing the largest influx of immigrant students since the beginning of the 20th century. Approximately 21.5 million new immigrants—documented and undocumented—settled in the United States in the years from 2000 to 2015. Less than 10% came from nations in Europe. Most came from Mexico, nations in South Asia, East Asia, Latin America, the Caribbean, and Central America (Camarota, 2011, 2016). The influence of an increasingly diverse population on U.S. schools, colleges, and universities is and will continue to be enormous.

Schools in the United States are more diverse today than they have been since the early 1900s, when a multitude of immigrants entered the United States from Southern, Central, and Eastern Europe. In 2014, the National Center for Education Statistics estimated that the percentage of students from ethnic minority groups made up more than 50% of the students in prekindergarten through 12th grade in public schools, an increase from 40% in 2001 (National Center for Education Statistics, 2014). Language and religious diversity is also increasing in the U.S. student population. The 2012 American Community Survey estimated that 21% of Americans aged 5 and above (61.9 million) spoke a language other than English at home (U. S. Census Bureau, 2012). Harvard professor Diana L. Eck (2001) calls the United States the "most religiously diverse nation on earth" (p. 4). Islam is now the fastest-growing religion in the United States, as well as in several European nations such as France, the United Kingdom, and the Netherlands (Banks, 2009; O'Brien, 2016).

The major purpose of the Multicultural Education Series is to provide preservice educators, practicing educators, graduate students, scholars, and policymakers with an interrelated and comprehensive set of books that summarizes and analyzes important research, theory, and practice related to the education of ethnic, racial, cultural, and linguistic groups in the United States and the education of mainstream students about diversity. The dimensions of multicultural education, developed by Banks (2004) and described in the *Handbook of Research on Multicultural Education* and in the *Encyclopedia of Diversity in Education* (Banks, 2012), provide the conceptual framework for the development of the publications in the Series. The dimensions are content integration, the knowledge construction process, prejudice reduction, equity pedagogy, and an empowering institutional culture and social structure. The books in the Multicultural Education Series provide research, theoretical, and practical knowledge about the behaviors and learning characteristics of students of color (Conchas & Vigil, 2012; Lee, 2007), language minority students (Gándara & Hopkins 2010; Valdés, 2001; Valdés, Capitelli, & Alvarez, 2011), low-income students (Cookson, 2013; Gorski, 2013), and other minoritized population groups, such as students who speak different varieties of English (Charity Hudley & Mallinson, 2011), and LGBTQ youth (Mayo, 2014). Several books in the Multicultural Education Series complement this book because they describe ways to reform teacher education to make it more responsive to social justice issues and concerns. They include *We Can't Teach What We Don't Know: White Teachers, Multiracial Schools* by Gary R. Howard; *Why Race and Culture Matter in Schools: Closing the Achievement Gap in America's Classrooms* by Tyrone C. Howard; *Learning to Teach for Social Justice*, edited by Linda Darling-Hammond, Jennifer French, and Silvia Paloma García-Lopez; and *Walking the Road: Race, Diversity, and Social Justice in Teacher Education* by Marilyn Cochran-Smith.

The first edition of this influential and bestselling book helped teacher education students and practicing teachers to acquire the knowledge, skills, and perspectives that enabled them to work more effectively with the rich and growing student diversity in U. S. and Canadian schools. This second edition has been enriched by the addition of a new chapter on class, enhanced pedagogical supports, and with additional examples from contexts outside the United States. Students will find the second edition of this excellent and visionary textbook challenging, enlightening, and empowering.

—*James A. Banks*

REFERENCES

Banks, J. A. (2004). Multicultural education: Historical development, dimensions, and practice. In J. A. Banks & C. A. M. Banks (Eds.). *Handbook of research on multicultural education* (2nd ed., pp. 3–29). San Francisco, CA: Jossey-Bass.

Banks, J. A. (Ed.). (2009). *The Routledge international companion to multicultural education.* New York, NY, and London, UK: Routledge.

Banks, J. A. (2012). Multicultural education: Dimensions of. In J. A. Banks (Ed). *Encyclopedia of diversity in education* (vol. 3, pp. 1538–1547). Thousand Oaks, CA: Sage Publications.

Banks, J. A. (Ed.). (2017). *Citizenship education and global migration: Implications for theory, research, and teaching.* Washington, DC: American Educational Research Association.

Camarota, S. A. (2011, October). A *record-setting decade of immigration: 2000 to 2010.* Washington, DC: Center for Immigration Studies. Retrieved from cis.org/2000-2010-record-setting-decade-of-immigration

Camarota, S. A. (2016, June). *New data: Immigration surged in 2014 and 2015.* Washington, DC: Center for Immigration Studies. Retrieved from cis.org/New-Data Immigration-Surged-in-2014-and-2015

Charity Hudley, A. H., & Mallinson, C. (2011). *Understanding language variation in U. S. schools.* New York, NY: Teachers College Press.

Chokshi, N. & Fandos, N. (2017, January 29). Demonstrators in streets, and at airports, protest immigration order. *The New York Times*. Retrieved from www.nytimes.com/2017/01/29/us/protests-airports-donald-trump-immigration-executive-order-muslims.html

Cochran-Smith, M. (2004). *Walking the road: Race, diversity, and social justice in teacher education*. New York, NY: Teachers College Press.

Conchas, G. Q., & Vigil, J. D. (2012). *Streetsmart schoolsmart: Urban poverty and the education of adolescent boys*. New York, NY: Teachers College Press.

Cookson, P. W. Jr. (2013). *Class rules: Exposing inequality in American high schools*. New York, NY: Teachers College Press.

Darling-Hammond, L., French, J., & García-Lopez, S. P. (Eds.). (2002). *Learning to teach for social justice*. New York, NY: Teachers College Press.

Eck, D. L. (2001). *A new religious America: How a "Christian country" has become the world's most religiously diverse nation*. New York, NY: HarperSanFrancisco.

Erlanger, S. (2017, March 29). Pillars of the West shaken by 'Brexit,' but they're not crumbling yet. *The New York Times*. Retrieved from www.nytimes.com/2017/03/29/world/europe/uk-brexit-article-50-analysis.html

Gándara, P., & Hopkins, M. (Eds.). (2010). *Forbidden language: English language learners and restrictive language policies*. New York, NY: Teachers College Press.

Gorski, P. C. (2013). *Reaching and teaching students in poverty: Strategies for erasing the opportunity gap*. New York, NY: Teachers College Press.

Haberman, M., & Chokshi, N. (2017, February 20). Ivanka Trump calls for tolerance after threats on Jewish centers. *The New York Times*. Retrieved from www.nytimes.com/2017/02/20/us/politics/ivanka-trump-jewish-community-centers.html?_r=0

Howard, G. R. (2016). *We can't teach what we don't know: White teachers, multiracial schools* (3rd ed.). New York, NY: Teachers College Press.

Howard, T. C. (2010). *Why race and culture matter in schools: Closing the achievement gap in America's classrooms*. New York, NY: Teachers College Press.

King, M. L., Jr. (1965, February 26). Sermon at Temple Israel of Hollywood. Retrieved from www.americanrhetoric.com/speeches/mlktempleisraelhollywood.htm

Lee, C. D. (2007). *Culture, literacy, and learning: Taking bloom in the midst of the whirlwind*. New York, NY: Teachers College Press.

Leonardo, Z. (2013). *Race frameworks: A multidimensional theory of racism and education*. New York, NY: Teachers College Press.

Mayo, C. (2014). *LGBTQ youth and education: Policies and practices*. New York, NY: Teachers College Press.

National Center for Education Statistics. (2014). *The condition of education 2014*. Retrieved from nces.ed.gov/pubs2014/2014083.pdf

O'Brien, P. (2016). *The Muslim question in Europe: Political controversies and public philosophies*. Philadelphia, PA: Temple University Press.

Painter, N. I. (2016, November 16). What Whiteness means in the Trump era. *The New York Times*. Retrieved from www.nytimes.com/2016/11/13/opinion/what-whiteness-means-in-the-trump-era.html?_r=0

Putnam, R. D (2015). *Our kids: The American dream in crisis*. New York, NY: Simon & Schuster.

Schlesinger, A. M. Jr. (1986). *The cycles of American history*. Boston, MA: Houghton Mifflin.

Shear, M. D., & Cooper, H. (2017, January 27). Trump bars refugees and citizens of 7 Muslim countries. *The New York Times*. Retrieved from www.nytimes.com/2017/01/27/us/politics/trump-syrian-refugees.html

Stiglitz, J. E. (2012). *The price of inequality: How today's divided society endangers our future.* New York, NY: Norton.

Suárez-Orozco, C., Pimentel, A., & Martin, M. (2009). The significance of relationships: Academic engagement and achievement among newcomer immigrant youth. *Teachers College Record, 111*(3), 712–749.

U. S. Census Bureau (2012). *Selected social characteristics in the United States: 2012 American Community Survey 1-year estimates.* Retrieved from factfinder2.census.gov/faces/tableservices/jsf/pages/productview.xhtml?pid=ACS_12_1YR_DP02&prodType=table

Valdés, G. (2001). *Learning and not learning English: Latino students in American schools.* New York, NY: Teachers College Press.

Valdés, G., Capitelli, S., & Alvarez, L. (2011). *Latino children learning English: Steps in the journey.* New York, NY: Teachers College Press.

Acknowledgments

We begin this text by acknowledging that we conduct our scholarship and teaching on the unceded ancestral territories of various Indigenous peoples, on what is today identified as Canada and the United States. It can be easy for us to dismiss how events from the past could matter to us here in the present. But studying the history of colonialism—the cultural, emotional, and physical genocide of peoples around the world—reminds us that to understand the injustices of today we must recognize their connection to injustices of the past. We offer our deepest respect to Elders both past and present.

We extend our heartfelt thanks to the friends and colleagues who have supported us with this project, especially those who so generously gave their time and expertise to read and offer feedback on various aspects of the book. Your collegial support, and willingness to push our thinking on issues taken up in the first and in this second edition have been invaluable. Specifically, we would like to thank Carolyne Ali-Khan, Kumari Beck, Rochelle Brock, Ann Chinnery, Sumi Colligan, Cheryl Cooke, Darlene Flynn, Paul Gorski, Aisha Hauser, Michael Hoechsmann, Rodney Hunt, Mark Jacobs, Byron Joyner, Yoo-Mi Lee, Darren Lund, Elizabeth Marshall, Anika Nailah, Deborah Terry-Hayes, Jason Toews, and Gerald Walton.

We thank the reviewers who have been involved in the first and second edition for their guidance and insightful suggestions.

Thank you to Katherine Streeter for her artwork.

Thank you to Brian Ellerbeck, Karl Nyberg, Lori Tate, and the entire publication team at Teachers College Press.

And finally, we extend our deepest appreciation to James Banks for his trust in us to produce a text worthy of joining the Multicultural Education Series, and for his lifelong courage and commitment to building a more just world.

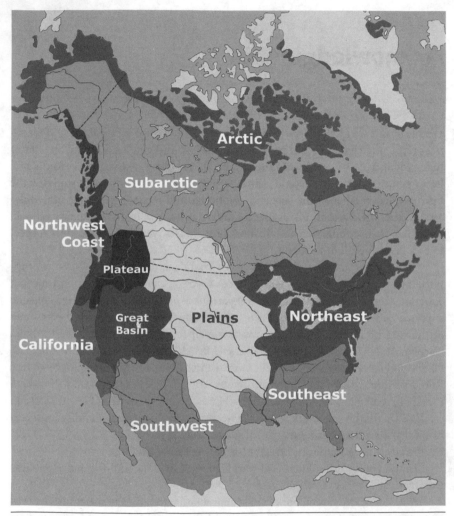

Source: en.wikipedia.org/wiki/File:Langs_N.Amer.png

Preface

We are educators who collectively bring over 2 decades of experience conducting research, teaching, writing, leading workshops, and facilitating discussions in the study and practice of social justice. We have led this work with elementary and high school students, undergraduate and graduate students, preservice and in-service teachers, and in the workplace for employees of government, university, nonprofit, and for-profit organizations. We have presented our research at national and international conferences, and within the disciplines of education, social work, cultural studies, women's studies, ethnic studies, and Middle East studies.

Through our experiences with wide-ranging audiences, we consistently see predictable gaps in peoples' understanding of what social justice is and what might be required to achieve it. We think of these gaps as a form of society-wide social justice illiteracy and argue that this illiteracy is not due to a lack of information alone. Rather, social *in*justice depends on this illiteracy; it is not benign or neutral, but actively nurtured through many forces and serves specific interests.

Social justice illiteracy prevents us from moving forward to create a more equitable society. Thus the primary objective of this book is to provide a foundation for developing social justice literacy. Using accessible language, addressing the most common misinformation, providing vignettes, definitions, exercises and reflection questions, our goal is to provide this foundation to a wide range of readers.

What Is Critical Social Justice?

Most people have a working definition of *social justice*; it is commonly understood as the principles of "fairness" and "equality" for all people and respect for their basic human rights. Most people would say that they value these principles. Yet seldom are the following questions discussed, and even less seldom are they agreed upon: What are those basic human rights? Have we already achieved them? If not, why not? How do we go about achieving them if we agree on what they are and why they haven't yet been achieved? From whose perspective is something fair and equitable? Might something be fair for one person while actually having an unfair outcome for another? What does *respect* actually mean in practice? While some say it is to treat others as *we* would like to be treated, some say that it is to treat others as *they* would like to be treated. Thus the *definition* itself is our first challenge.

The second challenge surfaces when we consider what it means to *practice* social justice. Generally, because most people see themselves as valuing social justice, most people also see themselves as acting justly in their lives. In response to questions about how they practice social justice, many would say that they treat everyone the same without regard to differences; because they do this, their actions are aligned with their values.

While these ways of conceptualizing social justice are very common, we see them as woefully inadequate. Indeed, a great deal of scholarship in social justice studies is focused on the gap between the *ideals* of social justice and the *practices* of social justice.

To clarify our definition, let's start with the concept *social justice*. While some scholars and activists prefer to use the term social justice in order to reclaim its true commitments, in this book we prefer the term *critical social justice*. We do so in order to distinguish our standpoint on social justice from mainstream standpoints. A critical approach to social justice refers to specific theoretical perspectives that recognize that society is *stratified* (i.e., divided and unequal) in significant and far-reaching ways along social group lines that include race, class, gender, sexuality, and ability. Critical social justice recognizes inequality as deeply embedded in the fabric of society (i.e., as structural), and actively seeks to change this.

The definition we apply is rooted in a critical theoretical approach. While this approach refers to a broad range of fields, there are some important shared principles:

- All people are individuals, but they are also members of social groups.
- These social groups are valued unequally in society.
- Social groups that are valued more highly have greater access to the resources of a society.
- Social injustice is real, exists today, and results in unequal access to resources between groups of people.
- Those who claim to be for social justice must be engaged in self-reflection about their own socialization into these groups (their "positionality") and must strategically act from that awareness in ways that challenge social injustice.
- This action requires a commitment to an ongoing and lifelong process.

Based on these principles, a person engaged in critical social justice practice must be able to:

- Recognize that relations of unequal social power are constantly being enacted at both the micro (individual) and macro (structural) levels.

- Understand our own positions within these relations of unequal power.
- Think critically about knowledge; what we know and how we know it.
- Act on all of the above in service of a more socially just society

Our goal in writing this book is to deepen our readers' understanding of the complexity of social justice and inspire readers to actively engage in critical social justice practice. We call this blend of understanding and action *critical social justice literacy.*

Chapter Summaries

We have brought together key concepts necessary for beginning to develop critical social justice literacy. Drawing on examples from Canada and the United States, the chapters are intended to be accessible to both Canadian and U.S. readers. We provide many familiar examples and have kept in-text citations to a minimum. We open each chapter with a quote that captures a familiar misconception that the chapter will address. The chapters are written to be building blocks; because each chapter builds upon the previous, they are best read in sequence. The issues are complex, political, and often emotionally charged, and if readers have difficulty understanding a key idea from one chapter, they may have difficulty carrying the idea forward into the next. For these reasons, the book has the following features:

- Definition Boxes in which we define key terms.
- Stop Boxes to serve as reminders of key ideas from previous chapters and to help with difficult or challenging concepts.
- Perspective Check Boxes to draw attention to alternative standpoints on examples used in the text.
- Discussion Questions and Extension Activities for those who are using the book in a class, workshop, or study group.
- Patterns related to specific dynamics of oppression and how to practice recognizing them.
- A Glossary of terms used in the book and guide to language use.

Detailed chapter summaries appear below.

Chapter 1: How to Engage Constructively in Courses That Take a Critical Social Justice Approach guides students using the book in a course context. We address some of the common challenges and present five guidelines or dispositions that can help ensure a constructive learning experience in the social justice classroom. These guidelines include how to reframe student beliefs and expectations about course grading and assessment.

Chapter 2: Critical Thinking and Critical Theory explains what it means to think critically about social justice. We explain the theoretical perspective known as *Critical Theory* and provide a brief sketch of key ideas relevant to our approach. The concept of *knowledge construction* is introduced. This chapter clarifies the difference between the *opinions* that readers already hold on a topic and the *informed knowledge* that we wish to provide and foster. We explain the importance of setting aside one's opinions and engaging with humility when encountering content that is personally challenging or politically charged.

Chapter 3: Culture and Socialization. This chapter explains what *culture* and *socialization* are and how they work. We introduce the relationship between being an individual and being a member of multiple social groups (such as race, gender, and class). The chapter explains how important it is for us to understand that our ideas, views, and opinions are not objective and independent, but rather the result of myriad social messages and conditioning forces. We take the reader beyond the common conception of parents and families as the sole forces of socialization and describe how other institutions work to form our worldviews. Examples are provided to illustrate the power of socialization and how it works as an unconscious filter shaping our perceptions.

Chapter 4: Prejudice and Discrimination unravels common misunderstandings of two key interrelated terms: *prejudice* and *discrimination*. The chapter examines prejudice as *internal*—thoughts, feelings, attitudes, and assumptions—and its relationship to discrimination, which is *external*—prejudice occurring in action. We explain that prejudice and discrimination cannot be humanly avoided; we all hold prejudices and we all discriminate based on our prejudices. We argue that the first step in minimizing discrimination is to be able to identify (rather than to deny) our prejudices.

Chapter 5: Oppression and Power explains how prejudice and discrimination are not the whole story. We move beyond individuals and take readers on an examination of prejudice and discrimination at the group level. We introduce the concept of *power*, which transforms group prejudice into oppression, and define terms such as *dominant group* and *minoritized group*. This chapter also explains the difference between concepts such as *race prejudice*, which anyone can hold, and *racism*, which occurs at the group level and is only perpetuated by the group that holds social, ideological, economic, and institutional power. The chapter explains the "ism" words (for example *racism, sexism, classism*) and how these words allow us to capture structural power as it manifests in particular forms of oppression.

Chapter 6: Understanding Privilege Through Ableism explains the rights, benefits, and advantages automatically received by being a member of the dominant group, regardless of intentions. From a critical social justice perspective, *privilege* is systemically conferred dominance and the institutional processes by which the beliefs and values of the dominant group are made "normal" and universal. While in some cases the privileged group is also the numerical majority, numbers are not the key criterion; the key criterion is social and institutional power. This chapter also explains related concepts such as *internalized oppression* and *internalized dominance,* and offers examples of how these dynamics work to hold existing relations of power in place.

Chapter 7: Understanding the Invisibility of Oppression Through Sexism traces a specific form of oppression—sexism—in order to illustrate how our ideas, views, and opinions are the product of interlocking and ongoing social messages in popular culture. We describe the ways in which such interlocking messages serve as barriers to seeing oppression and as such are central to how oppression is normalized.

Chapter 8: Understanding the Structural Nature of Oppression Through Racism traces a specific form of oppression in depth. *Racism* is discussed within the U.S. and Canadian contexts, and explained as White racial and cultural prejudice and discrimination, supported intentionally or unintentionally by institutional power and authority. Racism is illustrated through an examination of economic, political, social, and cultural structures, actions, and beliefs. We offer an in-depth understanding of racism as an entry point into building an in-depth understanding of how all oppressions are structural.

Chapter 9: Understanding the Global Organization of Racism Through White Supremacy. This chapter continues the examination of racism by identifying some of the ways in which racism adapts to and co-opts efforts to challenge it. We contrast multicultural education and antiracist education, introduce other concepts such as *Whiteness* and *White supremacy,* and end by addressing common misconceptions about racism. These misconceptions also function as another form of adaptation and co-optation.

Chapter 10: Understanding Intersectionality Through Classism begins with an examination of class oppression. We explain current economic relations of power, address concepts such as capitalism and socialism, wealth and income, as well as provide common class vernacular. The chapter also addresses the concept of *intersectionality* as an important theoretical development for understanding the multidimensional nature of oppression. We identify elements of class privilege, name common misconceptions about class mobility, and speak back to common classist narratives.

Chapter 11: "Yeah, But . . .": Common Rebuttals. Based on our experiences teaching these concepts in a variety of forums, we predict that readers will raise some common questions, objections, and critiques. This chapter addresses the most commonly raised issues. Drawing on all that has been discussed in previous chapters, we briefly but explicitly speak again to these issues.

Chapter 12: Putting It All Together. Understanding social justice means that an individual must be able to recognize how relations of unequal social power are constantly being negotiated at both the micro (individual) and macro (structural) levels, understand our own positions within these relations of unequal power, think critically about knowledge, and most importantly, *act* from this understanding in service of a more just society. The final chapter reviews key principles of critical social justice and offers some concrete suggestions for action.

We hope to take our readers on a journey that results in an increased ability to see beyond the immediate surface level to the deeply embedded injustice below; injustice that for so many of us is normal and taken for granted. Looking head-on at injustice can be painful, especially when we understand that we all have a role in it. However, in taking our readers on this journey we do not intend to inspire guilt or assign blame. At this point in society, guilt and blame are not useful or constructive; no one reading this book had a hand in creating the systems that hold injustice in place. But each of us does have a choice about whether we are going to work to interrupt and dismantle these systems or support their existence by ignoring them. There is no neutral ground; to choose not to act against injustice is to choose to allow it. We hope that this book gives our readers the conceptual foundations from which to act against injustice.

Prologue

A Parable: Hodja and the Foreigner

Once upon a time, a foreign scholar and his entourage were passing through a town in Anatolia. The scholar asked to speak to the town's most knowledgeable person. The townsfolk immediately called Nasreddin Hodja to come to meet the foreign scholar.

The foreigner did not speak Turkish, Persian, or Arabic, and Hodja did not speak any European languages, and so the two wise men had to communicate with signs while the townsfolk and the entourage watched in fascination.

The foreigner used a stick to draw a large circle in the sand. Hodja took the stick and divided the circle into two halves. The foreigner drew a line perpendicular to the one Hodja drew, and the circle was now split into four. He moved the stick to indicate first the three quarters of the circle, then the remaining quarter. In response, Hodja made a swirling motion with the stick on the four quarters. Then the foreigner made a bowl shape with his two hands held together side by side, palms up, and wiggled his fingers. Then, Hodja responded by cupping his hands with his palms down and wiggling his fingers.

When the meeting was over, the members of the foreigner's entourage asked him what they had talked about. "Nasreddin Hodja is a very learned man," he said. "I told him that the Earth was round and he told me that there was an equator slicing it in half. I told him that three-quarters of the Earth was water and one quarter of it was land. He said that there were undercurrents and winds. I told him that the waters warm up, vaporize, and move toward the sky, and to that he replied that they cool off and come down as rain."

The people of the town were also curious about how the conversation went. They gathered around Hodja. "This stranger has very good taste," Hodja explained. "He said that he wished there was a large tray of baklava. I said that he could only have half of it. He said that the syrup should be made with three parts sugar and one part honey. I agreed, and said that they all had to be well mixed together. Next, he suggested that we should cook it on blazing fire. And I added that we should pour crushed nuts on top of it."

Layers of the Parable

This story is from the tales of Nasreddin Hodja, a 13th-century Sufi sage. His wisdom stories often use humor to point out human failings and misunderstandings. What is relevant about this story for our purposes is the way it captures some of the key concepts in critical social justice literacy:

- Each of us has a culturally based worldview.
- We hold a common assumption that others share our worldview.
- We often assume that what we intend to communicate is what is received.

Because Hodja and the foreigner do not speak the same verbal language, they move to a form of sign language and assume that they share the same understandings of what is being signed. Although both men leave the exchange feeling satisfied, we realize that they have completely misunderstood each other. But if we go deeper than a simple misunderstanding, we might also see that they had completely different ways of organizing the world and what they valued within it. For the foreigner, the emphasis was on the elements of the Earth; he had a more scientific orientation. For Hodja, the emphasis was on sharing a meal; he had a more community orientation.

As their ideas about each other form and are communicated to their respective groups (the foreigner to his entourage and Hodja to his fellow townspeople), consider now that one of them is in the position to enforce his worldview upon the other; that is, consider what might happen when we add *power* to the encounter. Imagine the foreigner and his entourage are not just passing through, they are in town because their nation has just invaded Hodja's. The foreigner has been installed to govern Hodja's town and he now controls all of the land—land that Hodja and the townfolk have lived on and raised their food on all of their lives, as did their ancestors before them. But now Hodja must pay the foreigner large fees to use this land. The foreigner moves in and appoints his own people to key positions of government and sets up his culture's rules and social norms. The foreigner imposes these new rules and norms upon Hodja and the townspeople.

Which one of these men is going to need to learn to understand the perspective of the other? While they each have their own worldview and neither worldview is inherently superior, only one of them is in a position of power that enables him to impose his worldview on the other. Hodja and his community's ability to work and feed their families now depend upon the foreigner and his customs, language, and traditions, whereas the foreigner does not have to learn the town's customs, language, or traditions. Indeed, the foreigner, who now controls all of the resources needed for Hodja's livelihood, will profit from Hodja and the community's labor without ever having to learn to understand their perspective.

Now fast-forward from the 13th century to the 21st. Centuries of domination of the town and resultant conflicts have occurred. The descendants of the foreigner, who continue to control the town, benefit from the resources and power they have accumulated over the centuries. Meanwhile, the descendants of the townsfolk have had to change their entire way of life, customs, and even language in order to survive. The townsfolk try to pass their traditions on to their young children, but the children see little value in cultural traditions that don't seem to get them anywhere in society. Many of the foreigners' descendants are also frustrated. They can't understand why some townsfolk are so angry—after all, *they* weren't the ones who invaded the town centuries ago, and they don't see why the townspeople can't just get over it and assimilate so they can all live together in peace.

As we can see, there are many layers of complexity in this story, layers that have built up and been left unaddressed over generations. The foreigner's descendants see the situation as simple: Hodja's descendants should just let go of the past and move on. Hodja's descendants, however, see the situation as much more complicated. Until the historical, cultural, and ideological aspects of the foreigner's domination are addressed, no one can just "get over it." Indeed, they recognize that far from being over, the domination continues in newer forms. The suggestion that they could just move on reveals how little the foreigner's descendants understand the history of their town and their current position within society, based on that history. This story is meant to illustrate many of the complex issues that must be understood in order to develop critical social justice literacy.

CHAPTER 1

How to Engage Constructively in Courses That Take a Critical Social Justice Approach*

The struggle has always been inner, and is played out in outer terrains. Awareness of our situation must come before inner changes, which in turn come before changes in society. Nothing happens in the "real" world unless it first happens in the images in our heads.

—Gloria Anzaldúa (2009, p. 310)

Vocabulary to practice using: anecdotal evidence; platitude; mainstream society; peer review; objective; subjective

---

If you are reading this book, you are likely enrolled in a course that takes a critical stance. By *critical stance* we mean those academic fields (including social justice, critical pedagogy, multicultural education, antiracist, postcolonial, and feminist approaches) that operate from the perspective that knowledge is socially constructed and that education is a political project embedded within a network of social institutions that reproduce inequality.

Throughout your course, you will likely be studying key concepts such as *socialization, oppression, privilege,* and *ideology* and doing coursework that challenges your worldview by suggesting that you may not be as open-minded as you may have thought. You are encountering evidence that inequality not only exists, but is deeply structured into society in ways that secure its reproduction. You are also beginning to realize that, contrary to what you have always been taught, categories of difference (such as gender, race, and class) rather than merit alone, *do* matter and contribute significantly to people's experiences and life opportunities.

When confronted with evidence of inequality that challenges our identities, we often respond with resistance; we want to deflect this unsettling information

---

* A version of this chapter was previously published in the journal *Radical Pedagogy*, in 2014.

and protect a worldview that is more familiar and comforting. This is especially true if we believe in justice and see ourselves as living a life that supports it. Forms that resistance takes include silence, withdrawal, immobilizing guilt, feeling overly hopeless or overly hopeful, rejection, anger, sarcasm, and argumentation. These reactions are not surprising because mainstream narratives reinforce the idea that society overall is fair, and that all we need to overcome injustice is to be nice and treat everyone the same. Yet while comforting, these platitudes are woefully out of sync with scholarly research about how society is structured. The deeply held beliefs that inform our emotional responses make studying and teaching from a critical stance very difficult.

In addition to being asked to question ideology that is deeply internalized and taken for granted, critical engagement rarely provides concrete solutions. This ambiguity can lead to frustration, for our K–12 schooling (especially in Canada and the United States) has conditioned us to seek clear and unambiguous answers. Still, we pull various strategies together and offer an overall framework for critical engagement. We draw on research and our years of practice teaching social justice content and share the vignettes and guidelines that have been most effective for our own students. A list of key terms can be found at the beginning of this chapter. Practice incorporating these terms into your academic vocabulary.

An Open Letter to Students

Courses that address social justice and inequality through a critical lens often challenge mainstream understandings and thus bring to the surface patterns and tensions that other courses do not (Gallavan, 2000; Kincheloe, 2008). This is due, primarily, to two key reasons:

The first is that many of us are *underprepared to engage in the course content in scholarly ways*. Basic study habits, reading comprehension, writing skills, vocabulary, and critical thinking are often underdeveloped in college students. Ironically, much of this is due to structural inequalities that courses like these try to address. For example, political and economic pressures on schools to focus on standardized testing have resulted in moves away from intellectual curiosity, critical thinking, and engagement with ambiguity and toward creating conforming and compliant students who can memorize the "one right answer" to pass the test. Differences in the kinds of schooling we receive and the differential futures they prepare us for are based on structural inequalities related to our race, class, gender, and other social locations. These differentials affect our preparation for college and university-level engagement and are examples of the kind of inequalities that social justice–oriented courses address. The ultimate goal of social justice education is to enable us to recognize structural inequalities in ways that prepare us to change them. However, the sociopolitical context of schooling makes critical engagement challenging for many students, and this challenge is heightened when the topics under study are politically and emotionally charged.

This leads to the second reason that courses that address social justice and inequality bring to the surface patterns and tensions that other courses do not: *most of us have very strong feelings and opinions about the topics examined in social justice courses* (such as racism, sexism, and homophobia). These opinions often surface through claims such as:

"People should be judged by what they do, not the color of their skin"
"I accept people for who they are"
"I see people as individuals"
"It's focusing on difference that divides us"
"My parents taught me that all people are equal"
"I always treat everyone the same"
"I've been discriminated against so I don't have any privilege"
"Our generation is more open-minded"
"I have friends from all races and we are all fine with each other"
"I don't think race and gender make any difference—as long as you work hard"
"It's White males who are the minority now"
"Women are just as sexist as men"

While these opinions are deeply held and appear to be commonsense truth (and not opinion at all), they are predictable, simplistic, and misinformed, given the large body of research examining social relations. Yet, the relentless repetition of these ideas in the mainstream makes them *seem* true, and allows us to form strongly held opinions without being particularly educated on the issues. Indeed, where we are members of dominant groups (e.g., if we are male, White, cisgender, able-bodied), we will almost certainly have a superficial understanding because that is the primary message made available to us through mainstream society. Where we are members of minoritized groups (e.g., if we are women, Peoples of Color, transgender, People with disabilities), we may have a deeper personal understanding of social inequality and how it works, but may not have the scholarly language to discuss it in an academic context.

Further, it is a rare individual who is dominant in all key social groups, or conversely is minoritized in all key social groups. Yet messages that circulate in mainstream society do not prepare most of us to conceptualize or develop the language to discuss our intersecting identities in any depth. Take for example the intersection of race and class and consider a White woman who lives in poverty. While she will face many *class* barriers, she will not face *racism*. Yet a poor White woman—while not facing *racism*—will face barriers related to her gender—*sexism*—that a poor White man will not. For example, she will be more likely to be held responsible for the care of her children, she will be more likely to earn less than a man, and she will be more at risk for male violence, all of which increase the burden of poverty. Yet mainstream culture tends to present poverty as if there is a collective and shared experience of "the poor."

Without practice and study beyond what we absorb in our daily living, we are ill prepared to understand social group injustices. Therefore, our perspectives on issues like poverty and social inequality are necessarily lacking—and especially so if we ourselves are not poor. These perspectives include the idea that if we don't believe in social inequality, then we don't participate in it. Mainstream culture prevents us from understanding a central tenet of social justice education: Society is structured in ways that make us all complicit in systems of inequality; there is no neutral ground. Thus an effective critical social justice course will unsettle mainstream perspectives and institutional discourses, challenge our views about ourselves, what we think we know about society, how it works, and our place in it.

Unfortunately when we are new to the examination of social relations, we only know one way to respond to ideas studied in the course: "If the professor is saying that I participate in systems of injustice (such as racism), they are saying that I am a bad person (a racist)." Later, we should come to understand that this is *not* what our professors are saying, and that binary ways of conceptualizing these issues (good/bad, racist/not-racist) are part of what prevents us from seeing them.

In sum, the combination of underdeveloped academic skills, difficult theoretical concepts, and highly charged political content that is absent of complex analysis in mainstream culture, all of which is embedded within an institutional context that is structured to reproduce inequality, can make these courses challenging. Yet basing our knowledge on such sources as personal opinions, self-concepts, anecdotal evidence, hearsay, intuition, family teachings, popular platitudes, limited relationships, personal experiences, exceptions, and mainstream media is insufficient for understanding and responding constructively to social injustice.

Therefore, to maximize your learning of social justice content, we offer the following guidelines:

1. Strive for intellectual humility.
2. Recognize the difference between opinions and informed knowledge.
3. Let go of personal anecdotal evidence and look at broader societal patterns.
4. Notice your own defensive reactions and attempt to use these reactions as entry points for gaining deeper self-knowledge.
5. Recognize how your own social *positionality* (such as your race, class, gender, sexuality, ability-status) informs your perspectives and reactions to your instructor and the individuals whose work you study in the course.

Below we explain these guidelines in more depth and how they can help you engage constructively with social justice content.

A Story: The Question of Planets

Imagine: You are in a course that fulfills a university science requirement. The professor holds a PhD in astronomy. He has written several books, is widely published in academic journals, and has a national reputation in his field. The course objectives include defining terms used in modern astronomy and exposure to the practices, methodology, and concepts of the discipline. The professor is reviewing the assigned readings, which present the most established theories in the field. He overviews the scientific community's discussion of the number of planets and states that based on the criteria for what constitutes a planet, only 8 planets are officially recognized in our solar system.

One of the students raises his hand and insists that there are actually 9 planets because that is what he learned in school. He has seen many books with pictures of the planets, and there are always nine. As further evidence, he recites the mnemonic he learned to pass all his science tests: "My Very Educated Mother Just Served Us Nine Pizzas." He states that he had a map of the sky in his bedroom as a child and it showed 9 planets. Further, he says, his parents taught him that there were nine planets and many of his friends also agree that there are nine. He spent his childhood camping out and looking up at the sky and identifying constellations, so he has experience in astronomy. The professor tries to explain to the student that to engage with the planet controversy one must first demonstrate understanding of the criteria for what constitutes a planet, but he is cut off by the student, who declares, "Well, that's your opinion. My opinion is that there are nine."

The professor tries once more to explain that what he presents in regard to the number of planets is not his opinion, but knowledge based on the scholarly community's established criteria for what defines a planet. Although at one time astronomers believed that Pluto qualified as a planet, as with all disciplines, their knowledge evolved. With the discovery of new information and further study they now understand that Pluto doesn't meet the criteria of a planet, in large part due to its shape. This is not an opinion, the professor repeats, but astronomical theories that have resulted from ongoing research and study. The student replies, "I don't care if Pluto is square, diamond-shaped, or shaped like a banana, it's a planet, and there are nine planets."

How likely is it that the majority of the class thinks our hypothetical astronomy student is raising a credible point? Would the class admire him for standing up to the professor and expressing the same understanding they had (but were to hesitant to bring up)? Even if his peers did share his view, that would not make his argument valid. It is more likely that he would be seen as having some academic challenges, as somewhat immature, and perhaps even disrespectful. It may even be assumed that he might have trouble passing the class.

Guideline 1: Strive for Intellectual Humility

Our hypothetical student is representative of many students we encounter: He has not done the readings or has trouble understanding what he's read; he has limited knowledge but is resistant to increasing it; he clings to the same worldview he came into the course with; and he is overly confident about his position. Scholars have referred to these patterns as a form of *willful ignorance* (Baker, 1990; Dei, Karumanchery & Karumanchery-Luik, 2004; Schick, 2000). In our experience, students who have trouble understanding what they read seldom: re-read, read more slowly, use a dictionary to look up new words, or ask their professors to explain difficult passages. Standardized testing and the punishment and reward system of grades are major contributors to these habits, as they have created a school culture that rewards conformity and single, correct answers over intellectual curiosity and risk-taking. Yet critical social justice education demands a different kind of engagement than most of us have been prepared for in our previous schooling.

Another challenge to intellectual humility is that many of us see social science content as *soft science* and therefore *value-laden* and *subjective*. On the other hand, the natural sciences such as astronomy are seen as *hard science* and therefore *value-neutral* and *objective*. Because of the presumed neutrality of the natural sciences, we are unlikely to argue with astronomy findings until we have some mastery in the field—knowing that we might not fully understand the concepts and theories presented. We are more likely to focus on gaining a basic understanding and not on whether we agree or disagree. If we perform poorly on tests, we might feel frustrated with the professor or material as being too hard, but still recognize our own lack of knowledge as the primary cause of the poor performance.

Yet in the study of the social sciences—and particularly when the topic is social inequality—the behavior of our imaginary astronomy student is not unusual. In fact, it can be common for students to argue with professors prior to achieving mastery of the concepts and theories presented. Furthermore, students frequently cite anecdotal evidence to support their arguments and dismiss course content prior to engaging with the research. And unfortunately, students who "disagree with" social justice content *are* often taken seriously by classmates —even seen as a kind of hero for speaking up to the professor. Seeing the study of social inequality as a form of subjective scholarship, these students put it on par with their own personal opinions and dismiss it out of hand.

In academia (including the social and natural sciences), in order for an argument to be considered *legitimate* (e.g., such as how many planets there are, and whether racism exists), it must stand up to scrutiny by others who are specialists in the field. This scrutiny is called *peer review*. Peer review is the process by which theories and the research they are based on are examined by other scholars in the field who question, refine, deepen, challenge, and complicate the arguments, expanding the collective knowledge base of the field. Just as the astronomy professor's teachings are more than his personal opinions,

> 🖐 **STOP:** When we say that peer review makes an argument legitimate, remember that we mean this for academic contexts (such as a college or university course you might be taking). There are other forms of evidence that are legitimate. However, academic arguments such as those we present in this book must stand up to peer review.

social justice professors' teachings are more than their personal opinions. Both instructors are presenting concepts that have undergone peer review. The overall evidence, theories, arguments, and analysis presented in class are rooted in the peer review process.

Most of us have seldom previously encountered—much less understood enough to disagree with—the scholars we initially read, especially in introductory critical social justice courses. Although some of us may bring important firsthand experiences to the issues (such as being a member of a particular minoritized group under study), we too can benefit from grappling with any theoretical framework before debating it. For the beginner, grappling with the concepts is the first step. To facilitate doing so, practice the following:

- Read the assigned material carefully. Look up vocabulary words and terminology that are new to you (e.g., if there are terms used in this chapter that you do not know, start with the book's glossary). Accept that you may need to read all or part of the material more than once. Consider reading passages out loud or taking notes of key points as you read. Practice using new terms in class.
- If there are terms or concepts you are still unsure about, raise them in class. It is likely that you are not alone in your confusion. Assume that your instructors appreciate questions that demonstrate engagement and curiosity, rather than apathy and silence that make it difficult to assess student needs.
- Strive to see the connections to ideas and concepts already studied. This will help with your recall, critical thinking, and ability to see the big picture.
- Focus on understanding rather than agreement. Consider whether "I disagree" may actually mean "I don't understand," and if so, work on understanding. Remember, understanding a concept does not require that you agree with it.

- Practice posing questions. Because most students have been socialized to care more about getting the answers right and less about comprehension, we may fear that asking questions will reveal that we don't know the answers. Thus, we may make bold statements that lack intellectual humility. These statements could be more usefully framed as questions.
- Be patient and willing to grapple with new and difficult ideas. "Grappling with" ideas means to receive, reflect upon, practice articulating, and seek deeper understanding; grappling is not debate or rejection. The goal is to move us beyond the mere sharing of opinions and toward more informed engagement.

One place where grappling often falls short is in small-group work. For most instructors, the goal of small-group work is much more than students simply "sharing their ideas or opinions on X." Rather, it's an opportunity for students to spend time critically thinking through difficult ideas with the support of others in order to deepen understanding and share insights. In addition to the specific prompts and questions that the instructor has given, all of the following could be taken up in small-group work:

- Asking clarifying questions of each other
- Making connections to other readings
- Identifying key concepts and defining terms
- Generating examples that illustrate the concepts under study
- Identifying patterns
- Developing questions
- Questioning relationships between concepts
- Discussing the implications for your own life and work
- Practicing articulating the ideas introduced in the course using your own words, in order to clarify and increase your comfort discussing them with others
- Identifying and discussing challenging passages

Yet instructors often encounter small groups who are merely reinforcing their previous opinions, have moved on to engage in off-topic social banter, or are sitting in silence, checking email or texting because they are "finished" discussing the topic at hand. From an academic perspective, a small group should never be "done" talking about any topic they are given. Scholars have spent their careers developing these concepts, and a limited number of class minutes is not adequate to finish working through and understanding them. If you find yourself at a standstill, work through the bulleted list above, or ask your instructor for some prompts and check in about how you are doing in your comprehension.

Guideline 2: Everyone has an Opinion.
Opinions are Not the Same as Informed Knowledge

One of the biggest challenges to attaining Guideline 1—intellectual humility—is the emphasis placed in mainstream culture on the value of opinion. Mainstream culture has normalized the idea that because everyone has an opinion, all opinions are equally valid. For example, local news and radio shows regularly invite callers to share their opinions about questions ranging from "Do you think so-and-so is guilty?" to "Should immigration be restricted?" Reality shows invite us to vote on the best singer or dancer, implying that our opinions are equal to the opinions of professional dancers, singers, choreographers, and producers. While we *might* have an informed opinion, our response certainly does not depend on one. Thus we can easily be fooled into confusing *opinion* (which everyone has) with *informed knowledge* (which few have without ongoing practice and study).

Because of this socialization, many of us unwittingly bring the expectation for opinion-sharing into the academic classroom. However, in academia, *opinion is the weakest form of intellectual engagement.* When our comprehension is low and critical thinking skills underdeveloped, expressing our opinion is the easiest response. All of us hold opinions on a topic before we enter a course (as our astronomy student did), and these opinions don't require us to understand the issues or engage with the course readings at all. Therefore, expressing our opinions simply rehearses what we already think and doesn't require us to expand, question, or go beneath our ideas. If we aren't interested in reading what we have been assigned, or do not understand what we have read, the easiest thing to do is to point to a passage in the text and give a personal opinion about it (e.g., "I loved it when the author said that men dominate because it reminded me of an experience I had . . . ."), or use it to reject the reading out of hand (e.g., "The author said White people have privilege. I totally disagree with that because I know someone who didn't get a job because he's White!").

When we make claims based on anecdotal evidence with regard to the concepts studied—for example claiming, "Now there is reverse racism" —we are in effect expressing an opinion that is not supported by scholarly evidence. We would not use opinion in astronomy class and believe it unlikely that a student arguing that she or he disagrees with Stephen Hawking on a matter of astronomy would have her or his position taken seriously, much less feel free to make such a claim to begin with. Yet in the social justice classroom, scholars such as Peggy McIntosh, Michel Foucault, and Beverly Tatum are regularly disagreed with well before comprehension of their work is mastered. Consider how our astronomy student's understanding of planets—as well as his understanding of science as an ever-evolving field—could deepen if he was able to engage with current theories about what constitutes a planet. Unfortunately, our hypothetical student's attachment to his previously held beliefs precludes this possibility.

Because of these tendencies, professors who teach from a critical social justice stance sometimes "shut down" opinion-sharing (Sensoy & DiAngelo, 2014). This curtailing of the sharing of opinions in class is often perceived as breaking a social rule: "I have the right to my opinion and denying me that right is unfair." Of course we have a right to our opinions. But our academic goals are not to simply express our preexisting opinions; our goals are to engage with scholarly evidence and develop the theoretical tools with which to gain a more complex understanding of social phenomena. Yet let us be clear: We *do* want students to offer opinions in order to *reflect on and examine* them; opening one's opinions to examination is not the same as simply expressing them.

In order to move beyond the level of previously held opinions, practice the following:

- Reflect on your reasons for pursuing higher education. Many students would say they are going to university or college in order to secure a good career. However, your longevity and success in that career will depend on your critical-thinking skills and the depth and breadth of your general knowledge base. How might allowing your worldview to be stretched and challenged actually serve your future career interests?

- Recognize that you do not have to agree with concepts under study in order to learn from them. Let go of the idea that you must agree with a concept you are studying in order for it to be valid or worth learning.

- Practice posing open-ended questions rather than closed questions that invite yes/no responses or debate. Closed questions often begin with "Should" or "Do you agree" (e.g., "Should schools ban soda machines?" or "Do you agree that opportunity is not equal?"). The limitation of these questions is that the debate format does not leave much room for examining grey areas or grappling with complexities. Closed questions can also be answered with an easy yes or no, which prevents a nuanced engagement with complex issues.

- Practice developing quality questions. For example, using John Taylor Gatto's "Seven Lesson Schoolteacher" (2002), strong questions could include: "Consider Gatto's argument that all teachers teach the seven lessons. On a continuum from 'Yes absolutely' on one end, to 'No absolutely not' on the other, position yourself in relation to his argument. Explain why you have positioned yourself there." Use phrases such as, "Under what conditions . . ." and "To what extent . . ." when you ask questions. For example, "Under what conditions might we avoid teaching Gatto's lessons?" "To what extent does the school curriculum influence teacher autonomy?" Use the course readings to support your position. Questions connected to texts should require familiarity with the text to answer. For example, "Identify two of Gatto's seven lessons and find examples you have seen in schools."

If someone can respond to the question without ever having read the text, it is not a strong question. Questions may also ask people to re-imagine. For example, "Using the readings, design the ideal classroom. Describe the guidelines for student engagement in this ideal classroom. How would the curriculum and pedagogical activities be organized? How would you assess your goals?"

Guideline 3: Let Go of Anecdotal Evidence and Instead Examine Patterns

Anecdotal evidence is evidence drawn from hearsay or only personal experience, and thus anecdotal evidence is superficial, limited to interpretation, and not generalizable. For example, many of us have heard something similar to, "My cousin tried to get a job, but they hired an unqualified Black guy instead because they had to fill a quota." Because mainstream education and media seldom teach us how social inequality works, most of the evidence we rely on to understand issues of social justice is anecdotal. But the goals of college and university classes are to expand one's ability to make sense of everyday events, issues, and incidences. In other words, to offer new and more complex sense-making systems. One of the more important academic skills we can develop is the ability to apply a new sense-making framework to something we currently make sense of using another framework.

To illustrate this concept of frameworks, imagine that you have pain in your leg and go to your doctor. Your doctor would likely examine your leg, feel the bones and muscles, and perhaps take X-rays to identify the source of the pain. If, however, you went to an alternative (from a Western perspective) medical practitioner, such as a doctor of Traditional Chinese Medicine (TCM), she might have a completely different way of examining your body and identifying the source of the pain. She may begin by looking at your tongue and examining other parts of your body. A chiropractor might not examine your leg at all, but instead begin work on your spine.

If we are taking a course studying how humans understand the body and conceptualize healing, then we are less interested in which practitioner is "right" and which is "wrong" in their approach to identifying the source of your pain. We are more interested in the various frameworks each practitioner uses, the scholarly community that informs the ideas that practitioner draws on, and what each framework offers us in terms of understanding how the body works and how humans conceptualize illness and healing. Just as the TCM doctor offers a new way of understanding how your body works, the critical social justice framework offers us a new way of understanding how society works.

Another popular approach many of us take when we encounter a new and unfamiliar framework is to focus on one or two exceptions in order to disprove the framework under study. For example, when reading scholarship describing racism as structural, we may cite sensational examples such as Barack Obama as proof that "anyone can make it." We may also use personal stories to "prove" that structural oppression doesn't exist (or has now "reversed" direction), such as in the story above about the cousin who didn't get a job and believes this is because the company had to fill a racial quota. Although it is a common White myth that peoples of Color must be (unfairly) hired over Whites, it is false and problematic for at least three reasons. First, it's misinformed because hiring quotas are actually illegal. Affirmative Action in the United States or Employment Equity in Canada are not hiring requirements, but *goal systems for the hiring of qualified people who are underrepresented in a given field*. Second, all of the evidence demonstrates that peoples of Color are *discriminated against* in hiring, not preferred (Alexander, 2010; Bertrand & Mullainathan, 2004; Dechief & Oreopoulos, 2012). Third, the story above rests on an embedded racist assumption that the only reason a person of Color *could* have been hired over the cousin is because of a quota and not because the person of Color was in fact more qualified, or equally qualified but brought a needed perspective that the cousin did not.

Focusing on exceptions or unanalyzed personal experiences prevents us from seeing the overall, societal patterns. While there are always exceptions to the rule, exceptions also illustrate the rule. Yes, people from oppressed groups occasionally rise to the top in dominant society. But the historical, measurable, and predictable evidence is that this is an atypical occurrence. If we focus exclusively on those exceptional occurrences, we miss the larger structural patterns. Focusing on the exceptions also precludes a more nuanced analysis of the role these exceptions play in the system overall.

The following questions offer a constructive way to engage with the course content and support Guideline 3:

- How can using a critical framework expand my understanding of these phenomena? For example, let's say you are White and have spent time abroad. You have enjoyed the food and cultures of places such as China, Mexico, or Morocco, but have also felt discriminated against (ignored, stereotyped, made fun of) because you are White and from the United States or Canada. Why, you might wonder, aren't the locals more open to you when you are being so open to them—maybe even learning a bit of their language? You offer this anecdote as an example that illustrates that everyone *is* racist in some ways. Now imagine that you are grappling with a new framework to make sense of your experience. You are studying key concepts such as Whiteness, globalization, and hegemony. How can using this framework help you contextualize your experience within larger macrodynamics and apply academic concepts?

- Am I able to identify the larger group patterns at play in any individual situation? For example, if my best friend lives with a disability, I may assume that I am outside of ableism because I am open to this friendship when others are not. Yet *rather* than make me exempt from ableism, how can my friendship provide me with a view into the barriers faced by persons with disabilities? How can considering overall patterns help me recognize how my friendship is situated in relation to broader social dynamics—dynamics that intentions and individual practices alone do not overcome?

- Do I recognize that when I claim that my friend's disability is not an issue in our friendship, that I am sharing my own limited perspective, because my experiences are interpreted from my positionality as someone who is considered able-bodied? What might the risks be for my friend to disagree with me or try to give me feedback on unaware ableist assumptions I may be making? Do I have the skills to respond to this feedback without defensiveness and denial? Using another example, we often hear heterosexual students make claims such as, "There was one gay guy in our school and no one had an issue with him." Yet that "one gay guy" likely has a very different memory of school. Indeed, when we have students in our classes from minoritized groups, they invariably tell us of the misery of high school and all of the unconscious attitudes and behaviors from the dominant group that they had to endure. Our anecdotes are not universal, they are from a particular perspective; they will necessarily be filtered through our blind spots and thus are not sufficient evidence.

Guideline 4: Use Your Reactions as Entry Points for Gaining Deeper Self-Knowledge

Because social justice courses directly address emotionally and politically charged issues, they can be upsetting. For many of us, this is the first time we have experienced a sustained examination of inequality—especially where we are in dominant groups. Further, much of what is presented is counter to everything we have previously been taught. In addition, these courses typically ask us to connect ourselves personally to the issues under study, triggering patterns of resistance such as those previously discussed. For those of us who have experienced inequality in key dimensions of our lives, it can be painful to see the explicit resistance and hostility of classmates.

Although the frameworks used in these courses do not claim that people in dominant groups are "bad," many of us hear it that way because our current sense-making framework says that participation in inequality is something that only bad people do. Until we have a critical social justice framework—which requires a whole new paradigm of sense-making—we often find it difficult to remain open, especially if we're a member of a dominant group under study. Defensiveness, cognitive dissonance, and even feelings of guilt, shame, and grief are not uncommon. In some ways, these kinds of feelings indicate movement and change and although unpleasant, they are not necessarily problematic. The key to whether these feelings play a constructive or destructive role lies in what we do with them. We can, of course, use them as "proof" that the class content and approach "wrong" and reject all that we are being taught. But there is no growth for us in this reaction. Rather than allow these emotions to block our growth, we can use them as entry points into greater self-knowledge and content knowledge.

Conversely, where we belong to minoritized groups, these courses can surface emotions for different reasons. Feelings such as anger, frustration, shame, grief, and that we are under a spotlight are common and can also get in the way of our academic development. However, the analysis, evidence, and conceptual language offered by social justice education can provide the tools with which to challenge the relations of oppression that lead to these feelings. Indeed, the evidence and analysis presented should reveal that the challenges you have faced are not due to your own individual shortcomings but are in large part the product of socially organized structural barriers. As such, these barriers can be identified and acted against. In this way, rather than increase a sense of hopelessness and immobilization, courses such as this have the potential to empower.

Returning to our astronomy student, we can see that upon receiving information that challenged his worldview, he was unable to use his emotional reactions constructively. Instead, he categorically rejected the information, ending with a somewhat nonsensical claim that Pluto was still a planet, even if it was shaped like a banana. This is the equivalent to claiming that "I treat people the same regardless of whether they are 'red, yellow, green, purple, polka-dotted, or zebra-striped.'" Simplistic platitudes often surface when we are faced with evidence that fundamentally challenges our worldviews. For example, the evidence that racism not only exists, but is systemic and implicates everyone is a difficult idea for many of us. But popular platitudes such as "I don't care if you're purple" are problematic for at least two reasons: First, colorblindness is not actually possible—we *do* in fact see race and it *does* have social meaning and consequences. Second, people do not come in these colors and so claims about green, purple and polka-dotted people render race ridiculous and trivializes the realities of racism.

Social justice content can trigger strong reactions, but these reactions can be constructive if we use them as entry points to deeper self-awareness, rather than as exit points from further engagement.

Practice the following approaches to the course content in support of Guideline 4:

- How does considering the course content or an author's analysis challenge or expand the way I see the world?
- How have I been shaped by the issues the author is addressing? For example, if the author is talking about the experiences of the poor and I was raised middle class, what does their perspective help me see about what it means to have been raised middle class?

- What about my life in relation to my race/class/gender might make it difficult for me to see or validate this new perspective?
- What do my reactions reveal about what I perceive is at risk were I to accept this information?
- If I were to accept this information as valid, what might be ethically required of me?

Guideline 5: Recognize How Your Social Position Informs Your Reactions to Your Instructor and the Course Content

Positionality is the concept that our perspectives are based on our place in society. Positionality recognizes that where you stand in relation to others shapes what you can see and understand. For example, if I am considered an able-bodied person, my position in a society that devalues people with disabilities limits my understanding of the barriers people with disabilities face. I simply won't see these barriers, in large part because I don't have to—society is structured to accommodate the way I use my body.

Guideline 5 addresses the perception that the content of the class is subjective, value-based, and political, while the content of mainstream courses is objective, value-neutral, and unpartisan. We discussed this perception under Guideline 3 as it relates to common views on the social sciences. Here we want to consider this perception using the lens of positionality as it relates to the instructors of these courses. Because instructors of critical social justice content are more likely to *name* their positionality and encourage students to do the same, they are often seen as more biased. Mainstream courses rarely if ever name the positionality of the texts they study (for example, the idea that Columbus discovered America is from the colonizer's perspective, but certainly not from the perspective of Indigenous peoples). Unfortunately, because acknowledging one's positionality is a rare occurrence in mainstream courses, doing so reinforces students' perceptions of mainstream courses as objective and critical social justice courses as subjective. Yet all knowledge is taught from a particular perspective; the power of dominant knowledge depends in large part on its presentation as neutral and universal (Kincheloe, 2008).

In order to understand the concept of knowledge as never purely objective, neutral, and outside of human interests, it is important to distinguish between discoverable laws of the natural world (such as the law of gravity), and knowledge, which is socially constructed. By *socially constructed*, we mean that all knowledge understood by humans is framed by the ideologies, language, beliefs, and customs of human societies. Even the field of science is subjective (the study of which is known as the sociology of scientific knowledge). For example, consider scientific research and how and when it is conducted. Which subjects are funded and which are not (e.g., the moon's atmosphere, nuclear power, wind power, atmospheric pollution, or stem cells)? Who finances various types of research (private corporations, nonprofits, or the government)? Who is invested in the results of the research (e.g., for-profit pharmaceutical companies, the military, or nonprofit organizations)? How do these investments drive what is studied and how? How will the research findings be used? Who has access to the benefits of the research? As you can see, these are not neutral questions—they are always political, and they frame how knowledge is created, advanced, and circulated. Because of this, knowledge is never value-neutral.

To illustrate the concept of knowledge as socially constructed and thus never outside of human values and subjectivity, consider an example of a tree—a seemingly neutral object whose existence is simply a physical fact that can be observed. Yet notice that how we *see* the tree is connected to our meaning-making frameworks (and thus is not neutral at all). First, consider our perceptions of its *size*. A tree that looks big to someone who grew up on the East Coast might not look big to someone who grew up on the West Coast.

Next, consider our perceptions of its meaning or purpose; these will be shaped by our perspectives and interests. For example, an environmentalist might see a limited resource. A member of the Coast Salish nation might see a sacred symbol of life. A logger or a farmer might see employment. A scientist might see a specimen to be studied. Further, while it may appear that the logger and the farmer have shared interests, in fact their interests are opposite; the logger would see employment only if the tree is cut down, while the farmer would see employment only if the tree grows and bears fruit. Now let's add the layer of political power. Who owns the tree? Who has "the right" to cut it down and profit from it? Would the logger, tribal member, environmentalist and scientist all agree on this matter of ownership? Whose interests are served by the concept that nature can be owned at all? And who is in the position to impose this concept on others? Who takes the idea of ownership for granted and who doesn't? What kind of resources, institutions, and larger groups are behind each of these individuals and how do they influence whose interests will prevail?

Finally, how are these interests informed by the specific time and place in which they occur? What's considered valid scientific research today (from a Western perspective) is not the same as what was considered valid in the past. So while a tree may be an objective, factual, and real object that exists independently of humans, our understanding of it—and thus our interaction with it—cannot be separated from the cultural context we are currently embedded in. In other words, humans can only make meaning of the tree from the cultural frameworks into which they have been socialized. And so it goes for history, physics, and all fields studied in academia. Knowledge is always culturally informed and thus cannot be value-neutral.

Many educators use the metaphor of a fish in water to capture the all-encompassing dimensions of culture. A fish is born into water and so simply experiences the water as one with itself; a fish has no way of knowing that it is actually separate from the water. And although the fish *is* separate, it still cannot survive without water. In the same way that a fish cannot live without water, we cannot make sense of the world without the meaning-making system that our culture provides. Yet this system is hard to see because we have always been "swimming" within it; we just take for granted that what we see is real, rather than a particular perception of reality. For these reasons, social justice educators name our positionality (the currents and waters we swim in) in order to make the socially constructed nature of knowledge visible and to challenge the claim that any knowledge is neutral. Yet ironically, that naming is often used to reinforce the idea that social justice content and those who present it are driven by personal agendas and special interests, and thus less legitimate.

Because instructors who teach critical social justice courses often belong to minoritized groups and because they name these groups, they can be perceived as having a personal bias; they are viewed as if they only teach these courses because they are "minorities" and have an "axe to grind." Because the instructors are seen as simply pushing their personal agendas, students often feel more comfortable to explicitly disagree with the curriculum and pedagogy. Indeed, this challenge further illustrates how unimaginable our example of the astronomy student is. The instructor in our scenario is most likely a White male, as is the vast majority of higher education faculty (*Chronicle of Higher Education*, 2009). White males overall hold more social authority and are seen as more objective, and thus students are less likely to argue with them (Rudman & Kiliansky, 2000). That, along with the presumed neutral content of a subject like astronomy, means students respond to this instructor and the course as though they were value-neutral. In contrast, because the positionality of a woman of Color professor who teaches a social justice course is named, both she and the course are presumed to be value-driven.

Ultimately, one or two courses in our college or university schooling are not enough to brainwash us or deny us the ability to think freely. In fact, the opposite is true: The more depth, perspective, and complexity we can bring to bear on how we and others view and understand the world, the clearer, more nuanced, and ultimately freer our thinking can become.

Returning to our astronomy student, it isn't necessary for his positionality to align with the instructor's in order for him to consider the framework the instructor is using.

The following practices support Guideline 5:

- Identify your social positionality and stay attentive to how it informs your response to the course context (e.g., your race, class, gender). What limitations of awareness might you have as a result of that positionality? What are the things you can and can't see based on the social positions you hold or don't hold?

- Recognize the perspectives embedded in all texts (such as textbooks, newspaper articles, and TV news), especially those that don't explicitly name them. Are the ideas presented as if they have no perspective and apply universally to all people, regardless of social positionality? If so, practice seeking out and considering alternative perspectives informed by a range of positionalities.
- As you study the content of your course, it is important for you to continuously consider the interplay between your positionality and that of your instructor. If the instructor represents perspectives from key minoritized groups (women, peoples of Color, persons with disabilities, LGBTQ people), you could welcome the opportunity to hear perspectives seldom represented in mainstream education. Support the course for the opportunity it offers, rather than undermining it because the concepts are unfamiliar, uncomfortable, or difficult.

Grading

Grading in a course whose primary goal is to challenge social stratification is not without irony. Activist and scholar Audre Lorde (1984) captures this irony when she states that, "The master's tools will never dismantle the master's house." By this she means that in using the tools of the system we are more likely to uphold that system than to challenge it. As instructors, we recognize that by grading we are upholding an institution that ranks students hierarchically and such hierarchies are what we seek to challenge. Still, many of us choose to work within systems despite their constraints, so that we may better challenge them. The traditional grading system is one of those constraints we must work within.

Mainstream schooling places a tremendous emphasis on grades, and the prevalence of high-stakes testing has only intensified this emphasis. Grades convey powerful ideas about our presumed intellectual abilities and these ideas influence what education we will have access to (through tracking into gifted or special programs and ability grouping). We are placed into academic tracks as early as 1st grade and these tracks have very real consequences for the kinds of careers we will have access to later in life (Anyon, 1981; Oakes, 1985). Thus an understandable but regrettable outcome of tracking based on grades in K–12 schooling is that we may care more about the grades we receive than about the knowledge we gain.

The focus on grades often shapes our very identities and sense of self-worth, further complicating the dynamics of grading. This identity is often reinforced outside of school as we earn praise or punishment from our families based on our grades. While some students who have not been successful within this system come to feel fortunate just to earn a C, students who have generally been successful by the measure of grades often feel entitled to As. It is not uncommon for these students to claim, "I am an A student!" Students with such an identity may feel frustrated—even personally slighted—when receiving grades that challenge this identity.

Although we as instructors are aware of the complexities and contradictions of grading, we are also deeply invested in student comprehension of the course concepts. The grading system is one of the primary tools we must use to both measure and communicate our assessment of this comprehension. We encourage students to keep the following in mind when considering the dynamics of grading:

In Order to Grade Comprehension, Instructors Must See Demonstration of Comprehension. Whether in assignments or in class participation and discussion, we must *demonstrate* understanding. Comprehension can be demonstrated in written, verbal, and active forms (such as presentations and projects).

Assessing our comprehension verbally is generally done through class discussions and question and answer sessions. However, assessing comprehension verbally can be challenging for instructors if students don't speak up in class. For example, how many times have you witnessed your instructor posing a question to the whole class only to be met by silence? Looking out into a room full of students, most of whom are not responding, instructors are left to assume that these students cannot answer the question. Students sometimes say later that they did not respond because the answer was "so obvious" that it did not require a response. Yet how can our instructors know that we understand if we do not respond when questions are posed in class, even if the answers to those questions seem obvious?

Another common explanation for silence is that someone has already said what we were thinking. Yet from an instructor's perspective, it is fine to repeat (or better yet, to build on) an idea that another student has already stated. No two people will say it exactly alike, and it is important to practice articulating these concepts in your own words in order to develop your critical social justice literacy. Any statement can be expanded, deepened, or in other ways supported. At the minimum, if students build on what others have said, instructors can gain a sense of how many students are thinking similarly, or struggling with understanding key ideas. This is valuable information for instructors in terms of assessing the collective understanding of the group as well as the comprehension levels of individual students. For these reasons, we encourage students to give some kind of verbal response when asked questions in class, even if it is to say that one does not know, is not sure, or only has a partial answer.

In regard to demonstrating understanding in written work, we evaluate this work by assessing how well written, organized, and clear it is, and how well the submitted work meets the goals of the assignment. The work should at minimum be proofread for errors, use academic language, avoid colloquialisms, conform to a standard style of citation, use inclusive language, and stay within the guidelines of the assignment description. These are all baseline indicators of the degree of student achievement in a written assignment. Perceptive integration of course readings and lectures in a student's own words, relevant use of examples, and insightful connections can transform an adequately written assignment into an excellent (or "A") assignment. These criteria are usually communicated to students in either the course syllabus or assignment description. Thus in order to most accurately grade comprehension, we must see evidence of comprehension in both verbal participation and written work.

Effort Is Not the Same as Understanding. When students are worried about their grades or are making a case for the grade they believe they should receive, they often claim that they "worked really hard." These students feel that they should be rewarded for that hard work with an A. The reason this argument rarely makes much headway with instructors is because we are grading student *demonstration* of understanding of content, not the perceived degree of effort expended to achieve it.

Consider this analogy: I am taking swimming lessons. My goal is to compete in an upcoming match. I see myself as putting in a lot of effort by making the time to show up for practice, following my coach's instructions, and swimming the number of laps I am assigned. My coach, however, expects that I will attend lessons and complete my practice sessions; thus, they are focused on other things, such as how I hold my body while swimming, my breathing pattern, hip and shoulder movements, smoothness of stroke, and speed. In the end, my coach will determine whether I am ready to compete. This determination will be made based on my demonstrated ability that I am ready, regardless of the degree of effort it takes me to reach that point, and certainly not on the mere fact that I showed up for my lessons and got in the pool.

In a similar way, we are grading students on the degree of demonstrated understanding of studied concepts and not on perceptions of effort, especially because what we as instructors see as effort and what a student sees as effort are often not the same. For some students, showing up to class, listening, and handing in assignments are viewed as evidence of a level of effort that should we rewarded with an A. For instructors, this level of effort qualifies as the minimum expectation for all students. Still, we are not grading on how hard a student works but on the outcome of that work.

The following are common student rationales we hear for why they should get a grade higher than what was assessed:

"I worked really hard."
"I am an A student."
"I came to all the classes."
"I listened."
"I spent hours doing the readings."

"I talked in class discussions."

"I handed in all my assignments."

"I have never thought about these things before."

"I'm really interested in these issues."

"I've had other courses like this one so I already know all this."

"I have to get a good grade or I will have to drop out."

"I have been going through a lot of personal issues this semester."

"I learned so much in this class."

Student rationales such as these are familiar to many instructors, and we understand that they are driven by genuine anxieties about grades. However, we urge our students to challenge this anxiety because it thwarts the process of authentic learning.

A final note on grading: Students often believe that the reason they received a poor grade was because the instructor didn't like something they said in class, or because they disagreed with the instructor. Every institution has an appeal process for students who feel they have not been graded fairly by an instructor. This makes it very difficult to lower a student's grade just because of something they said. While classroom assessments have some degree of subjectivity, an instructor must account for a grade they gave in terms of guidelines for the assignment, as well as in terms that are clear to a mediating third party. Because of this accountability, an instructor's grading criteria are usually clearly stated in the syllabus or on assignments.

Conclusion

Many college and university courses provide opportunities that are rare in any other dimension of life: critical engagement with new ideas; opportunity to hear and consider multiple perspectives; expansion of our capacity to understand and talk about complex social issues; guidance in the examination of our identities, socialization, and meaning-making frameworks; and tools to work toward a more just society. Unfortunately, a fixation on grades minimizes these opportunities. We find that students who let go of their attachment to grades and put their energy into sincerely grappling with the content tend to do well. Worrying about grades detracts from the ability to focus on content and can become a kind of self-fulfilling prophecy. The following reflection questions may be useful in lessening this attachment:

- Am I willing to consider that I may not be qualified to assess my performance in a course, especially one in which new concepts are being introduced?
- Do I expect an A in all of my courses, and if so, why? Is it because I have always received As, or is it because I have demonstrated mastery of cour concepts?

- When I ask my instructor, "How am I doing?" am I asking them to provide me with valuable feedback about what my performance conveys about my comprehension and how it might be improved, or am I asking them to tell me what grade I will receive?

We sincerely hope that our students find our courses valuable in terms of the knowledge and insight gained. It has been our experience that this is most likely achieved when students focus more on mastery of content than on the final grade.

Discussion Questions

1. If I weren't worried about my grade, how would my engagement in this course shift?
2. Which of the various guidelines detailed in this essay are the most challenging to me, and why? How can I meet these challenges?
3. What degree of responsibility am I willing to take for getting the most out of this course (e.g., coming to class prepared and having completed the reading, engaging in large-group discussions, not dominating discussions, asking questions for clarity, speaking respectfully in class, and using academic rather than colloquial discourse)?
4. What degree of responsibility am I willing to take to support my peers in getting the most from this course (e.g., engaging in discussions, not dominating discussions, listening respectfully when others speak and building on their ideas, taking the small-group discussions seriously, coming to class prepared and having completed the reading)?
5. Many students think about higher education solely as a stepping-stone to employment, and thus the only knowledge that is worthwhile is knowledge they see as directly connected to getting a job. We ask you to consider what other kinds of skills higher education can provide, and how these skills are also connected to future employment. If you think beyond a strictly vocational approach, what skills do citizens in a global democracy need? How are these skills also important to any future work you do?

CHAPTER 2

Critical Thinking and Critical Theory

"Everyone has a right to their opinion."

This chapter explains what it means to think critically about social justice. We explain the theoretical perspective known as "Critical Theory" and provide a brief overview of key ideas relevant to our approach.

Vocabulary to practice using: ideology; critical theory; social stratification; positionality; socially constructed; Enlightenment; positivism

---

Many of the concepts we present in this book are politically and emotionally charged. In order to help readers engage with these concepts most effectively, this chapter will review what it means to take a critical (as opposed to layperson's) perspective.

The term *critical* has several meanings. The most common meaning is to find fault, to judge, or to criticize. However, this is not the way we use the term here. When we use critical, we refer to an intellectual skill of analysis—critical thinking—as well as to a body of scholarship—Critical Theory. *Critical thinking* is a general approach, which means to think with complexity, to go below the surface when considering an issue and explore its multiple dimensions and nuances. *Critical Theory* is a scholarly approach that analyzes social conditions within their historical, cultural, and ideological contexts. Critical Theory is a complex theoretical perspective, and mastery requires ongoing study and practice. However, even a preliminary understanding of its principles can offer tools for thinking critically about knowledge.

Two Dimensions of Thinking Critically About Knowledge

One of the persistent myths of mainstream society is that the knowledge we study in schools is factual and neutral. Yet we know that knowledge evolves over time and is dependent on the moment in history and the cultural reference point of the society that accepts it. Thinking critically involves more than just acquiring new information in order to determine which facts are true and which false. It also

23

involves determining the social, historical, and political *meaning* given to those facts. This determination includes assessing the investment various groups may have in furthering or challenging those meanings in any particular historical moment. For example, there was a time when it was not widely understood that the Earth is round. Common sense might tell us that it is flat, and anyone looking out over a vast landscape would have this sense confirmed. Yet when scientific reasoning and more accurate technological methods for measuring the Earth emerged, the knowledge or "fact" that the Earth is flat was rewritten so that now we teach students that the Earth is spherical—or round.

Thus one dimension of thinking critically about knowledge is *the acquisition* of new information that may challenge our common sense (such as looking out the window and seeing what we believe is a flat landscape). In other words, to think critically means to continuously seek out the information that lies beyond our commonsense ideas about the world. Yet knowledge also involves understanding *the meaning* given to information (such as the meaning given to the journeys of explorers such as Columbus that are presumed to have debunked the idea of a flat Earth). We must understand what the political investments are in that meaning—in other words, who benefits from that knowledge claim and whose lives are limited by it?

Thus, thinking critically not only requires constantly seeking out new knowledge, but also understanding the historical and cultural context in which knowledge is produced, validated, and circulated. For example, while many might believe (and were perhaps taught in school) that people thought the Earth was flat until Columbus set sail for India, the reality is that many civilizations knew the Earth was round prior to Columbus. These civilizations included the ancient Greeks, Muslim astronomers, early Christian theologians, ancient Indian scholars, and Maya, Aztec, and Inca Indigenous peoples of what is today known as North, Central, and South America. Why, then, are we so familiar with the idea that everyone believed in a flat Earth until Columbus set sail? What are the cultural, political, and social investments in fostering this idea?

Considering the first dimension of thinking critically (acquisition of new information), we would first seek new knowledge about other societies and their contributions (such as ancient Indigenous, Indian, and Islamic scientists). Now considering the second dimension of thinking critically (the meaning given to that "flat Earth until Columbus" knowledge), we would ask questions about the social and historical context of that knowledge. For example, in what contexts has the knowledge of societies other than European been hidden? Critical thinkers might argue that obscuring this knowledge promotes the idea of progress as a line moving from ancient and non-European societies (Indigenous, Indian, Islamic) to European and then to North American societies.

Practicing thinking critically helps us see the role of ideology in the construction of knowledge about progress. It challenges the belief that knowledge is simply the result of a rational, objective, and value-neutral process, one that is removed from any political agenda. The notion of value-free (or objective) knowledge was central to rationalizing the colonization of other lands and peoples that began in the 15th century. For example, if we believe that Columbus was simply an explorer and trader, we reinforce the idea of discovery as outside of political and ideological interests. The promotion of this idea has allowed dominant culture to ignore the genocide of Indigenous peoples and the transatlantic slave trade that his "discoveries" set in motion.

Just as our commonsense understanding would have had us convinced that the Earth is flat (validated by looking out our windows), many of the arguments that we make in this book may also counter commonsense understandings. For example, common sense would tell us that because we do not believe in discrimination, we do not engage in it. However, most discrimination is unconscious and takes place whether we intend to discriminate or not, despite genuinely held beliefs in fairness and equity. If we think critically about this idea that we do not discriminate, we would discover that this belief is inaccurate. There is a great deal of research in the dynamics of discrimination that demonstrates again and again the power of discrimination to elude conscious awareness (Dovidio, Glick, & Rudman, 2005; Greenwald & Krieger, 2006). Were we to consider the impact of the idea that we do not discriminate, we might discover that this idea actually allows discrimination to continue. Thus those who benefit from societal patterns of discrimination may be invested in not understanding the actual nature of discrimination.

Thinking critically requires the ability to recognize and analyze how knowledge is socially constructed and infused with ideology. Critical thinking is not just acquiring new knowledge (today we know the Earth is round and not flat), it is also understanding the social meaning given to that knowledge (our social and political investment in the idea that before the Age of Discovery all people believed the Earth was flat).

A Brief Overview of Critical Theory

Our analysis of social justice is based on a school of thought known as Critical Theory. Critical Theory refers to a body of scholarship that examines how society works, and is a tradition that emerged in the early part of the 20th century from a group of scholars at the Institute for Social Research in Frankfurt, Germany (because of this, this body of scholarship is sometimes also called "the Frankfurt School"). These theorists offered an examination and critique of society and engaged with questions about social change. Their work was guided by the belief that society should work toward the ideals of equality and social betterment.

Many influential scholars worked at the Institute, and many other influential scholars came later but worked in the Frankfurt School tradition. You may recognize the names of some of these scholars, such as Max Horkheimer, Theodor Adorno, Jürgen Habermas, Walter Benjamin, and Herbert Marcuse. Their scholarship is important because it is part of a body of knowledge that builds on other social scientists' work: Emile Durkheim's research questioning the infallibility of the scientific method, Karl Marx's analyses of capitalism and social stratification, and Max Weber's analyses of capitalism and ideology. All of these strands of thought built on one another. For example, scientific method

STOP: From a critical social justice framework, informed knowledge does not refer exclusively to academic scholarship, but also includes the lived experiences and perspectives that marginalized groups bring to bear on an issue, due to their insider standing. However, scholarship can provide useful language with which marginalized groups can frame their experiences within the broader society.

(sometimes referred to as "positivism"—the idea that everything can be rationally observed without bias) was the dominant contribution of the 18th-century Enlightenment period in Europe. Positivism itself was a response and challenge to religious or theological explanations for "reality." It rested on the importance of reason, principles of rational thought, the infallibility of close observation, and the discovery of natural laws and principles governing life and society. Critical Theory developed in part as a response to this presumed infallibility of scientific method, and raised questions about whose rationality and whose presumed objectivity underlies scientific methods.

Efforts among scholars to understand how society works weren't limited to the Frankfurt School; French philosophers (notably Jacques Derrida, Michel Foucault, Pierre Bourdieu, and Jacques Lacan) were also grappling with similar questions (this broader European development of Critical Theory is sometimes called "the continental school" or "continental philosophy"). This work merges in the North American context of the 1960s with antiwar, feminist, gay rights, Black power, Indigenous peoples, The Chicano Movement, disability rights, and other movements for social justice.

Many of these movements initially advocated for a type of liberal humanism (individualism, freedom, and peace) but quickly turned to a rejection of liberal humanism. The logic of individual autonomy that underlies liberal humanism (the idea that people are free to make independent rational decisions that determine their own fate) was viewed as a mechanism for keeping the marginalized in their place by obscuring larger structural systems of inequality. In other words, it fooled people into believing that they had more freedom and choice than societal structures actually allow. Many of these social justice activists critiqued these societal structures and argued that social institutions were organized in ways that perpetuated the marginalization of women, and of Black, Indigenous, Chicano, disabled, and LGBT peoples. Many of these revolutionary movements were led by young activists, and their ideas were in part informed by the theoretical and scholarly literature they were studying in universities. The politics of the social justice movements aligned with academic research showing that society is structured in ways that marginalize some to the benefit of others.

This broad-brush sketch of Critical Theory is not the whole story. Critical Theory neither begins in Europe nor ends in the United States and Canada. Critical Theory's analysis of how society works continues to expand and deepen as theorists from indigenous, postcolonial, racialized, and other marginalized perspectives add layers to our collective understanding. Thus, to engage in a study of society from a critical perspective, one must move beyond common sense–based opinions and begin to grapple with all the layers that these various, complex, and sometimes divergent traditions offer.

📖 **Social Stratification:** The concept that social groups are relationally positioned and ranked into a hierarchy of unequal value (e.g., people without disabilities are seen as more valuable than people with disabilities). This ranking is used to justify the unequal distribution of resources among social groups.

✋ **STOP:** "I'm looking out the window and there's a rock there, what do you mean there's no human objectivity? A rock is a rock. I see it with my eyes." Yes, you see a rock, but the meaning, placement, and function of the rock is dependent upon human *subjectivity*—what you believe about what a rock is and where it should be; what you have been taught about rocks. For example, when is a rock an expensive gem and when is it something you toss aside to clear a path? When does a rock add beauty to your home and when does it make your home dirty?

In this book, our goal, rooted in Critical Theory, is to increase our readers' understanding of these factors:

- Different levels of thinking: opinion versus critical thinking, layperson versus scholarly
- Political and ideological aspects of knowledge production and validation
- Historical context of current social processes and institutions
- Process of socialization and its relationship to social stratification
- Inequitable distribution of power and resources among social groups

Why Theory Matters

Many people outside of academia find theory uninteresting. Theory often seems unnecessarily dense and abstract, far removed from our everyday lives. But, in fact, all of us operate from theory. Whenever we ask "how" or "why" about anything, we are engaged in theorizing; theory can be conceptualized as the learned cultural maps we follow to navigate and make sense of our lives and new things we encounter. Everything we do in the world (our actions) is guided by a worldview (our theory).

If you are a teacher, you might believe that theory is irrelevant to your practice, but let's consider a common scenario: Several students regularly come to school without a lunch. Your response will depend on where you see the problem located and what you see as your role in the problem (that is, how you theorize, or make sense of, what's going on). If you theorize that the problem is about individual families, that the students lack a lunch because their families don't have the resources to attend to their children's needs, you might direct the students to the free and reduced lunch program (perhaps assuming the family does not know about such programs). If you theorize that the problem is structural, you might see the students' lack of lunch as representative of issues that go beyond the family and advocate at the governmental level. In fact, we can take free and reduced lunch programs for granted today because people became involved and worked to address some of the structural aspects of childhood poverty.

Consider the theoretical distinction between locating the problem in the individual (it's each family's responsibility to provide for their own children) versus the collective (it's a social responsibility to ensure that all children are provided for). These two theoretical frameworks will result in very different ways of making sense of, and responding to, the problem. Neither is neutral, but both will impact the problem in profoundly different ways (for example, some countries with a more collectivist approach, such as Japan and Finland, automatically provide school lunch for all children, not just low-income children. In so doing, they remove the stigma associated with special programs).

The way we make sense of our world (or our theories about the world) is often invisible to us. But we cannot address issues of critical social justice without first examining the maps we are using to identify the problem and conceptualize its solutions. Further, awareness of our theoretical maps can lead to fundamental change in our behaviors. This is why understanding theory is not only relevant but also essential for social change to occur.

Knowledge Construction

One of the key contributions of critical theorists concerns the production of knowledge. Given that the transmission of knowledge is an integral activity in schools, critical scholars in the field of education have been especially concerned with how knowledge is produced. These scholars argue that a key element of social injustice involves the claim that particular knowledge is objective, neutral, and universal. An approach based on critical theory calls into question the idea that objectivity is desirable or even *possible*. The term used to describe this way of thinking about knowledge is that knowledge is socially constructed. When we refer to knowledge as socially constructed we mean that knowledge is reflective of the values and interests of those who produce it. This concept captures the understanding that all knowledge and all means of knowing are connected to a social context.

In understanding knowledge as socially constructed, critical educators guide students along at least three fronts:

1. Critical analysis of knowledge claims that are presented as objective, neutral, and universal; for example, Christopher Columbus's "discovery" of America
2. Critical self-reflection about their own social perspective and subjectivity; for example, how the Columbus myth and the teacher's racial identity influence what they know and teach about the history of North America
3. Developing the skills with which to see, analyze, and challenge ideological domination; for example, rewriting existing school lesson plans or curricula to reflect the complexities of the myth of discovery and the political investments in this myth

In these ways educators who teach from a critical perspective guide their students in an examination of the relationship between their frames of reference and the knowledge they accept and reproduce. Of course this is no easy task because for many Westerners the ideal of positivism (that European science followed rules and thus its findings are indisputable) is very powerful and deeply entrenched. It is challenging to guide people in a critical examination of knowledge that they have been taught is indisputable. Thus what critical educators often begin with is an examination of students' own social positions and the relationship between those positions and the knowledge that they have.

For this reason the concept of *positionality* has become a key tool in analyzing knowledge construction. Positionality asserts that knowledge is dependent upon a complex web of cultural values, beliefs, experiences, and social positions. The ability to situate oneself as knower in relationship to that which is known is widely acknowledged as fundamental to understanding the political, social, and historical dimensions of knowledge. Positionality is a foundation of this examination.

James Banks is one scholar in education who has made significant contributions to the understanding of knowledge as socially constructed. Banks (1996) explains that the knowledge we create is influenced by our experiences within various social, economic, and political systems. Thus who we are (as knowers) is

intimately connected to our group socialization (including gender, race, class, and
sexuality). For example, consider the Columbus story. Whose racial perspective is
reflected in the idea that the continent was
"discovered"? Which racial groups may be
invested in this story? Which racial groups
may be invested in challenging it? Asking
questions such as these develops a clearer

> 📖 **Positionality:** The rec-
> ognition that where you stand
> in relation to others in society
> shapes what you can see and
> understand about the world.

picture of how "*what* you know" is connected to "*who* you are" and "*where* you
stand."

Banks's knowledge typology has become a classic framework used by critical
educators to help unravel how knowledge is validated. According to Banks, there
are five types of knowledge:

Personal and cultural knowledge refers to the explanations and interpretations people acquire from their personal experiences in their homes, with their
family and community cultures. Personal and cultural knowledge is transferred
both explicitly, such as direct lessons taught by family members on what constitutes politeness (e.g., "make eye contact with your elders"), as well as implicitly
through messages such as what isn't talked about (e.g., race or money).

Popular knowledge refers to the facts, beliefs, and various character and
plot types that are institutionalized within television, movies, and other forms of
mass-mediated popular culture. Concepts such as the ideal family, normal relationships, and which kinds of neighborhoods are dangerous are all standardized
through ongoing representations in popular culture. Because popular knowledge
is widely shared, it serves as a common vocabulary and reference point. For instance, you might remember where you were when you heard about the death
of Prince or David Bowie. If you asked, many people would know what you were
referring to and be able to say where they were too.

Mainstream academic knowledge refers to the concepts, paradigms, theories,
and explanations that make up the traditional and established canon in the behavioral and social sciences. This type of knowledge is based on the belief that there is
an objective truth and that with the right procedures and methods it is possible to
attain this truth. For example, many university courses teach theories that explain
the psychological, physical, and intellectual development of children as a cohesive
group. This development is said to occur through predictable stages that can be
named, studied, and applied to all children, regardless of socioeconomic status,
race, or gender identity.

School knowledge refers to the facts and concepts presented in textbooks, teachers' guides, and other aspects of the formal curriculum designed for use in schools. School knowledge also refers to teachers' interpretations of that knowledge. A critical component of school knowledge is not only what *is* taught, both explicitly and implicitly, but also what *is not* taught. School knowledge can also be thought of as *canonized knowledge* that has been approved or officially sanctioned by the state, for example, through textbooks or standardized tests. Many students are socialized to not question the textbook, but rather to accept it uncritically. Questioning school knowledge is often penalized (grades, test scores, tracking, and reprimand) in ways that have deep and lasting consequences.

Transformative academic knowledge refers to the concepts and explanations that challenge mainstream academic knowledge and that expand the canon. Transformative academic knowledge questions the idea that knowledge can ever be outside of human interests, perspectives, and values. Proponents of transformative academic knowledge assume that knowledge is not neutral and that it reflects the social hierarchies of a given society. Transformative academic knowledge recognizes that the social groups we belong to (such as race, class, and gender) necessarily shape our frame of reference and give us a particular—not a universal—perspective. Therefore, each of us has insight into some dimensions of social life but has limited understanding in others.

Example of Knowledge as Socially Constructed

Let's examine knowledge construction through a specific example. In what is considered to be a seminal study on social class, Jean Anyon (1981) asked elementary aged students to respond to variations on the simple question, "What is knowledge?" Their answers revealed that their definitions were largely dependent on which social class positions they held (see Figure 2.1).

Children who attended schools that served primarily poor and working-class families most often said that knowledge was "remembering things," "answering questions," and "doing pages in our workbooks." Children who attended affluent schools serving primarily upper-class families said things such as "you think up ideas and then find things wrong with those ideas," "it's when you know things really well," and "figuring out things."

As can be seen from these responses, how these students conceptualized knowledge was shaped by the intersection between their social class and the institution of schooling. This institution provides students with very different education based on their position in society and the resources they have access to. This is profoundly significant because the kind of knowledge we receive in schools has concrete implications for our later positions in life.

Figure 2.1. Jean Anyon Study

Question	Working-class schools	Middle-class schools	Affluent professional schools
What is knowledge?	"To know stuff." "Doing pages in our books and things." "Worksheets." "You answer questions." "To remember things"	"To remember." "You learn facts and history." "It's smartness." "Knowledge is something you learn."	"You think up ideas and then find things wrong with those ideas." "It's when you know something really well." "A way of learning, of finding out things." "Figuring out stuff."
Where does knowledge come from?	"Teachers." "Books." "The Board of Ed." "Scientists."	"Teachers." "From old books." "From scientists." "Knowledge comes from everywhere." "You hear other people talk with the big words."	"People and computers." "Your head." "People—what they do." "Something you learn." "From going places."
Could you make knowledge, and if so, how?	No. (15) Yes. (1) Don't know. (4) One girl said, "No, because the Board of Ed makes knowledge."	No. (9) Yes. (11) "I'd look it up." "You can make knowledge by listening and doing what you're told." "I'd go to the library." "By doing extra credit."	No. (4) Yes. (16) "You can make knowledge if you invent something." "I'd think of something to discover, then I'd make it." "You can go explore for new things."

Thinking Critically About Opinions

It is important to distinguish between *opinions*, which are often based in common-sense understandings, and *critical thinking*, which is based on expertise through study. Unfortunately, popular culture promotes the idea that all opinions are equal. Although popular culture is not an educational space per se, it does play an important role in normalizing the idea that all opinions are equally valid.

However, critical thinking is not simply having different opinions; critical thinking results in an informed perspective after engaging with new evidence and accounting for multiple layers of complexity. Simply having an opinion is not predicated on any accounting for new information or understanding of complexity; popular opinions tend to be superficial and anecdotal and do not require that we understand an issue at all. For example, although someone might disagree that social injustice exists, to be credible they must root their argument in an understanding of the knowledge that has already been established and demonstrate how their opinion brings new evidence for consideration. From a scholarly perspective, offering anecdotal evidence that social injustice does not exist (e.g., "In today's society, everyone has an equal opportunity to succeed, regardless of race, class, or gender") is equivalent to the claim, "I looked out my window and the Earth doesn't look round to me." To argue that there is no longer social injustice and have validity, one must be aware of existing knowledge in the field. From an academic perspective, knowledge claims must stand up to scrutiny by peers who are specialists in the subject. This process is called *peer review*, and it is the cornerstone of how academic knowledge is evaluated. Claims about social injustice made within the academic community have undergone peer review. Although there are debates within this community, peer scholars have found the arguments to be relevant and worthy of engagement.

In this book, we ask our readers to grapple with the claims we present, rather than strive to maintain the opinions they already hold. We use the term *grappling* to capture the process of critical thinking: reflecting upon new information, seeking deeper clarity and understanding, and practicing articulating and discussing an issue. Grappling requires engagement with intellectual humility, curiosity, and generosity; grappling is not dependent on agreement. The goal of education is to expand one's knowledge base and critical thinking skills, rather than protect our preexisting opinions. Of course we have a right to our opinions, but there will be no personal or intellectual growth for us if we are not willing to think critically about them. We urge our readers to remember this as we proceed to raise some challenging and politically charged issues.

Discussion Questions

1. Explain in your own words the difference between "critical thinking" and "opinion."

2. What does it mean to say that knowledge is socially constructed? Give some examples.
3. What do the authors mean when they say that "what you know" is connected to "who you are"?

Extension Activity

1. Choose a newspaper article, textbook passage, novel, film, commercial, or other text. Identify which of the various forms of knowledge (personal/cultural knowledge, popular knowledge, school knowledge, mainstream academic knowledge, transformative knowledge) manifest in the text, and describe how.
2. a. Read Chapter 1 of Howard Zinn's *A People's History of the United States: 1492–Present* (New York: HarperCollins, 1980) or Bill Bigelow and Bob Peterson's *Rethinking Columbus: The Next 500 Years* (Milwaukee, WI: Rethinking Schools, 1998).
   b. Watch the film *Pocahontas* (Walt Disney Pictures; Burbank, CA: Walt Disney Home Entertainment, 1997). Using the text and the film as a window into knowledge construction, reflect upon the following questions:
      » Which story of first contact is most often taught in schools? How is it taught?
      » Whose interests are served by "school knowledge" about first contact?
      » How do these texts illustrate the concept of knowledge as socially constructed?

Patterns to practice seeing:

1. What kinds of knowledge are presented as fact and which are presented as opinion? How is this difference conveyed to us?
2. How do families tend to feel about what school their children go to? What are all of the different processes and options related to school choice? What does this say about the idea that all knowledge is equal?

CHAPTER 3

Culture and Socialization

"I don't think about people's race, class, or gender. I just see people as human."

This chapter explains the process of socialization and the interplay between our individuality and our membership in social groups (such as race, gender, and class). We also explain how important it is for us to understand that our ideas, views, and opinions are not simply individual, objective, and independent, but rather are the result of social messages and conditioning forces. We describe how, in addition to our families, institutions and other social forces work together to influence our worldview. Examples are provided to illustrate the power of socialization and how it works as an unconscious filter shaping our perceptions.

Vocabulary to practice using: dominant culture; binary; normalized (norm, normative); gendered; racialized; minoritized

---

Imagine that you are in a class or workshop and your instructor makes any one of the following statements:

"White people receive the message that they are more important and more valuable than people of Color."
"Members of the middle and upper classes have an easier time getting into universities and getting jobs."
"When men enter women-dominated fields, they quickly rise to the top to positions of leadership over the women."
"Heterosexuals publicize their sexuality daily in a multitude of ways."

Several people in the class, perhaps including yourself, hear this and have an immediate defensive reaction: "Wait a minute, you can't generalize like that! You don't know me, and you definitely don't know what obstacles I faced getting into college. I was taught to see everyone as equal. I have a female boss! I don't talk about my sexuality in public!"

Such reactions are common when discussing politically charged issues such as race, class, gender, and sexuality. But defensiveness is triggered by more than a difference of opinion about what the instructor is saying. In order to understand the instructor's statements and why they so often cause defensiveness, we have to have a thorough understanding of culture and socialization.

> ✔ **PERSPECTIVE CHECK:** Of course, some members of this class may be excited to hear the instructor make these statements precisely because they challenge dominant ideas and/or affirm their own experiences.

What Is Culture?

Each one of us is born into a particular time, place, and social context—into a particular *culture*. Culture refers to the characteristics of everyday life of a group of people located in a given time and place. Some of these characteristics are visible and easily identified by the members of the culture, but many (indeed most) of them are below the surface of everyday awareness.

> 📖 *Culture:* The norms, values, practices, patterns of communication, language, laws, customs, and meanings shared by a group of people located in a given time and place.

The iceberg illustration presented in Figure 3.1 is a helpful visual representation of culture. While we may be able to identify superficial elements of culture (such as food, dress, and music), deeper levels of culture (such as notions of modesty and concepts of time) are more difficult to see. Like a fish that is immersed in water from the moment of consciousness and thus cannot know that it is separate from the water, we too are immersed from birth in the deep water of our culture.

What Is Socialization?

Socialization refers to our systematic training into the norms of our culture. Socialization is the process of learning the meanings and practices that enable us to make sense of and behave appropriately in that culture. Notice the massive depth of the iceberg under the water and how many aspects of socialization are below the surface—not consciously thought about; we just *know* when someone is "friendly," or is "acting weird," or has "poor hygiene." We know because we have been socialized into the norms of our culture, norms that regulate these aspects of social life, and if our friends have been socialized this way too, getting along is easy. Socialization begins at birth and continues throughout life. Indeed, the

Figure 3.1. The Iceberg of Culture

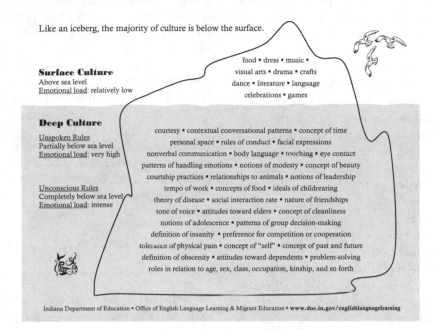

Like an iceberg, the majority of culture is below the surface.

Surface Culture
Above sea level
Emotional load: relatively low

food ▪ dress ▪ music ▪
visual arts ▪ drama ▪ crafts
dance ▪ literature ▪ language
celebrations ▪ games

Deep Culture

Unspoken Rules
Partially below sea level
Emotional load: very high

Unconscious Rules
Completely below sea level
Emotional load: intense

courtesy ▪ contextual conversational patterns ▪ concept of time
personal space ▪ rules of conduct ▪ facial expressions
nonverbal communication ▪ body language ▪ touching ▪ eye contact
patterns of handling emotions ▪ notions of modesty ▪ concept of beauty
courtship practices ▪ relationships to animals ▪ notions of leadership
tempo of work ▪ concepts of food ▪ ideals of childrearing
theory of disease ▪ social interaction rate ▪ nature of friendships
tone of voice ▪ attitudes toward elders ▪ concept of cleanliness
notions of adolescence ▪ patterns of group decision-making
definition of insanity ▪ preference for competition or cooperation
tolerance of physical pain ▪ concept of "self" ▪ concept of past and future
definition of obscenity ▪ attitudes toward dependents ▪ problem-solving
roles in relation to age, sex, class, occupation, kinship, and so forth

Indiana Department of Education ▪ Office of English Language Learning & Migrant Education ▪ **www.doe.in.gov/englishlanguagelearning**

Source: www.homeofbob.com/literature/esl/icebergModelCulture.html

forces of socialization are gathering even before birth, when our families begin to project their hopes, dreams, and expectations onto our lives.

One of the clearest examples of this cultural education is the process of gender socialization. Consider the first question most people ask expectant parents, "Is it a boy or a girl?" Why do we ask this question? We ask because the answer sets in motion a

> ✔ **PERSPECTIVE CHECK:** What's below the surface is often easier to see when the deep culture you have been socialized into does not match the deep culture you are currently navigating. for example, if there is a difference between your home culture and your school or work culture.

series of expectations and actions. For example, if parents are informed that they are having a girl, they may begin to buy clothes and decorate the room in preparation for their daughter's arrival. The colors they chose, the toys they buy, their expectations for her future, will all be informed by what that culture deems appropriate for girls.

But even our conception of what girls and boys are is rooted in our culture. Although sex and gender are often used interchangeably, they mean different things. *Sex* refers to the biological, genetic, or phenotypical markers that are used to categorize us into female and male bodies: genitals, body structure, hormones, and so on. These markers are related to reproduction. *Gender,* on the other hand, is what it *means* to have that body in a given culture. Gender refers to the roles, behaviors, and expectations our culture assigns to those markers: how you are supposed to feel and act based on whether your body is seen as female or male. Males are expected to learn to "act like a man"—they are trained into *masculinity*; and females are expected to learn to "act like a woman"—they are trained into *femininity*.

When we fit neatly into these binary categories, scholars sometimes use the prefix "cis" to describe us. *Cis* is Latin for *same* and indicates that one's gender assignment and identity are the same or in agreement. Another way to think about this is that a person who is cisgender is not transgender. People who are transgender have a gender identity that is different from their assigned sex at birth. A transgender woman is someone who was identified as male at birth but whose gender identity is female and lives, or desires to live, her life as a woman. A transgender man is someone who was identified as female at birth but whose

Cisgender: The term for people whose gender assignment at birth and subsequent socialization are the same as their identity.

Transgender: The term for people whose gender assignment at birth is different from their gender identity.

Genderqueer, Genderfluid, nonBinary: People who do not identify in binary terms and /or whose gender identity and expression is fluid and dynamic.

✓ **PERSPECTIVE CHECK:** Of course this binary construct is the dominant construct in Western society. In other cultures, there are "third" or alternate gender identities that are normalized, such as two spirit or Muxe in Indigenous traditions, Hijra from South Asian traditions, or Kathoey from Asian traditions (among many others). These traditions show that societies around the world have grappled with the complexity of gender and sexuality identity and expression for millennia.

gender identity is male and lives, or desires to live, his life as a man. (And there are some people who don't want to be in either of the gender categories; they are nonbinary.) One thing we all have in common, regardless of our gender identity, is that we live in a society that is set up to enforce the gender roles imposed on us from birth. Cisgender and transgender people have this in common, though they will undoubtedly have different experiences and feelings about being socialized as boys or girls during childhood, following a prescribed script throughout adolescence about what it means to achieve manhood or womanhood, and existing as adults in a structure where compulsory gender norms continue to be imposed. We acknowledge that the terms we use here—"man," "woman," "male," "female"—are neither natural nor unchanging. What we aim to communicate by using these terms, limited and inadequate as they may be, is the power of socialization; what society tells us it means to be a man or a woman, a boy or a girl, male or female, how it tells us, and what the consequences are. Thus, we use the terms men and women to illustrate the process of socialization within a cisnormative gender binary and how that socialization is rooted in sexism.

More often than many people realize, babies are born with variant sex characteristics that are not easily understood as being female or male, or with a combination of both female and male genitals (Bergvall, Bing, & Freed, 1996; Fausto-Sterling, 2000). Gender in many cultures is a binary system that insists on male/female opposites, and this binary has profound meaning and consequences. Because of this, doctors routinely opt to surgically and hormonally "correct" any variations and assign one or the other sex and gender status to the child even though many of these babies are healthy at birth. Through medical intervention, the bodies of sex-variant babies are reshaped into what is considered normal for a male or female and therefore understandable in terms of gender binaries.

Because we are taught that sex and gender differences are natural, we rarely notice how much we have been socialized into them. Indeed, as the title of a popular book from the 1990s tells us, men are from Mars and women are from Venus: so fundamentally different that they don't even come from the same planet. Yet in fact, there are actually fewer, rather than more, differences between women and men (Fausto-Sterling, 1992). However, because society is invested in the differences (in maintaining the different social statuses of women and men), the research that validates difference between women and men is the research that gets promoted.

Like gender, many other aspects of our socialization are also invisible to us. For example, how close do we stand when talking to someone? How do we know when someone is standing too close? And how do aspects of socialization (such as age, social class, religion) and context (such as at a party, in the office, or at home) influence our assessments of whether or not someone is standing too close? The norms of our culture are most often invisible until they are violated.

Cultural Norms and Conformity

Let's consider the example of grooming norms to illustrate the power of cultural socialization. Imagine it is a hot summer day and you are having lunch in an outdoor café. You notice an attractive couple sitting at the table next to you. Just like many others, they are wearing shorts and tank tops, enjoying the warm weather. At some point, the man raises his arm to flag down the waiter. The café's busy, and the waiter doesn't notice. After a few minutes of being ignored, the woman raises her arm in an attempt to get the waiter's attention, and you see that she does not shave under her arms and has a thick patch of black underarm hair.

Many people would feel a sense of shock; some might even lose their appetite. You might point it out to your lunch mate, and tell your friends about it later that day. However, thinking back to when the man raised his arm, you might realize that you did not have any reaction at all to his unshaved armpits. In fact, they didn't even register. Yet underarm hair is completely natural to the adult human body—male *and* female. Why would the woman's hair disgust many of us, but not the man's? It is because we have been socialized to see underarm hair as inappropriate for women. This socialization is so effective that we actually have a physical reaction when the norm is violated. Further, this norm is specific to dominant culture in Canada and the United States. In a different social context (or place or time), underarm hair on women would appear natural, perhaps even sexy, to most people.

This leads to another key aspect of socialization—our beliefs need not be inherently *true* to have very real consequences. For example, it is not inherently true that underarm hair on women is disgusting. But if that is the norm in our culture, it will be true in its impact; we will still *feel* disgusted and this disgust will seem natural and appropriate. So despite not being inherently true, the effect and consequences of our socialization are real. Similarly, while the colors blue and pink are simply colors that occur in nature and are not naturally male or female, once we assign that meaning to them, they become real in their consequences. Any male who has worn pink (in the wrong shade or to the wrong place) will know this firsthand; young males in particular actually risk physical harm if this norm is violated in certain spaces. (Why then, you might ask, can a girl wear blue without risking violence? To understand why, you must understand social power, which we address in Chapter 5.)

> ✔ **PERSPECTIVE CHECK:** Of course trans and genderqueer peoples face additional social threats and even violence when they transgress social expectations. These additional risks are amplified if they are trans people of Color.

On an abstract level most people grasp the concept of socialization. However, applying it personally to our *own* lives is more challenging. We live in a culture that teaches us that human objectivity (or independence from socialization) is not only possible, but that it can be readily attained through simple choice. In other words, if I *want* to be an individual who is not influenced by the forces of socialization around me, then I can just decide that I *am* an individual who is not influenced by those forces; it is presumed that this decision is all that it takes to break away from the undertow of socialization. Yet this breakaway from socialization is much more challenging than it may appear. There are social, psychological, and material rewards for conformity, such as social acceptance, being treated as "normal" by family, peers, and superiors, and even opportunities for career progression.

Conversely, there are also penalties for not conforming. Take our example of the woman with the underarm hair; while she has the right to not shave under her arms, she also has to deal with the consequences of that choice. For example, she will face looks of disgust, pressure from family and friends, and questions about her sexuality and her hygiene; this choice may even be cause for censure in the workplace. That is, by not playing by the rules, she jeopardizes her status as a "normal" member of that society. And the penalties do not necessarily go away if the woman has greater social power. For instance, female celebrities who do not shave their armpits are routinely criticized, mocked, and insulted on social media for their choice. Thus the social norms of a given culture, whether we conform to them or choose to challenge them, are powerful and unavoidable. Of course this still assumes that we can readily identify aspects of our socialization we want to change. Much of our socialization is so internalized and taken for granted that we don't even see it as a choice—we just believe that it's natural to feel and act the way we do.

Consider one of many studies of its kind regarding discrimination in hiring (Bertrand & Mullainathan, 2004). Seeking to understand the well-documented patterns of inequality between Whites and Blacks in the U.S. job market in terms of rate of employment and pay, researchers at the University of Chicago conducted a large study. These researchers responded to over 1,300 help-wanted ads in Boston and Chicago newspapers by sending out close to 5,000 resumes. While the qualifications on the resumes were consistent, they randomly assigned stereotypically White-sounding names, such as Emily Walsh or Greg Baker, to half of the resumes, and stereotypically Black-sounding names, such as Lakisha Washington or Jamal Jones to the other half. Resumes with White-sounding names received 50% more callbacks than the resumes with stereotypically Black-sounding names, regardless of the employer, occupation, industry, or size of the company.

The researchers also investigated how improvements in credentials affected the callback rate. While the resumes with White-sounding names received 30% more callbacks when the credentials improved, there was no significant improvement in callback rates for the applicants with Black-sounding names. In other words, there were no benefits to Black applicants for improving their credentials. The discrimination stayed consistent and did not vary across occupations, region, or industry; even when the applications of people perceived as Black were *more* qualified, they were still discriminated against. Although race was the focus of the study, it is virtually impossible to separate race from class, gender, and presumed religious affiliation.

While this study along with others of its kind (Gaddis, 2015; Kang, DeCelles, Tilesik, & Jun, 2016; Oreopoulos, 2011) provides clear evidence that racial discrimination is alive and well, it raises another question: What happened when the human resource workers screened these resumes? They were likely not aware that they were discriminating, and would probably have vigorously (and sincerely) denied any suggestion to the contrary. They would not be intentionally lying when they denied discriminating, and herein lies the power of socialization: We often have no idea that we are discriminating. What we see appears to be the truth; that is, *this* batch of applicants appears to us as more qualified than *that* batch. But we have interpreted these resumes through our racial filters, filters that have been activated as soon as we read the names. When we read the resume and see, for example, the name Lakisha Washington, a name

> ✋ **STOP:** While many of us believe that we treat everyone the same, this is not possible. Countless studies show that humans are not and cannot be objective (independent from our socialization) about one another. This socialization drives us to discriminate. Most of our discrimination is not conscious, but real nonetheless. There are ways to help us minimize this discrimination, but they cannot help us if we refuse to accept that we don't in fact treat everyone equally.

traditionally associated in our culture with Blacks, our racial filters are triggered. We are now unconsciously reading her resume through these filters, which are filled with the assumptions and expectations about her qualifications that we have absorbed from the culture at large.

Whether we are aware of these filters or not, we have associations based on names that cause us to see some in a more favorable light than others. Because dominant culture constantly reinforces the idea that Blacks are underqualified, even when the qualifications of an already qualified applicant with a Black-sounding name were *increased*, the resume readers still perceived them as unqualified. In other words, the facts are not enough to trump the socialized beliefs.

In the case of Lakisha, this happens instantaneously and is almost always unconscious—we will simply interpret her resume in a way that fulfills our expectations that she is less qualified based on assumptions about her race and class. Names such as Emily Walsh or Greg Baker don't trigger the same set of racial filters because they are associated with dominant culture and thus are neutral in terms of racial association (since Whites in mainstream culture are not racialized, it is peoples of Color who "have" race). The unconscious racial filters for these names allow us to interpret their resumes as from "normal" candidates, and thus we can take in the facts of their qualifications with different (more positive) bias. Regardless of the race of the readers of these resumes themselves, names convey ideas about race (and gender and class) to everyone, and these ideas are often unconscious, yet still play a powerful role in the presumed "fit" of one candidate over another.

This is both the power of our filters and the dilemma of our denial that they exist; if we can't see (or admit) that this is happening, we can't stop doing it or put protections in place to help minimize it. For example, because studies of this kind

Figure 3.2. Frame of Reference Glasses Diagram

provided powerful proof of racial discrimination, many companies now block out the names on resumes before sending them to hiring committees in order to protect against unaware bias.

In order to develop critical social justice literacy, we must be able to see how our ideas, views, and opinions are not objective and independent, but rather the result of myriad social messages and conditioning forces. The first layer of socialization we might easily identify is our family. While our families do indeed form the first unit through which we learn language, values, and behaviors, our parents and families are not the sole or dominant forces of socialization. There are many other socializing forces including schooling, media, and religion, which also wield great authority. Thus the common conception that families are the sole forces of socialization is an incomplete view because our families themselves are products of socialization. In order to critically reflect on the forces of socialization that shape us, we must understand the role of broader society.

"You" in Relation to the "Groups" to Which You Belong

Humans are social beings who depend on the humans around us to make sense of our world. A useful metaphor for understanding how we learn to make sense of our world is to think of our culture as a pair of glasses that we wear at all times (see Figure 3.2). Just like the fish is always immersed in water, we are always wearing our cultural glasses and cannot ever truly take them off. There are two significant parts to these glasses: the frames and the lenses. The frames are the "big picture" (macro) norms—what everyone in that culture is taught from birth. The lenses constitute the individual (micro) perspective.

At the frame (macro) level, for example, in the culture of mainstream United States and Canada, we are all taught that pink is for girls and blue is for boys, that democracy and free market capitalism are the best forms of government and economic policy, and that we should strive to be independent from others. Regardless of whether or not we personally agree with these teachings, we all receive them through social institutions like schools, government, and the mass media.

For example, even if as parents we want to challenge traditional gender roles and intentionally avoid dressing our daughters in pink or sons in blue, we still receive the message in mainstream culture whenever we watch TV, walk through the toy aisles in stores, or order a Happy Meal at McDonald's and are asked if we want the "girl" or "boy" toy. In fact, many parents who try to avoid traditional gender teachings find it to be a losing battle, given the relentless messages children receive from everything else around them; we are constantly being pressured to follow the norms of society.

The social groups we are born or develop into are part of the frames of our glasses. For example, when we are born we are socialized according to whether we are male or female, rich or poor, able-bodied or with a disability. While group divisions are not in reality this clear-cut, the macro level of society organizes groups into simple either/or groupings (called *binaries*). For every social group, there is an opposite group. One cannot learn what a social group *is*, without also learning what the group *is not*. Thus the frames of our glasses are the big picture ideas about social groups. Although there are many, the primary groups that we name here are: race, class, gender, sexuality, ability status/exceptionality, religion, and nationality.

Figure 3.3 is intended to help readers begin the process of identifying several of their key social group memberships. Despite these limitations, our intention is that readers use this chart for the purpose of beginning to understand the relevance of race/ethnicity in society at large.

We develop our ideas about people in terms of their race, class, gender, sexuality, ethnicity, religion, ability, and citizenship from the culture that surrounds us, and many of these ideas are "below the surface" or below the conscious level. But we all rely on shared understandings about these social groups because we receive messages collectively about them from our culture. The frameworks we use to make sense of race, class, or gender are taken for granted and often invisible to us.

Race and ethnicity are examples of how complex and interrelated these categories can be. While race and ethnicity are related in important ways and often used interchangeably, they

✓ **PERSPECTIVE CHECK:** We have based the list in Figure 3.3 on categories of identification that are collected by the Canadian and U.S. governments. However, these categorizations do not reflect the complexities of race and ethnicity as experienced in society. For example, in Figure 3.3 we have included Latino/Hispanic under the category of race despite the fact that this is not technically a singular racial group; it includes many racial groups. We have included it because of the very real racialized experiences that occur for people who are identified as Latino/Hispanic.

Figure 3.3. Group Identities

Group identities

Group	It is unavoidable that some groups have not been listed. If your group has been left out, please write it in.
Race	Perceived as Person of Color
	Perceived as White
Race detailed	Asian (e.g., Chinese, Japanese, Korean ancestry)
	South Asian (e.g., Indian, Sri Lankan, Nepalese ancestry)
	Black (e.g., African, Caribbean ancestry)
	Bi- or multiracial (parents and/or grandparents of mixed racial ancestry)
	Indigenous (e.g., Cherokee, Inuit, Dakota ancestry)
	Native Hawaiian/Pacific Islander (e.g., Samoan, Guamanian, Fijian ancestry)
	White (e.g., Irish, French, Ashkenazi Jewish ancestry)
	Hispanic or Latino/a (e.g., Puerto Rican, Cuban, Mexican ancestry)
Class	Poor, Working Poor, Working Class, Lower Middle Class, Middle Class, Professional Class, Upper Class, Owning/Ruling Class
Gender	Cis-Women, Cis-Men, Transgender, Genderqueer
Sexuality	Lesbian, Bisexual, Gay, Two Spirit, Heterosexual
Religion	For example: Hindu, Buddhist, Jew, Christian, Muslim, Atheist
Ability	For example: Able-bodied, people with physical disabilities, people with developmental disabilities, exceptionality
Nationality	Indigenous, Immigrant (perceived non-status), Citizen (perceived)

are not interchangeable. *Race* is a socially constructed system of classifying humans based on particular phenotypical characteristics (skin color, hair texture, and bone structure). *Ethnicity* refers to a group of people bound by a common language, culture, spiritual tradition, and/or ancestry. Ethnic groups can bridge national borders and still be one group (such as the Cree community, which straddles the United States and Canada). At the same time, ethnic groups can live within the same national borders and not share the same ethnic identity. For example, "British" refers to people of English, Scottish, and Welsh ancestry who live in the United Kingdom of Great Britain. However the English, Scottish, and Welsh are distinct ethnic groups. As well, British can refer to citizens of Great Britain who may have racial and ethnic heritages other than English, Scottish, or Welsh—such as African, Asian, or Arab.

As this example shows, race and ethnicity interact in complex ways with language and citizenship. For those new to the study of critical social justice, mastering these complexities is of secondary importance. Of primary importance is the ability to understand these categories as *socially constructed* and reflective of a particular political and cultural context. This does not mean that we dismiss categories of race and ethnicity because they are unstable; rather we must understand the larger dynamics that their instability is related to and the impact of those larger dynamics on our lives (this will be discussed in more depth in Chapter 7).

There are also important interactions between race and ethnicity, and internal and external dynamics of identity; how one personally *identifies* versus how one *is identified* by others. In other words, how I see myself versus how others perceive me. While how we see ourselves and how others see us may not be the same, they are in fact, inseparable, because how our identities develop is shaped by how others see and respond to us. Sociologist Charles Cooley (1922) called this interconnection the "looking glass self" to capture the idea that we come to know who we are in large part through the process of what others reflect back to us. The looking glass self includes the concept that the process of learning to know who we *are* is shaped by learning who we are *not*.

We now return to the analogy of the "frame of reference" glasses. As we said previously, the lenses constitute the individual (micro) perspective. These are our unique experiences that make us "one of a kind"—our birth order, our family, our personality—the "prescription" lens that fits in the frame. Yet no one is *simply* an individual. We are all members of multiple social groupings and widely circulating social messages about those groupings. To understand your personal cultural glasses, you have to explore the interplay or relationship between your frames and your lenses. A primary challenge in developing critical social justice literacy is to understand the relationship between you as an individual and the social groups you belong to; the interplay of positionality. From a critical social justice framework, when we say the words "men," "women," "heterosexuals," "middle class," and so on, we are speaking about specific social group positions and histories.

If we are resisting the very notion of having to identify ourselves in terms of social groups, such as our race or gender, this too provides insight into our collective socialization. In Western society we are socialized to prioritize our individuality. Yet, although we *are* individuals, we *are also*—and perhaps fundamentally— members of social groups. These group memberships shape us as profoundly, if not more so, than any unique characteristic we may claim to possess.

Consider how one of the key aspects of individuality is one's preference for certain food, music, and dress styles. However, these preferences are never simply one's internally-driven likes or dislikes. It is no coincidence that popular shows of the day (whether it be the *Twilight* movie franchise or the Netflix series *Stranger Things*) influence which names rise to the top of "most popular name" lists. Think back to when other iconic figures from popular culture influenced hairstyles of the time (Pam Grier, Farrah Fawcett, Jennifer Aniston, Justin Bieber). Conversely, seeking names that are "different" is also a function of culture—you are still reacting to the culture at large. Without the popular names, your different name (different from what?) would not have the same meaning.

> 📖 **Dominant Group(s):** The group(s) at the top of the social hierarchy. In any relationship between groups that define one another (men/women, able-bodied/disabled, young/old, White/Black), the dominant group is the group that is valued more highly. Dominant groups set the norms by which the minoritized group is judged. Dominant groups have greater access to the resources of society and benefit from the existence of the inequality.

The point is, while parents may have preferences for particular names, and any individual may have a preference for a particular hairstyle, it is not simply a matter of preference. There are predictable patterns of group behavior we can observe and study. And we can make predictions about your preferences based on your class, race, gender, and so on.

Returning to our opening vignette, hopefully you now have a better idea of what was meant by the instructor's statements when she said for example that, "Members of the middle and upper classes have an easier time getting into universities and getting jobs." The instructor was not making claims about each *individual person* in these groups, but about *patterns among social groups*. These patterns are longstanding, measurable, and well documented. The fact that these kinds of statements often cause defensiveness speaks to the way they challenge Western elevation of the individual over the group. We have been taught that social group memberships such as race, class, and gender do not and should not matter, and thus must be minimized and denied.

Specifically, the instructor is challenging a societal norm by moving past individual difference and instead focusing on shared dynamics between members of social groups. She is also challenging a norm connected to our elevation of the individual—the idea that people should be seen as unique, and thus it is inappropriate to generalize. And finally, she is naming the dominant group in each of these examples, which violates assumptions that dominant groups are neutral and that difference lies with the "other."

Discussion Questions

1. Key careers tend to be organized in ways that are gendered (police and firefighters tend to be men, while teachers and nurses tend to be women). How would the authors explain this pattern?

2. According to the authors, why do so many people feel immune to the forces of socialization?
3. How does the concept of *socialization* challenge the idea of *individualism*?
4. Many sociologists say that in part how we come to know ourselves is by knowing who we are not. Sociologist Charles Cooley described this process as the "looking glass self" to capture the idea that it is what others reflect back to us that teaches us who we are—that is, our ideas about ourselves are based on how we see ourselves (people like us) in relation to others (people not like us). What kind of people did you learn were different from you? In which ways were they different? How were you taught about this difference? If you were told that everyone was the same, did the implicit messages of your environment match this explicit message? For example, what key groups (such as the elderly, people with disabilities, people of different social classes than your own, people from different religious groups, people from different racial groups) were you segregated from? As you reflect on this question, consider implicit (unspoken) messages as well as explicit (direct) messages.

Extension Activities

1. "Act like a boy or girl." This is a popular diversity exercise intended to draw out the forces of gender socialization.

   Divide the group into men and women (if someone doesn't identify with either category, ask the person to choose a group depending on either how mainstream society would categorize him or her or which group he or she most identifies with or has the most insight into).

   Now, imagine that an alien has landed in your group. This alien comes from a planet where gender is organized very differently. The job of this alien is to "get by," "blend in," and learn about human society. The alien has already received treatments to "look" human, but has no idea how to "act like a boy" or "act like a girl" in order to pass. As a group, generate a list of instructions for your alien about how to "act like a boy" (if you are the men's group) and how to "act like a girl" (if you are the women's group).

   Your list should include verbs. Consider settings like school, work, family gatherings. Remember, the goal of your alien friend is to blend into mainstream society and understand its basic customs, not to challenge them.

   Ask the groups to write their lists on the board or chart paper, then draw a box around each list. As the groups share their lists of instructions, ask the following questions:

   » How do we "know" these rules? (Even if we personally reject them or think they are silly, notice that we must still know what they are in order to refuse them.)

» Since these are learned behaviors, what would it mean to "unlearn" them? Is this possible? How would we do this?

» What are the costs of stepping outside of your gender script? That is, what happens when you don't "act like a boy"? Are there some areas (settings? places? with certain company?) where there is more permission to act in ways outside the script? In what settings is it less ok?

» It should be obvious that many of the things on the list are rather absurd and limiting to our lives. What keeps us in line? In other words, what are the penalties for stepping too far out of these boxes? What do we get called or seen as?

Return to your groups to discuss this question: What doors would be open to you that are not open to you now, if we were truly free of gender roles? Bring the groups back together to share the results of their discussion of this last question. Notice if there is a difference in enthusiasm between the men and the women in terms of eliminating gender roles. Why are men usually less interested in eliminating gender roles?

2. a. Read Simon Weisenthal's *The Sunflower: On the Possibilities and Limitations of Forgiveness* (New York: Schocken, 1976).

   b. Watch the film *The Question of God: Sigmund Freud & C. S. Lewis* (C. Tatge & D. Lasseur, Producers; C. Tatge, Director; Alexandria, VA: Tatge-Lasseur Productions, 2004).

   c. Using the text and the film as a window into socialization, reflect upon the following questions:

      » How would you answer Wiesenthal's question on forgiveness?

      » What framework are you using to address the question?

      » How did you acquire this framework?

      » Why might so many others answer such a question very differently?

      » How can religious debates help us identify our cultural frameworks?

Patterns to Practice Seeing

1. Practice identifying patterns at the *group* (rather than individual) level. For example, in workplace meetings or other public spaces, practice seeing which groups are included and which are not.

2. Practice naming people by their key social groups. For example, "Tina, a white able-bodied cis-woman, went to the store." Notice your own as well as others' levels of comfort.

CHAPTER 4

Prejudice and Discrimination

"I was taught never to judge a book by its cover."

This chapter explains two key interrelated terms: prejudice and discrimination. We explain that prejudice and discrimination cannot be avoided; we all hold prejudices and we all discriminate based on our prejudices. We argue that the first step in minimizing discrimination is to be able to identify (rather than deny) our prejudices.

Vocabulary to practice using: prejudice; discrimination; implicit bias

Imagine that you are on a hiring committee to identify the best candidate to join your school faculty. Ms. Hardy, the principal who chairs the committee, reports that there are too many applicants for the one position and that the committee needs to thin out the applicant pool. As she is distributing the files for review, she says, "Oh, here's a male applicant. We definitely want to consider this one, since we have so few male teachers at our school." As she says this, she is thinking, *I really want to get some male teachers in here; just the other day a parent was complaining that there weren't any male role models for the boys.*

Liz, a teacher on the committee, thinks, *Oh great, a man. That's all we need. He'll probably be the vice principal by next year;* and says, "Yes, but there are many other dynamics associated with what a candidate brings."

Wendy, another teacher, thinks, *I hope he's gay; men teaching at the elementary level usually are. He'll probably be a blast to work with;* and says, "Yeah, we should look closely at his application. And it would be so great to have more diversity around sexual orientation too."

Mary, another teacher, thinks, *Uh-oh, he's probably gay . . . that's going to be an issue for a lot of the parents;* and says, "Yes, but we should consider how the candidate fits the culture of our students' families. In the past, we've had problems around gay teachers."

Liz exclaims, "Whoa, this is prejudice!"

Everyone is stunned by this charge. Wendy retorts, "That's a terrible accusation! We have a process here, and policies that we will follow to ensure that every candidate is evaluated fairly. Besides, Mary and I don't have a prejudiced bone in our bodies!"

What is Prejudice?

This vignette illustrates some of the many complicated dimensions associated with critical social justice. While most people want to be fair, we can't help but have preconceived notions—prejudices—about other people based on their social groups (in this case, the candidate's gender). At the same time, we often feel deeply hurt and insulted when someone suggests that we have prejudices at all, let alone that they are showing. To gain a more complex understanding of the

> 📖 **Prejudice:** Learned prejudgment about members of social groups to which we don't belong. Prejudice is based on limited knowledge or experience with the group. Simplistic judgments and assumptions are made and projected onto everyone from that group.

dynamics in the above vignette, we must first examine the relationship between two interrelated concepts: *prejudice* and *discrimination*.

Prejudice is learned prejudgment toward social others and refers to *internal* thoughts, feelings, attitudes, and assumptions based on the groups to which they belong. While everyone has prejudices based on distinctive experiences that are unique to them—for example, someone got into a legal dispute with a cashier and now doesn't trust cashiers—here we are concerned with the collective prejudices we learn from the culture at large about our own and other social groups.

These prejudices can be either positive or negative. However, they are always unfair, because they are not earned by the individual but granted or imposed based on ideas about the group that the individual belongs to. For example, *I prefer to teach math to Chinese heritage students because I assume they will do well on the math test, and I don't like to teach math to White female students because I assume they will do poorly.* While the prejudice I have toward the Chinese heritage students appears to be positive, it is still unfair in that it isn't earned, will interfere with my ability to make valid assessments, and sets one racial group up against others.

Prejudice manifests in attitudes about an individual, but it is based on our ideas about the group to which that individual belongs. Prejudice is part of how we learn to sort people into categories that make sense to us (boy/girl, old/young, rich/poor). Although this is a process necessary for learning, our categorizations are not neutral. We are socialized to perceive and value these categories differently.

For example, take the categories of "attractive" and "unattractive." While there is some variation in opinion between people, on the level of collective socialization, there are sanctioned norms of beauty constantly communicated to us through major institutions such as the entertainment industry. Media-based representations present a consistent image of who the attractive people are, what they look like, and what we can do to look more like them (if you doubt this, just scan the magazine rack at your local grocery store).

Most of us are acutely aware that there are social benefits that go with being in the "attractive" group and social penalties for being in the "unattractive" group. These benefits and penalties are communicated to us *explicitly*—effusive praise for a celebrity's beauty, magazine covers featuring the "100 Most Beautiful People," the "20 Hottest Bodies," the open ridicule of unattractive people, more praise for us when we "dress up"—and *implicitly* through larger salaries, career advancement, better evaluations, and other research-documented benefits that accrue to those considered attractive (Hamermesh & Parker, 2005; Rhode, 2010).

These definitions are not natural but are specific to a given cultural context. They change over time and our perceptions change with them, indicating the learned nature of our prejudices. For example, in the United States Marilyn Monroe was once considered one of the most beautiful women in the world. However, while she might still epitomize the White, blonde ideal of feminine beauty, she would be considered overweight today and therefore would not have the beauty status that she held over 50 years ago.

Prejudices begin as stereotypes. While many use these terms interchangeably, there are important nuances. *Stereotypes* refer to reduced or simplified characteristics attributed to a group. For example, if we ask someone to describe Americans and Canadians, they may answer that Americans are industrious, independent, and like fast food, while Canadians are polite, love hockey, and end their sentences with "eh." When we ask what elementary school teachers are like, we may have ideas that they are nurturing and loving. These kinds of simplifications are either a set of characteristics *attributed to* a group (elementary school teachers are nurturing), or a feature of some members of a group that *stands out* (Canadian speech, American eating habits).

People often say that there is always a kernel of truth to stereotypes, but this belief has more to do with the ways in which stereotypes work and less to do with their validity. For example, although some Canadians end some of their sentences with "eh," most Canadians do not. Yet this distinction is what helps us make sense of the category "Canadian" as distinct from the category "American." This is especially easy to see in the realm of media where having, for example, a character say "eh" establishes that character as Canadian. For an American watching these movies, this stereotype is reinforced again and again. Because many Americans may not know many Canadians, we don't have much else to draw on and over time come to believe this is how Canadians talk. The stereotype is now formed in our minds and will appear to be true because we are drawing on the fixed representation we have seen so regularly. When we encounter people who don't fit the stereotype, we either don't notice or we view these people as exceptions. On the other hand, when we encounter people who do fit the stereotype, even if we encounter them very rarely, they stand out to us and reinforce the stereotype as true. Therefore, if we hold this stereotype and visit Canada, we will notice any Canadian we hear say "eh" and disregard the countless Canadians we meet who don't, thus reinforcing our belief in this particular stereotype.

Prejudice comes into play when we add values to our stereotypes. Let's put stereotypes together with values, using the example of "elementary school teacher." If I am a parent going to meet my son's 2nd-grade teacher for the first time, I would expect to meet a female (as the vast majority of elementary teachers are female). If instead I meet a male, I may wonder if he is gay (a common stereotype about

> ✔ **PERSPECTIVE CHECK:** If I am a gay parent, or have close relationships with many gay people whom I advocate for, I am more likely to be informed and educated on the issues and thus not have the same worry.

male elementary school teachers) and worry that if he is, he will be an inappropriate role model for my son (a common prejudice about gay men). This worry develops from the interaction between stereotypes about male elementary school teachers and the values associated with those stereotypes in our culture, leading to a prejudicial attitude that my son's gay teacher will be an unsuitable role model.

Notice how conceptions about the teacher are interwoven in important ways with conceptions about gender roles. These conceptions are important because they are the basis of our evaluations for what is "normal"; every teacher we encounter who does not match our internal definition of "teacher" will be evaluated differently than the "normal" teachers who do match them. These evaluations don't just distinguish between who is deemed normal and who isn't, but also influence our assessments of other important social values such as character. When we assign character values, our stereotypes have moved into prejudice.

Many of us think that we don't hold prejudicial thoughts against people. Because we think this, we see ourselves as free of prejudice. But the process is much more complicated. The reality is that no one can avoid prejudice because it is built into our socialization. All humans have prejudices, but they are so normalized and taken for granted that they are often very difficult to identify. This is one of the challenges of critical social justice literacy: developing the critical thinking that would enable us to bring our prejudices to the surface and reflect upon and challenge them. Yet society tells us that it is bad to have prejudices, and thus we feel pressure to deny them.

However, because social acceptance of prejudices varies over time, we don't feel compelled to deny all of our prejudices. In fact, when we hold prejudices against certain groups—groups that it is socially acceptable to hold prejudices against—we often don't see them as prejudices at all, but as facts. For example, not too long ago it was socially acceptable for White people to openly admit holding prejudicial beliefs about Black people, which they saw as justified because most White people believed that Black racial inferiority was simply *true*. Today this belief is understood to be untrue, and to admit to holding such a belief is no longer considered acceptable in most circles. However, admitting to prejudices against people considered overweight (especially women) *is* currently acceptable. And in fact, not only are these prejudices acceptable, but many magazines, for example, openly ridicule women perceived as overweight.

While there are health risks to obesity, the beauty and entertainment industries are invested in selling us the *idea* of fat as ugly, as undisciplined, and as worthy of contempt. These ideas allow us to rationalize our prejudice. The economic interest in maintaining these prejudices is so deep that they are marketed to all people. Consequently, girls who have not even reached puberty are socialized into a culture of dieting, and very few people feel satisfied with their bodies regardless of their size or health (Grogan, 2016; Levin & Kilbourne, 2008). These industries relentlessly present the image of the ideal body, and this ideal has become increasingly unattainable and in some contexts (such as the modeling industry) unhealthy. In fact, the image is so unrealistic that the magazine cover models themselves don't actually look like the images presented; images are routinely digitally modified to reshape their bodies, decrease their weight, enhance their breasts, remove their pores, and more. This leads to deep body dissatisfaction, which in turn translates into billions of dollars for the beauty and diet industries.

What is Discrimination?

The term *discrimination* has multiple meanings, including having discriminating (or refined) taste in music or food. In critical social justice studies, we use it to refer to action based on prejudices toward social others. How we *think* about groups of people determines how we *act* toward them;

> **Discrimination:** Action based on prejudice toward social others. When we act on our prejudgments, we are discriminating.

Discrimination occurs when we act on our prejudices. Our prejudice toward others guides our thoughts, organizes our values, and influences our actions. These prejudgments, when left unexamined, necessarily shape our behaviors. Once we act on our prejudices, we are *discriminating*. Acts of discrimination can include ignoring, avoiding, excluding, ridicule, jokes, slander, threats, and violence.

Consider this example: You are at a play and you notice that the person in the seat next to yours is fumbling with her program. You turn to look at her and realize that she is blind, which is signaled to you by the white cane by her side. Once you realize that she is blind, she is placed in your mind into a new social category that triggers a new set of possible responses to her. These responses could range from ignoring (because you are not sure of the proper way to communicate with someone who is blind) or avoidance (if you find her blindness discomfiting), to an offer of help (based on an assumption that she will need it). If you decide to offer your assistance, you may, without even realizing it, speak more slowly than you normally would to an adult stranger, reflecting a common (but unaware) assumption that a visual impairment also implies cognitive impairments.

> ✓ **PERSPECTIVE CHECK:**
> The example discussed in the text assumes the perspective of an able-bodied person who has not thought deeply about ableism. If you come from the perspective of a person with a disability (or have a person with a disability in your life whom you advocate for), you are more likely to be informed on the issue and thus interact more constructively.

While you might insist that you would never interact differently with a blind person than with anyone else, research supports the prediction that you would (Dovidio, Glick, & Rudman, 2005; Greenwald & Krieger, 2006). That doesn't make you a bad person; our prejudices and the discriminatory behaviors they produce are often not consciously known to us. Nor do we have to be aware of them in order for them and their effects to be real.

The prejudice that leads to the differential treatment we name here—either ignoring/avoiding the blind woman or offering unsolicited help and speaking as if to a child—is not unique to us, and can be predicted precisely because of that fact. The messages that reinforce prejudice toward blind people are everywhere and affect all of us. This prejudice in turn informs our behavior. Consider representations of people with disabilities in media. Inspirational heroes are valorized for having "overcome" the tragedy of disability; horror movies wherein the villain's ability to scare victims is connected to "freaky" eyes or disfigurements of the body; and admonishments to children to avoid activities that could cause them to go blind (implying that this would be the worst possible condition to have).

When we add the fact that most sighted people don't know any blind people (because in our society most blind people are separated out and sent to special schools and workplaces), you ensure the likelihood of problematic ideas and interactions. Notice that blind people (and people with other perceived exceptionalities) are both highly *visible* in the ways their blindness is amplified in films and popular culture, and at the same time *invisible* in that they are often separated from the mainstream. This dynamic sets us up to rely on misinformation and starts the cycle of prejudice and discrimination. We are not saying every person will discriminate in these specific ways against the woman in the theater, but many will. In addition, given the dynamics of prejudice and discrimination, our own personal assessment of whether we will is simply not reliable.

All Humans Have Prejudice and Discriminate

Just as all people have prejudices, learned from socialization, all people discriminate. So, the blind woman in our previous example may also have prejudices against us because we are sighted. Based on her previous experiences with sighted people, she may assume that we are ignorant about people with disabilities and that we will be condescending toward her. Thus if we attempt to speak to her, she may ignore us; she is discriminating against us based on her prejudice toward us. However, her prejudice and discrimination against us will not have the same impact as ours against her will (we will discuss why in Chapters 5 and 6).

If we all have our prejudices, can we avoid discriminating? Without conscious effort, this is highly unlikely; because prejudice informs how we view others, it necessarily informs how we act toward others. This action may be subtle—as subtle as avoidance and disinterest. But this lack of interest is not accidental or benign; it is socialized and results in not developing relationships—in this case, with people with disabilities. However, while we can't avoid prejudice, we can work to recognize our prejudices and gain new information and ways of thinking that will inform more just actions.

A key aspect to challenging our prejudices is challenging the social segregation that is built into the culture; the more educated we become about people who are different from us and the more relationships we build with them, the more likely we are to have constructive responses when interacting with other members of their group. This education requires more than knowing one or two individuals in the past and in a limited way, such as having a coworker or neighbor who is blind. If we engage in ongoing study and education, while also building wide-ranging and authentic relationships with people who are blind, we are more likely to have an informed rather than superficial response to the woman in the theater.

In order to get a sense of the power of our deep-structure, below-the-surface socialization in terms of our ideas about and actions toward others, consider this thought experiment. You are going about your day and engaging in conversations with the following people: your friends, your romantic partner, your children, and your supervisor. You might be joking with your friends, sweet-talking with your romantic partner, speaking with formality to your supervisor, and talking irritably with your children. Now add a layer of context: your friends in the classroom before class versus on the weekend at the bar; your romantic partner while walking across campus versus alone in your dorm room; your children when they are celebrating an accomplishment versus struggling with a disappointment; and your supervisor when you are receiving positive feedback on your work versus when you are explaining a series of missed deadlines.

In each of these scenarios you are weighing the value of the social group of the other person in relation to the value of your own social group. These relational values inform how you speak—your tone, the words you use, and even your facial expressions. The navigations we make are the result of our socialization about groups and do not generally occur at the conscious level. You don't need to pause and figure out how to switch gears from your friends to your supervisor; your awareness of the value relations are so internalized that you shift gears effortlessly.

Awareness of ourselves as socialized members of a number of intersecting groups within a particular culture in a particular time and place (social location or positionality) will increase our critical social justice literacy. We need to see the general patterns of our socialization and be aware of ourselves in shifting contexts. In other words, we need to step back and become aware of ourselves shifting gears and examine the assumptions underlying these shifts and the behaviors they set in motion. When interacting cross-culturally with members of less familiar groups, the codes we rely on are more likely to be based on stereotypical assumptions and messages. A key goal of critical social justice literacy is to raise our awareness of these patterned codes. When we are more conscious of them, we are more equipped to change them when they are based upon misinformation.

Returning to the vignette of the search committee that opens this chapter, we can see that this scenario illustrates several dynamics related to the key concepts of prejudice and discrimination. First, every person in the room had prejudices about a male elementary school teacher. These prejudices were both negative (the candidate is less suitable because he is male) and positive (the candidate is more suitable because he is male). While the members of the hiring committee necessarily also held stereotypes, assumptions, and value judgments (prejudices) about female teachers, these prejudices were invisible, unremarkable, and taken for granted because female teachers are the norm in the elementary grades. Only the male teacher stood out to them. In other words, for someone to be seen as *not* suitable for the job based on their social group membership, someone else has to be seen *as* suitable for the job, based on their social group membership.

Second, each person tried to present this prejudice in a way that she believed was more socially acceptable than simply stating it bluntly. This indicates her awareness of the belief that it is wrong to be prejudiced.

And third, when someone pointed out the prejudice, others became defensive and insisted that no one in the group had any prejudice whatsoever. This illustrates the belief that it is possible to *avoid* prejudices altogether. Mary's final statement that they had policies and procedures that would prevent any prejudicial evaluations leads us to the next chapter.

Discussion Questions

1. According to the authors, all people have prejudice and all people act (discriminate) based on their prejudices. Explain this process.
2. What is necessary in order to minimize the effects of our (discriminatory) actions based on our (prejudiced) ideas about social groups?

Extension Activities

1. Generate a list of actions (verbs) and personality attributes (characteristics) that people in various occupations perform and have.

    For example:

Teacher	Environmentalist
Police officer	Dentist
Soldier	Counselor
Librarian	Stay-at-home parent
Scientist	Housekeeper
Farmer	Car wash attendant

    What is the picture in your mind that you have of the person who holds that occupation? What gender, race, and class is that person? Does the person have a visible disability? Is she or he someone who will observe religious/holy days? If so, which ones?

    Then compare your list with others' lists. What are the implications of these pictures in our minds for the ways we might behave toward the person? And what are the implications of the awareness of these pictures in our mind for the ways we might behave toward the person?

2. Get a magazine and choose 10 photos of people. Swap your photos with others (so you are working with a different set). Sort the people in the photos according to each of these questions. Then pick one question, and rank all 10 photographs for that attribute, for example, from "smartest" to "not the smartest."

    1. Who's the smartest?
    2. Who's the wealthiest?
    3. Who's the most religious?
    4. Who reads a lot?
    5. Who's careful with money?
    6. Who's a stay-at-home parent?
    7. Who's the most likely to feel included in society?
    8. Who's the most likely to feel isolated?
    9. Who's the most likely to be put in charge?
    10. Who's the most likely to travel freely anywhere in the world?

    Now interview two people (other than those engaged in the activity with you), asking them to do what you did.

    What patterns do you notice in the responses? How did an awareness of your prejudices (or preconceived ideas) influence the decisions you made in response to each of the questions?

Patterns to Practice Seeing

1. How do people often respond when their prejudices are pointed out?
2. What kind of person is most often depicted in media as prejudiced? How are they depicted? What kinds of people are depicted as free from prejudice?

CHAPTER 5

Oppression and Power

"You can only be oppressed if you let yourself be oppressed."

This chapter introduces the concept of power, which transforms group prejudice into oppression. We explain the difference between concepts such as "race prejudice" (which anyone can hold) and "racism," which only the dominant racial group can impose. The chapter introduces the "ism" terms (e.g., racism, sexism, classism) and explains how these terms allow us to capture the dynamics of prejudice, discrimination, plus structural power at the group level.

Vocabulary to practice using: hegemony; power; oppression; internalized dominance; internalized oppression

---

Let's return to the hiring committee vignette in Chapter 4. Regardless of the final choice the committee makes, it is impossible for the candidate's gender *not* to play a role in the decision. Of course gender would play a role in the decision even if the committee had not openly discussed it, as our imaginary committee did. Gender would also play a role whether or not the committee was aware that it did. We all view people through the socialized lenses of group memberships—theirs and ours. This socialization is *always* at play.

For example, gender socialization influences every aspect of our perceptions and evaluations, both of ourselves and others. Returning to the glasses metaphor introduced in Chapter 3, gender is one of our key lenses. We are *always* wearing these lenses, and in the example of the hiring committee, always reading the resumes through them. We don't notice the lenses—or they are unremarkable— when all of the resumes have matched what we expect to see in terms of gender. Because the open position is one traditionally held by women, we assume that we are reading women's resumes. As soon as we come across a resume that does not match this assumption—one that is not normal for the context—we become conscious of the lens, or conscious of gender. We now begin to interpret the candidate's qualifications based on our gender expectations for male elementary school teachers.

Again, this does not mean that we were not interpreting the other resumes from our expectations for females, but because our expectations matched the resumes of female candidates, we are not aware that we are doing this; our gender lens is invisible to us because seeing the resumes of female applicants for this position is normal. Gender becomes consciously relevant only when we come across a resume that does not match what we expect to see.

If the candidate is not hired due to prejudice against him as a male, this will constitute discrimination but not oppression. However, if he is not hired because of prejudice against him based on an assumption that he is gay, this will constitute oppression. To put it another way, Mary (who is prejudiced against a *gay* candidate) is enacting oppression, but Liz (who is prejudiced against a *male* candidate) is not. Why?

To understand, we must build on the concepts of prejudice and discrimination by adding an understanding of oppression and power. But before we begin this discussion, let's revisit an important element of critical thinking introduced in Chapter 2. Our distinguishing between the results of Mary's prejudice and Liz's prejudice unsettles common ideas about fairness and will likely seem unfair to many people, at least initially. But we remind readers that the way we have been taught to think about these relationships hides their operation in society. In this book we are providing a critical theory framework that is different from the one mainstream socialization provides; a critical theory framework is based on solid scholarship, study, and practice.

What Is Oppression?

To oppress is to hold down—to press—and deny a social group full access and potential in a given society. *Oppression* describes a set of policies, practices, traditions, norms, definitions, and explanations (discourses), which function to systematically exploit one social group to the benefit of another social group. The group that benefits from this exploitation is termed the *dominant* (or agent) group, and the group that is exploited is termed the *minoritized* (or target) group.

Oppression is different from prejudice and discrimination in that

📖 **Oppression:** The prejudice and discrimination of one social group against another, backed by institutional power. Oppression occurs when one group is able to enforce its prejudice and discrimination throughout society because it controls the institutions. Oppression occurs at the group or macro level, and goes well beyond individuals. Sexism, racism, classism, ableism, and heterosexism are specific forms of oppression.

prejudice and discrimination describe dynamics that occur on the individual level and in which all individuals participate. In contrast, oppression occurs when one group's prejudice is *backed by legal authority and historical, social and institutional power.*

Common shorthand within the discipline is:

Prejudice > Discrimination

Prejudice + Power = Oppression

Oppression involves institutional control, ideological domination, and the imposition of the dominant group's culture on the minoritized group. No individual member of the dominant group has to do anything specific to oppress a member of the minoritized group; the prejudice and discrimination is built into the society as a whole and becomes automatic, normalized and taken for granted.

The example of women's suffrage (gaining the right to vote) in the United States and Canada illustrates several distinguishing features of oppression. Women of course played a primary role in the struggle for suffrage; they had to organize and fight to gain the vote. Yet ultimately, the ability to grant women suffrage rested in the hands of men; women could not grant themselves the right to vote because they did not hold *institutional power.* Only men could actually grant suffrage to women because only men held the institutional positions of power necessary to do so. Hence, while both groups could be prejudiced against the other, men's prejudice took on a much more powerful and all-encompassing form.

Because men controlled all of the major institutions—government, media, economics, religion, medicine, education, police, and military—the collective effect of men's prejudice was radically different. Men as a group infused their prejudice into the very fabric of society. Prejudice is often unconscious, so this would happen whether or not men intended to or were aware that they were doing this. Because men made the rules, the rules reflected their prejudices and served their interests. For example, because scientists began with the premise of female inferiority, their research questions and the interpretation of their findings were informed by that assumption (Harding, 1991; Tuana, 1993). Because they were in the position to disseminate their findings, they further reinforced and rationalized their superior positions. All other institutions (also controlled by men) were constructed in ways that normalized male superiority (Tuana, 1989): The clergy preached male superiority from the pulpit and rationalized it through the Bible; doctors used the male body as the reference point for health; psychiatrists based definitions of mental health on male norms for emotions and rationality; and male professors taught men's history, ideas, and concerns.

The term for male centrality is *androcentrism.* Androcentrism is not simply the idea that men are superior to women, but a deeper premise that supports this idea: the definition of males and male experience as the standard for *human*, and females and female experience as a deviation from that norm.

Androcentrism remains invisible in all contexts except when we are specifically referring to women, for example: women's literature, women's movies (or "chick flicks"), women's basketball, and women's rights. "Men"

> **Androcentric:** Male centered. The centering of society on the interests, needs, norms, patterns and perspectives of men.

(as a group) are the invisible reference point that women are measured against, and because women do not fit the norms of men, they appear inferior. In this way, male superiority is rationalized, normalized, disseminated, and reinforced through every social institution. Returning to our suffrage example, because oppression is one group's prejudice plus the power to enforce that prejudice throughout society, even if individual men believed women should have the right to vote, as men they still benefited from women's exclusion. Thus oppression need not be personal, and intentions are irrelevant in terms of having privilege and advantage.

Social Stratification

In Chapter 3 we discussed how individuals belong to various social groups. For the purposes of understanding *socialization*, we described how important it is for individuals to recognize the significance of these social groupings. For the purposes of understanding *oppression*, we must also understand that these groups are given different value in our society. This process of assigning unequal value is called *social stratification*.

All major social group categories (such as gender) are organized into binary, either/or identities (e.g., men/women). These identities depend upon their dynamic relationship with one another, wherein each identity is

> ✓ **PERSPECTIVE CHECK:** Figure 5.1 is not intended to imply that these are the only forms of oppression in society. For example, we have not included oppressions such as adultism, ageism, linguicism, or sizeism, nor have we separated out the way that anti-Semitism is both a form of religious oppression and also ethnic oppression. Our intention is not to deny the reality of these forms of oppression but rather to provide a starting point for those new to the recognition of group membership and social positionality.

defined by its opposite. The category "men" can have no meaning without an understanding of a category called "women." Not only are these groups constructed as opposites, but they are also ranked into a hierarchy. This means that one group (men) is positioned as more valuable than its opposite (women). The group that is positioned as more valuable—the dominant group—will have more access to the

Figure 5.1. Group Identities Across Relations of Power

Minoritized/Target Group	Oppression	Dominant/Agent Group
Peoples of Color	Racism	White
Poor Working Class Middle Class	Classism	Owning Class
Women; Transgender; Genderqueer	Sexism	(cis)Men
Gays; Lesbians; Bisexuals; Two Spirit	Heterosexism	Heterosexuals
Muslims; Buddhists; Jews; Hindus; and other non-Chris- tian groups	Religious Oppression Anti-Semitism	Christians
People with Disabilities	Ableism	Able-bodied
Immigrants (perceived)	Nationalism	Citizens (perceived)
Indigenous Peoples	Colonialism	White Settlers

resources of society. The group that is positioned as less valuable—the minoritized group—will have less access to the resources of society. The terms used to describe these relationships of inequality between dominant and minoritized groups usually ends in "ism." Figure 5.1 illustrates the historical and current relationships between some of these key social groups in Canada and the United States and the term for that specific form of oppression.

As you read down the table, you will probably find yourself in both dominant and minoritized group positions (i.e., falling sometimes on the left side and sometimes on the right side of the oppression column). One is not simply a man, but a cisgender man, a White man, or a man of Color; or a working-class White man, perhaps a working-class gay White man, or a heterosexual Christian able-bodied man of Color—and each of these identity positions intersect in important ways.

In the case of women's suffrage, we can see how these intersecting group identities add more layers of complexity. Women's suffrage is a more complicated story when we add the dimensions of class and race. White women of the upper classes led the initial movement for women's suffrage in both Canada and the United States (Davis, 1981; Devereux, 2005; Newman, 1999). In Canada, racial exclusion in suffrage was not removed until the 1940s and did not extend the right to vote freely to Indigenous peoples until the 1960s. In the United States, Black women did not have full access to the right to vote until the Voting Rights Act of 1965. So

Figure 5.2. Dolores Huerta (b. 1930)

Huerta is a pioneering labor and civil rights leader, and the cofounder (with Cesar Chávez) of the United Farmworkers of America. In 1955 she became involved with a grassroots organization (the Community Service Organization) that was fighting police brutality in the community and pushing for improved public services. It was there at CSO that she met Cesar Chávez. Together they became involved in supporting farm workers, and she played a central role as cofounder, organizer, and leader for the movement. She led some of the most important peaceful demonstrations and public boycotts, spoke out against the harmful effects of pesticides, organized field strikes, and lobbied for changes to policies to support workers. All of her efforts helped win recognition for farm workers' rights. She was also significantly involved in the feminist movement, and challenged gender discrimination within the farm workers movement.

Today, the Dolores Huerta Foundation pursues its mandate to motivate and organize sustainable communities in order to attain social justice.

Note. Photo available at https://feminismandreligion.com/2012/11/02/dolores-huerta-si-se-puede/

while the women we commonly refer to as suffragists were oppressed *as women*, they were privileged as *White* women: Their race was made neutral and natural to the exclusion and marginalization of women of Color, as they were held up as representing *all* women. For example, one of the key issues of suffragists was entry into the workforce. But of course women of Color had long been working outside the home. Their interests may have been better served by calls for economic justice. The life and work of Dolores Huerta (Figure 5.2) embodies the concept of intersectionality.

Understanding the "isms"

In order to understand how oppression works and why it is different from discrimination, we must understand that oppression involves pervasive, historical, and political relationships of unequal power among social groups. It is more than an individual, situational, or momentary interaction. Scholars capture this large-scale, historical, political, and pervasive relationship through the "ism" words, such as: racism, sexism, heterosexism, classism, ableism. In the study of social stratification, when scholars use the "ism" words, we are not referring primarily to individual acts of discrimination, which all people can commit. Rather, we are referring to specific forms of oppression.

The "ism" words give us the language to discuss these specific forms of oppression and include in the discussion the reality of unequal social and institutional power between dominant and minoritized groups. In this way, we avoid denying power dynamics by reducing oppression to individual acts of discrimination and claiming that these acts are comparable, regardless of who commits them. From this perspective, "reverse racism" or "reverse sexism" are mis-

✋ **STOP:** Discrimination and the "isms" (e.g., sexism and racism) are not the same thing. All people have prejudice and discriminate, but only the dominant group has the social, historical, and institutional power to back their prejudice and infuse it throughout the entire society. Thus these terms cannot be used interchangeably.

nomers and do not exist because racism and sexism (or any form of oppression) refer to power relations that are historic, embedded, and pervasive—they are not fluid and do not flip back and forth; the same groups who have historically held institutional power in the United States and Canada continue to do so.

For example, despite suffrage and women's numerical majority, in 2017 women in the United States are only 19% of the House and Senate seats, 33% of the Supreme Court, 18% of mayors, 8% of governors and have never held the highest office, the presidency. In Canada, women constitute 52% of the population, and in 2015 Canada's new Prime Minister Justin Trudeau gained wide praise for appointing a 50/50 gender-balanced Cabinet. Despite this important move, women are still under-elected to federal posts, making up only 26% of members of parliament (MPs) in the House of Commons. Thus, many of the 24 standing House committees (such as Environment, Health, Industry Science and Technology, National Defence, Public Safety, Veterans Affairs) are without equal (even marginal) female MP representation simply because there aren't enough elected women MPs to go around. These committees play important roles in the evaluation of legislation that's before the House, and these committees make decisions that impact women's lives (Taber, 2016; Equal Voice, 2014; Parliament of Canada, 2017). The only one of the 24 standing House committees with a female majority is the Status of Women committee (Taber, 2016). In 2015, across Canada women represented 28% of city councillors, and 18% of mayors (Federation of Canadian Municipalities, 2015).

The United Nations has concluded that a critical mass of at least 30% of women is needed before government policies begin to reflect women's priorities and shift governmental management style and organizational culture (Tarr-Whelan, 2009). In 2017 Canada and the United States were 62nd and 104th respectively in an international ranking of women's representation in 193 federal parliaments (dropping from their positions as 50th and 72nd respectively in 2010) (Inter-Parliamentary Union, 2017). In fact, the number one country in terms of women holding office is Rwanda (with women holding 61% of seats); Sweden, Spain,

Argentina, Philippines, Algeria, and Afghanistan all rank higher than Canada or the United States. Our North American neighbor Mexico outranks both countries by far with its position at #8 on the list, between Sweden and Finland, with 43% of federal seats held by Mexican women. While numbers do matter, oppression isn't simply the result of a numerical majority (e.g., women are the majority of the world, as are poor and working class people, yet they don't hold institutional power). Oppression is a multidimensional imbalance of social, political, and institutional power that builds over time and then becomes normal and acceptable to most people in the society. There are four key elements of oppression.

Oppression is historical. The underrepresentation of women in government is not simply the result of the last federal election in a given country. Women's exclusion from government in the United States and Canada well into the 21st century illustrates their long-term overall exclusion as citizens, guaranteeing that they would have no role in deciding how society would be organized or governed. The cumulative effect of this exclusion cannot be corrected in a single election nor within one generation. The institution of government itself—its processes and practices—have been established by men; if tomorrow only women were appointed to government, they could not govern outside the rules that men had established. To reshape the institution and its norms and practices would take generations of effort (and be solidly resisted all along the way). (White) women received the right to vote in the early 20th century in Canada and the United States but injustice between men and women did not end the day suffrage was granted. In fact, victories enacted through law, while important, often work to slow progress because they mislead people into believing that a single change has solved the issue. For example, in 2013 key protections in the U.S. Voting Rights Act were struck down, illustrating the tenuous nature of civil rights advancements in the face of deeply embedded systems of oppression.

Oppression is ideological. Ideology, as the dominant ideas of a society, plays a powerful role in the perpetuation of oppression. Ideology is disseminated throughout all the institutions of society and rationalizes social inequality. Thus oppression cannot be remedied through law alone. Oppression is embedded within individual consciousness through socialization and rationalized as normal; once people are socialized into their place in the hierarchy, injustice

> 📖 **Ideology:** The big, shared ideas of a society that are reinforced throughout all of the institutions and thus are very hard to avoid believing. These ideas include the stories, myths, representations, explanations, definitions, and rationalizations that are used to justify inequality in the society. Individualism and Meritocracy are examples of ideology.

is assured. Oppressive beliefs and misinformation are internalized by both the dominant and the minoritized groups, guaranteeing that overall each group will play its assigned role in relation to the other, and that these roles will be justified as natural. When we believe the social hierarchy is natural, it is difficult to see our positions within it as unequal at all. Not all women were invested in gaining suffrage or saw themselves as oppressed without it. The suffrage movement had to convince other women, as well as men, that it was an issue of rights (although only men had the institutional power to actually grant suffrage to women).

Oppression is institutional. Government is only one of many institutions that men dominate. Men also dominate all other major institutions of society (military, medicine, media, criminal justice, policing, finance, industry, higher education, religion, and science). These institutions are interconnected and function together to uphold male dominance across the whole of society. Using our suffrage example, while male government officials denied women the right to vote, all the other institutions of society were also dominated by men and worked simultaneously with government to block suffrage. Male doctors claimed that women did not have the physical capacity to engage in politics, male psychiatrists claimed that women did not have the capacity for rational thought necessary for suffrage, male clergy preached that a woman's place was in the home and ordained by God *him*self—a male God who only spoke to men and whom only men could speak for, male journalists published editorials critiquing suffrage, male police officers shut down demonstrations and made arrests, and male judges determined punishments (Bem, 2004; Green, 1997). Women were not in a position to use any institutions in the service of suffrage and could only rely on a few sympathetic men who could present their case for them or allow them limited opportunities to present it for themselves.

Oppression is cultural. Oppression is embedded in all dimensions of culture. Referring to the iceberg diagram from Chapter 3, consider how the norms of what constitutes deep culture (the unspoken and unconscious rules) are gendered and manifest in government processes and policies. These norms privilege men. Women who do enter politics are most successful when they are able to demonstrate their ability to fit into the androcentric (male-centered) culture. Demonstrating their fluency with the norms of androcentric culture demands that women conform with the deep structure rules of masculine culture (e.g., don't show emotions, show only "appropriate" levels of care for family responsibilities, don't name sexism). While demonstrating this fluency, women simultaneously enact the deep structure rules of "their own" culture. Thus minoritized group members carry the extra burden of duality. W. E. B. Du Bois (1903/1989), speaking about race, coined the term "double consciousness" to capture this burden of having to perform the dominant culture's norms as well as your own. Because none of these conditions

of oppression apply to men, there is
no oppression against men *as men*
and therefore no "reverse" sexism
(although there *is* oppression against
men where they also inhabit oppressed positions, e.g., *working class*
White men or *gay Asian* men or *elderly Sikh* men).

Men may be a numerical minority in a given context and experience
short-term and contextual discrimi-

STOP: There is no such thing as
reverse racism or reverse sexism (or
the reverse of any form of oppression). While women can be just as
prejudiced as men, women cannot
be "just as sexist as men" because
they do not hold political, economic,
and institutional power.

---

nation. For example, men in elementary education are the minority in number
and may experience feelings of isolation and disconnection from cultural norms
in elementary school, and they may experience discrimination and exclusion from
the women with whom they work. However, this is not oppression, because, while
these feelings and experiences may be painful, they are individual, temporary, and
situational, and do not have the necessary elements to constitute oppression. The
historical, ideological, institutional, and cultural dimensions of schooling are still
androcentric and will reward and advance men over women. Men are most often
in positions of authority over women, advance faster than women—even in female
dominated fields—and are consistently paid more for the same work across multiple sectors (Budig, 2002; McMurry, 2011; Bishu & Alkadry, 2017).

Precisely because the care of children is associated with women, early childhood education is naturally seen to be the responsibility of women, perceived as
little more than advanced babysitting with very low status. As children grow older,
more male teachers and masculine approaches to schooling appear. For example,
values associated with primary education such as play, community, cooperation,
and sharing virtually disappear in the higher grades, as values such as rationality,
independence, and competition take over. As well, the status of teaching increases
in the higher grades because more men are present, and subject areas increase in
status when they are associated with men: mathematics, science, and philosophy
over literature, drama, and art.

Marilyn Frye (1983) illustrates the interlocking forces of oppression through
the metaphor of a birdcage. If you come up close and press your face against the
bars of a birdcage, you will have a myopic view of the bird inside; your perception of the bars will be limited. If you turn to look closely at just one wire in the
cage, you cannot see the other wires. If your conception of what is before you is
determined by this limited view, you could look at that one wire and be unable to
see why the bird could not escape by simply flying around the wire. Even if you
slowly moved around the cage and closely inspected each wire, one at a time, you
still could not see why the bird would have trouble going past any particular wire
and flying away. But if instead of the close-up view, you step back and take a wider

view, you begin to see how the wires come together in an interlocking pattern, a pattern that works to hold the bird in place. It now becomes clear that the bird is surrounded by a network of systematically related barriers. In isolation, none of these barriers would be that difficult for the bird to get around, but because of their connections to one another, they are as confining as solid walls.

It is now possible to grasp one of the reasons why oppression can be hard to recognize: We have been socialized into a limited view, focusing on single situations, exceptions, and anecdotal evidence, rather than on broader, interlocking patterns. Although there are always exceptions, the patterns are consistent and well documented; the experience of oppressed people is that their lives are confined and shaped by forces and barriers that are not accidental, occasional, or avoidable, but are systematically related to each other in such a way as to restrict and penalize their movement. In this way, oppression gives everyone a distorted view of how society works.

Dominant groups have the most narrow or limited view of society because they do not have to understand the experiences of the minoritized group in order to survive; because they control the institutions, they have the means to legitimize their view ("I worked hard for what I have, why can't they?"). Minoritized groups often have the widest view of society, in that they must understand both their own and the dominant group's perspective—develop a double-consciousness—to succeed. But because they are in the margins, the view of minoritized groups is seen as the least legitimate in society, dismissed via phrases such as "they just have a chip on their shoulder, . . . complain too much, or . . . want special rights." In order to understand the power of these phrases we must understand language as political.

Language is not a neutral transmitter of a universal, objective, or fixed reality. Rather, language is the way we *construct* reality, the framework we use to give meaning to our experiences and perceptions within a given society. Language is also cultural, making it dependent on the historical and social moment in which it is used (e.g., colorblindness as a means to end racism is a discourse that would not have made sense before the civil rights movement). Furthermore, language is not just words; it includes all of the ways we communicate with others. Discourses include not only what we say, but also what we *don't* say (how we learn what lies under the surface of the iceberg). The scholarly term for language in all of its dimensions is *discourse*.

Take the word "tree," a seemingly neutral term. Yet notice that how we *see* the tree is connected to our frame of reference. A tree that looks big to someone who grew up on the East Coast might not look big to someone who grew up on the West Coast. A logger might see employment, an environmentalist might see a limited resource, and a member of the Coast Salish nation might see a sacred symbol of life. Each of these "ways of seeing" is a discourse and connects to other discourses (consider the politics between the logger and the environmentalist, and the environmentalist and the Coast Salish member). These politics are rooted in the meaning the tree has for each group, and the investments that result from those meanings.

Discourses, because they shape how we think about and relate to one another, shape relations of power. For example, the discourses of the dominant group about the minoritized group will always represent the dominant group's interests and thereby reinforce their meaning-making framework. Dominant discourses socialize us into seeing our positions in the hierarchy as natural. Scholars use the terms *internalized dominance* and *internalized oppression* to refer to this acceptance of our socialization (Adams, Bell, Goodman, & Joshi, 2016; Freire, 1970; Nieto, Boyer, Goodwin, Johnson, Collier Smith, & Hopkins, 2010; Tappan, 2006).

> **Discourse:** The academic term for meaning that is communicated through language, in all of its forms. Discourses include myths, narratives, explanations, words, concepts, and ideology. Discourses are not universally shared among humans; they represent a particular cultural worldview and are shared among members of a given culture. Discourse is different from ideology because it refers to all of the ways in which we communicate ideology, including verbal and nonverbal aspects of communication, symbols, and representations.

Internalized Dominance

Internalized dominance refers to internalizing and acting out (often unintentionally) the constant messages circulating in the culture that you and your group are superior to the minoritized group and thus entitled to your higher position.

Examples include:

- Rationalizing privilege as natural ("It's just human nature—someone has to be on top.")
- Rationalizing privilege as earned ("I worked hard to get where I am.")
- Perceiving you and your group as the most qualified for and entitled to the best jobs ("She only got the position over me because she's Black.")
- Living one's life segregated from the minoritized group yet feeling no loss or desire for connections with them (e.g., patterns of White flight rationalized as "I want my kids to grow up in a good neighborhood where they can play outside with their friends.")
- Lacking an interest in the perspectives of the minoritized group except in limited and controlled doses (e.g., during ethnic authors week, or holidays such as Chinese New Year) or when it appears to benefit the dominant group ("I want my child to experience diversity.")

- Feeling qualified to debate or explain away the experiences of minoritized groups ("I think you are taking this too personally, I don't think that's what he meant.")

Internalized dominance manifests in our daily actions through what psychologist Derald Wing Sue (2010) termed *microaggressions*. By definition, microaggressions are everyday slights, insults, and insensitivities from dominant group members to minoritized members. These messages are expressed through statements

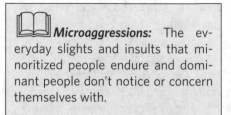
Microaggressions: The everyday slights and insults that minoritized people endure and dominant people don't notice or concern themselves with.

and actions that remind the minoritized person of their lesser status. Examples of microaggressions are asking a multiracial person, "What are you?", telling an older woman, "I bet you were beautiful when you were young," and telling a person of Color, "I don't see you as Black."

Internalized Oppression

Internalized oppression refers to internalizing and acting out (often unintentionally) the constant messages that you and your group are inferior to the dominant group and thus deserving of your lower position.

Examples include:

- Believing that dominant group members are more qualified for and deserving of their positions
- Seeking the approval of and spending most of your time with members of the dominant group
- Behaving in ways that please the dominant group and do not challenge the legitimacy of its position
- Silently enduring microaggressions from the dominant group in order to avoid penalty
- Having low expectations for yourself and others associated with your group
- Believing that your struggles with social institutions (such as education, employment, health care) are the result of your (or your group's) inadequacy, rather than the result of unequally distributed resources between dominant and minoritized groups
- Harshly criticizing members of your group who do not assimilate to dominant norms ("Pull up your pants!" "Speak English!")

Internalized dominance and oppression create observable social group patterns in members of dominant and minoritized groups. While there will always be exceptions, these patterns are well documented, recognizable, and predictable (Adair & Howell, 2007). Figure 5.3 illustrates common characteristics of members of each group as a result of their group's overall position in society. It illustrates the common patterns for each side of the social hierarchy, as well as how they fit perfectly together to hold each group in place.

Hegemony, Ideology, and Power

Hegemony refers to the control of the ideology of a society. The dominant group maintains power by imposing their ideology on everyone. Recall that ideology refers to the stories, myths, explanations, definitions, and rationalizations that are used to justify inequality between the dominant and the minoritized groups. The key element of hegemony is that it enables domination to occur with the consent of the minoritized group—rather than by force. If people believe that they deserve their unequal positions—that these positions are fair and natural—no force is necessary. In other words, the minoritized group accepts their lower position in society because they come to accept the rationalizations for it. Hegemony, then, includes the ability to define and impose self-discipline on others in ways that serve dominant group interests.

> 📖 **Hegemony:** The imposition of dominant group ideology onto everyone in society. Hegemony makes it difficult to escape or to resist "believing in" this dominant ideology, thus social control is achieved through conditioning rather than physical force or intimidation.

As explained earlier, in order to oppress, a group must hold institutional power in society. In this way, the group is in the position to impose their worldview on others and control the ideas (ideologies), political rules (the technical mechanisms), and social rules for communication (discourses) that we are all taught (socialized) to see as normal, natural, and required for a functioning society. This domination is historical (long-term) and normalized.

Power in the context of understanding social justice refers to the ideological, technical, and discursive elements by which those in authority impose their ideas and interests on everyone. Michel Foucault's (1977/1995) analysis of a 19th-century prison structure may be helpful for understanding the concept of power. The panopticon shown in Figure 5.4 is a design unveiled in 1843 in which the cells of a prison were located around the circumference of a circle with a tower in the center and a guard located in the tower. The key to the panopticon design is the funneling of light in ways that create strategic darkness and blindness. Much

Figure 5.3. Patterns of Internalized Dominance and Internalized Oppression

an individual from the DOMINANT GROUP	an individual from the MINORITIZED GROUP
Defines rules, judges what is appropriate, patronizes	Feels inappropriate, awkward, doesn't trust perception, looks to expert for definition
Is seen as, and feels, capable of making constructive changes	Is seen as, and feels, disruptive
Assumes responsibility for keeping system on course; acts without checking in with others	Blames self for not having capacity to change situation
Self-image of superiority, competence, in control, entitled, correct	Self-image of inferiority, incompetent, being controlled, not entitled, low self-esteem
Presumptuous, does not listen, interrupts, raises voice, bullies, threatens violence, becomes violent	Finds it difficult to speak up, timid, tries to please Holds back anger, resentment, and rage
Seeks to stand out as special	Feels secure staying in the background, feels vulnerable when singled out
Assumes anything is possible, can do whatever one wants, assumes everyone else can too	Feels confined by circumstances, limits aspirations, sees current situations in terms of past limits
Initiates, manages, plans, projects	Lacks initiative, responds, deals, copes, survives
Sees problems and situations in personal terms	Sees problems in social context, results of system
Sees experiences and feelings as unique, feels disconnected, often needs to verbalize feelings	Sees experiences and feelings as collectively understood and shared, no point in talking about them
Sees solutions to problems as promoting better feelings	Sees solutions to problems in actions that change conditions
Thinks own view of reality is the only one, obvious to all, assumes everyone agrees with this view; disagreements are result of lack of information, misunderstandings, and/or personalities	Always aware of at least two views of reality, their own and that of the dominant group
Views self as logical, rational; sees others as too emotional, out of control	Often thinks own feelings are inappropriate, a sign of inadequacy
Believes certain kinds of work below their dignity	Believes certain kinds of work beyond their ability
Does not believe or trust ability of others to provide leadership	Does not believe has capacity for leading
Unaware of hypocrisy, contradictions	Sees contradictions, irony, hypocrisy
Fears losing control, public embarrassment	Laughs at self and others; sees humor as way of dealing with hypocrisy
Regards own culture as civilized, regards others' as underdeveloped, disadvantaged; turns to other culture to enrich humanity while invalidating them by calling them exotic	Feels own culture devalued; uses cultural forms to influence situation; humor, music, poetry, etc. to celebrate collective experience and community; sees these as being stolen

Source: Adapted from Adair & Howell (2007), with permission

Figure 5.4. The Panopticon

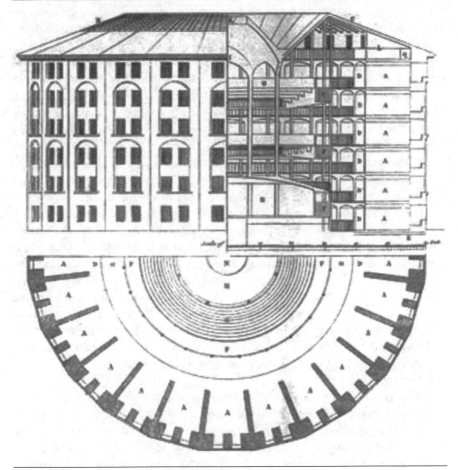

Source: www.moyak.com/papers/Panopticon.jpg

like the effects of being onstage with the lights shining in your eyes, the prisoners in the cells could not see the tower guard watching them. The prisoners were constantly visible to the central tower while they themselves were blinded—never knowing when they were being watched. Thus the guard could monitor the prisoners without the prisoners knowing when, or even *if*, they were being observed.

This model produced a type of *self*-policing, a self-imposed mechanism for control and supervision. In other words, the prisoner becomes fearful of the threat of the ever-watching eye of authority. Not knowing when that eye will be turned on him, he begins to monitor himself in order to avoid penalty. This structure of surveillance produces a conforming and passive prisoner.

Foucault argued that the panopticon was a metaphor for the ways in which power is transmitted, normalized, and internalized through social institutions such as prisons, military, hospitals, and schools; a metaphor for how these institutions socialize us into compliance with norms that serve controlling group interests. Those who have the motivation, authority, and resources to design, institute, and enforce the panopticon are those who hold institutional power in a society. These power relations are in place well before our birth, and we might think of ourselves as born into a cell that already exists and is waiting for us.

However, Foucault did not see these relations as fixed and unchangeable but rather as constantly reproduced and negotiated in society. This means that we have the ability to challenge power, but first we must see and understand how power works.

Consider the example of schools. Schools train students to conform to a set of self-disciplining measures by structuring students' time and handing out rewards and punishments such as grades, honors, tracked placements, detentions, and expulsions. While this seems normal to us, the organization of the school is not neutral. Through its structures, the school regiments and monitors all activities such as what will be studied; when, how, and for how long it will be studied; how proficiency will be demonstrated; how intelligence will be defined and measured; when (and often what) students will eat; when they will rest; when they will play; when they may use the bathroom; and when they will go home. The structures that regulate schools are also regimented and monitored. The principal oversees the activities within the school, while the school trustees or district officials monitor and regulate the schools in the district, and the relevant government bodies (state, provincial, federal, ministry of education) monitor and regulate the institution of schooling at large.

The school also mandates the continuation of this regimen beyond its walls and into the home through homework, expectations for parent involvement, parent-teacher conferences, and parent participation in fieldtrips and other activities. Punishments are also given out in this domain. These punishments include the evaluation and assessment of parents as either "good" or "bad" based on their participation in these activities. These evaluations have consequences for students and their families. These consequences determine the degree to which families are included or marginalized within the system and the extent to which children can remain connected to their families and still succeed in conforming to the norms and requirements of the school. If we expand our discussion of school to include institutions of higher education such as universities, we can see how federal grant agencies and the research they choose to fund can also be seen as structuring education.

Another key way that power circulates is through the mechanisms of *knowledge* and how knowledge is constructed, validated, and taught. There are at least two forms of knowledge that are important for understanding how power circulates in schools. The first is our everyday understanding about how schools work, or knowledge *about* school. This form of knowledge is important because it is a form of taken-for-granted *cultural capital* (social resources other than money) that not all families possess equally. For example, immigrant families, Indigenous families, non-native English speakers, and parents who did not complete school often do not have enough understanding about how schools work to help their children navigate the system, or to challenge it when it has treated their children unfairly. When they do challenge the school, their voices do not carry as much weight.

However, knowledge about how the structure works is only part of the story. The other important kind of knowledge is knowledge *within* school. This kind of knowledge includes how students should behave and conform; how learning is defined, tested, and measured; what topics are worthy of study and from whose perspective; what topics and perspectives will be rendered nonexistent; and how the creation and justification of "tracks" label and separate students into categories such as "advanced" and "special." These categories dictate the kind of knowledge that students will have access to, which in turn translates into the kinds of opportunities they will have in later life. This knowledge also shapes their sense of place in society, for example, as either those who *manage* others or those who are *managed by* others. Thus knowledge within the school benefits some students at the expense of others, while being presented as neutral, logical, and normal.

To illustrate that school knowledge is not neutral, revisit the study by Jean Anyon that was described in Chapter 2 (Anyon, 1981). Anyon asked children from three different kinds of schools—working-class, middle-class and affluent-professional—to define knowledge. Their responses, summarized in Figure 2.1, reveal the differences in what kind of education the children receive, and how this education will direct their future and the kinds of work—or place in society—for which they are being prepared. The structures in place between groups of people limit mobility in very significant ways. While there is always the possibility of an individual working-class child moving beyond the limited education she's been given, clearly this will take a great deal of effort. Conversely, because this system benefits the affluent child, she will be less invested in removing these barriers for others. In fact, she (and those who advocate for her) will most often resist removing these barriers.

Returning to the hiring committee in the beginning of Chapter 4, we may now understand why Mary (who is prejudiced against a gay candidate) is demonstrating oppression but Liz (who is prejudiced against a male candidate) is not. Mary's discrimination against gay people is backed by historical, ideological, cultural, and institutional power in all major institutions in society. Indeed, in the United States there is no federal protection against discriminating against a gay candidate. In other words, this hiring committee could openly state that they are not hiring this candidate because he is gay. In Canada, while federal protections do exist, they cannot be taken for granted because they are regularly challenged and must continually and actively be defended.

On the other hand, Liz's discrimination against men is not backed by historical, ideological, cultural, or institutional power. Indeed, if the man gets hired, he will be more likely to rise to a position of leadership over the very women who hired him. Why, we might ask, are men who enter women's fields more likely to rise to positions of leadership in the organization, while women who enter male-dominated fields are unlikely to rise to positions of leadership in the organization? To understand this we must understand internalized dominance and internal-

> ✋ **STOP:** Remember that both groups in a social relationship receive the same messages about their positions; the minoritized group is also taught to see the dominant group as more deserving of or suitable for leadership.

ized oppression. The forces of socialization are powerful. Once the message of our superiority or inferiority is internalized, very little outside force is needed in order to ensure that we will play our social roles. Of course the messages about where our group belongs continue to circulate in the culture all around us and reinforce what we have internalized, but the fundamental acceptance is complete by an early age. Men will tend to see themselves in positions of leadership and expect to be in these positions, and women will support this tendency because they will also tend to see and expect men to be in these positions.

Women will also tend to be more comfortable with men in positions of leadership (recall the common patterns from Figure 5.3). For example, as instructors, we often see these dynamics play out in class. Even when there is one male in a group of women for a small-group discussion, he will invariably be the spokesperson for the group when it comes time to report out. When this pattern is pointed out, the women often say, "But we wanted him to be our spokesperson" or "We asked him to be our spokesperson." We would argue that this perfectly illustrates the power of internalization. Wanting a man to speak for you as a woman does not negate the impact of this pattern; it demonstrates both prescribed roles. Most often, the male as spokesperson happens automatically; in other words, there is no discussion of who will actually report out, it is just assumed that it will be the male. The women see themselves as choosing this, even in cases where no explicit decision was made—because at a very deep level, they *are* choosing the men to lead. This is how both groups play their roles in keeping oppression in place. That we chose members of the dominant group to lead does not negate that this choice is informed by the dynamics of oppression. Rather, the predictability of this choice confirms the dynamics of internalized oppression and internalized dominance. These dynamics play a powerful role in moving men up in female-dominated fields, while limiting women's movement up in male-dominated fields.

We must also remember that we are never solely one group; we occupy multiple and intersecting group identities. The disadvantages of one membership do not cancel out the advantages of another. In other words, if our candidate is in fact a gay man, the disadvantages of being gay would not cancel out the advantages of being male. A key project of critical social justice is to help untangle the complex ways these locations work together to hold oppression in place.

Discussion Questions

1. The authors argued that Mary (who was prejudiced against a presumed gay candidate) was enacting oppression, but Liz (who was prejudiced against a male candidate) was not. Review the reasons for this distinction. Why was Mary enacting oppression but Liz not?
2. In your own words, explain the authors' argument that there is no such thing as a reverse form of oppression (i.e., no "reverse racism" and no "reverse sexism").
3. How does the example of women's suffrage illustrate the difference between discrimination and oppression?

Extension Activities

1. a. Working with a partner with whom you share a dominant group identity, draw on experiences from your own life in order to generate examples of how internalized dominance (as a member of the group identity you share) manifests. Begin by thinking about privileges that you take for granted every day, and how those privileges may be affecting minoritized group members in relation to you.
    b. Next, working with a partner with whom you share a minoritized group identity, generate a list of examples of how internalized oppression manifests in your life. Draw on your lived experiences to generate specific examples of internalized oppression. (If you have no minoritized identity, choose a different dominant identity and repeat 1a.)
    c. As a whole group, discuss which task was easier to do. What does this reveal about how internalized oppression and internalized dominance work?
2. Research the life of Dolores Huerta (see Figure 5.2). Write an essay that describes how her life and work exemplify the intersection of identities, including race, class, and gender.

Patterns to Practice Seeing:

1. When are people's group identities most often named (e.g., race, gender, sexuality, ability)? Consider movie directors, teachers, movie stars, writers, etc. Which group identities are most likely to be named, and which are not?
2. Pay attention to participation patterns in class discussions and other group settings. Which group members tend to speak first and most often? How do these patterns change depending on the topic under discussion?

CHAPTER 6

Understanding Privilege Through Ableism

"No one's handed me anything. I've worked hard for what I have."

This chapter explains the privileges automatically received by being a member of the dominant group. From a critical social justice perspective, privilege is defined as systemically conferred dominance and the institutional processes by which the beliefs and values of the dominant group are "made normal" and universal. While in some cases, the privileged group is also the numerical majority, the key criterion is social and institutional power. This chapter also extends the discussion of related concepts such as "internalized oppression" and "internalized dominance," and offers examples of how these dynamics work to hold existing relations of power in place.

Vocabulary to practice using: internalized dominance; internalized oppression

A female prime minister was strategizing with her all-male cabinet about how to address a string of recent sexual assaults on women throughout the city. Someone suggested a 9:00 p.m. curfew, which the cabinet thought was a good idea. The prime minister also nodded her head in agreement, "Yes. No men will be allowed out after 9:00 p.m." Her cabinet was shocked and said that was unfair, it was women who should stay in after 9:00 in order to ensure their safety. They only had the best interest of women in mind, they insisted, and the curfew was for their own good. The prime minister replied, "It is men who are committing these assaults, not women. Why should women's movements be restricted?"

Imagine from a woman's perspective what it would be like to walk freely throughout a city at night with no fear of sexual assault from men. But also notice whose movements are assumed to need restricting and who would be blamed for being in the wrong place at the wrong time were an assault to occur. In Chapter 5 we discussed the relationship between dominant and minoritized groups. In this chapter, we examine a key aspect of that relationship for the dominant group: privilege.

What Is Privilege?

The academic definition of *privilege* used in critical social justice may be different from how our readers know the word in everyday usage. Consider by way of analogy how most people use the word *average* to mean ordinary. In contrast, mathematicians would use the term average to specifically describe the mean, median, or mode of a series of numbers. In mathematical usage the average is the sum of all the numbers divided by the total number of items (the mean), the number in the middle when a series of numbers is ranked lowest to highest (median), or the number that occurs the most frequently in a series (mode). As you can see, while the lay usage ("ordinary") may be loosely related, the mathematical usage has much greater specificity.

Similarly, the lay usage of *privilege* means to be *lucky,* to have *fortunate* opportunity and to benefit from this luck and opportunity. These definitions suggest that privilege is a positive outcome of happenstance. However, when academics use the term in describing how society works, they refer to the rights, advantages, and protections enjoyed by some at the expense of and beyond the rights, advantages, and protections available to others (Kimmel & Ferber, 2016; Johnson, 2006). In this context, privilege is not the product of fortune, luck, or happenstance, but the outcome of advantages some have and others do not. Because dominant groups occupy the positions of power, their members receive social and institutional advantages; thus one automatically receives privilege by being a member of a dominant group (e.g., cis-men, Whites, heterosexuals, the able-bodied, Christians, upper classes).

In Chapter 3 we described our immersion into our cultural socialization as similar to a fish immersed in water. While the fish is moving through the water, the water is also moving around the fish. Even when the fish is simply floating without expending effort, currents still affect its movement. When you are swimming in open water, your outcome (where you end up and how long it takes you to get there) is not determined solely by the effort you expend, but in larger part by the particular current you are in.

If the water is moving *against* you rather than with you, the amount of effort it takes to move forward is enormous. Yet this effort results in only the smallest increments of advancement. On the other hand, if the current is *with* you, swimming is almost effortless. With minimal effort, you can quickly travel a great distance and are seldom aware of the current at all (we are much more likely to be aware of the current when we have to swim against it). Privilege is like having this powerful current propelling you forward throughout your life.

While this metaphor may be useful for understanding privilege, we do not want to reinforce the idea of privilege as natural or an outcome of luck and happenstance; privilege is neither. Privilege is socially constructed to benefit members of the dominant group. Further, structures of privilege are not just artifacts of a racist, sexist, or classist past; privilege is an ongoing dynamic that is continually reproduced, negotiated, and enacted. An example is *The Bell Curve* (Herrnstein & Murray), a bestselling book published in 1994 that argued that there were genetic differences in intelligence among racial groups, a perspective that is in line with the scientific racism that legitimized the enslavement, extermination, genocide, and colonization of racialized groups around the world. Geneticists have debunked this "fact," yet books such as these continue to be published and widely read (Gould, 1981/1996; Nisbett, 1998).

Another more recent example is the research into the "causes" of homosexuality and how that research is used to justify the denial of privileges and opportunities to same-sex partners and gay and lesbian people. Still another is the immensely popular writing of Ruby Payne (2005), who promotes the idea of a "culture of poverty." She argues that those who are at the bottom of society are there because they are culturally deficient—that is, they lack the attitudes or work ethic necessary to "get ahead" in society. Perspectives such as these are sometimes referred to as *cultural deficit theory.*

In this chapter we want to unravel two interrelated dynamics that are central to understanding social and institutional privilege: the *external and structural* dimensions and the *internal and attitudinal* dimensions. We will use the example of ableism to examine how these dimensions of privilege play out.

> 📖 **Cultural Deficit Theory:** The explanation that minoritized groups do not achieve in society because they lack the appropriate cultural values (e.g., "They just don't value education") or because their culture is deficient in some other way.

External and Structural Dimensions of Privilege

Are you left-handed? If so, you may notice how left-handed people are marginalized by social norms: the desks in classrooms, the shape of scissors, the locations of buttons on carry-on handles, a camera's shutter release button, and even the standard way one is taught to strum a guitar or swing a hockey stick. It is possible that you may not have noticed these things, or perhaps they don't seem significant to you, even if you are left-handed. It may even be the case that left-handed people prefer to use these "normal" tools, having become used to doing things "backwards." And perhaps there are some right-handed folks who, just for fun, like to use lefty tools to see how it feels for a while. Yet it is still the case that only right-handed people have automatic *structural privilege* (i.e. unearned advantages)—because they were born right-handed in a social world that was designed for people like them.

Moving on from left-handedness to consider a case with higher stakes, think about how ableism operates (*ableism:* the oppression of peoples with disabilities).

Those of us whose bodies fit the fluid social category called "normal" can go through entire days, weeks, and months never having to consider (for example the physical) barriers that limit access to our environment. How we will get to a certain event, whether we can enter a building, or how we will be seated at the coffee shop, can all be taken for granted. Even if a building is considered accessible, there is often only a single entrance providing access to a limited part of the space, such as the top of a large lecture hall. Such limits segregate people who use wheelchairs or other tools for mobility. They would likely have the worst view and difficulty hearing the questions posed to the speaker, and would have difficulty being heard or seen were they to pose questions. Those of us who are able-bodied can take access for granted because the social and physical environment was set up to accommodate our bodies, giving us social privilege and enabling us to not have to think about life without such "rights."

"But," you may wonder, "aren't there more people *without* disabilities than people *with* disabilities? Shouldn't social institutions accommodate the majority?" While in some cases the privileged group is also the numerical majority, that is not the key criterion. For example, the following dominant groups do not constitute a numerical majority: Men, the upper classes, and White South Africans under apartheid. The key criterion is institutional power; a focus on numbers hides this reality.

As the example of ableism illustrates, privilege has the following external and structural dimensions:

- The integration of dominant group norms into the structures of society
- The construction of what's normal and not-normal by the dominant group
- The invisibility of privilege for the dominant group

The integration of group-based norms into the structures of society. As we explained in Chapter 5, oppression is a deeply embedded system that operates on multiple levels at all times. The result of this system is consistent unearned privileges and advantages for the dominant group, regardless of any one individual member's intentions. As with our male who sympathized with suffragists but still benefited from an androcentric system that granted him the vote (elevating and imposing *his* ideas and beliefs over womens'), intentions are irrelevant to receiving privilege. Even if a male disagreed with denying women the right to vote, and even if a male worked for women's suffrage, he still lived in a society that automatically granted him privileges that were denied to women.

Similarly, in the example of ableism, since many of the things taken for granted as basic rights for able-bodied people (such as access to buildings and transportation) cannot be taken for granted by people with disabilities, they become privileges for the able-bodied. It is not necessary to do anything in order to receive these privileges; it isn't even necessary to agree that we should receive them.

Simply as a result of living in a society that defines some bodies as normal and some as abnormal, and then devalues the abnormal, those defined as normal (the dominant group) gain unearned benefits. Having always had these benefits, we come to see them as natural, inevitable, and something to which we are entitled (if we see them at all).

As an example of the structural integration of dominant norms, consider how cities and towns are designed. Prior to the 1990s, curb cuts (the place where the sidewalk slopes to the street), or tactile paving (textured surface to assist the visually impaired) did not exist. For able-bodied people, the need for curb cuts would not cross our minds—we can simply step up or off the curb. But for people with limited mobility, or who use wheelchairs or other technology, the absence of curb cuts severely limits access. Because a basic component of oppression is segregation between the dominant and minoritized groups, people with disabilities were not "at the table" and therefore their perspectives and interests were missing from the city planning decisions that so profoundly affect their lives. For many cities, the incorporation of curb cuts into city planning became law only with the enactment of the Americans with Disabilities Act (ADA) of 1990. This simple change in structure opened the physical environment to people with disabilities in profound and life-changing ways. Yet it took decades of activism from people with disabilities and their allies to get the ADA passed. Since then, cities have come to see that curb cuts are beneficial not only to people with disabilities, but to the elderly, the very young, people pushing strollers, bicyclists, and many others (however, the ADA is not consistently enforced and many buildings remain inaccessible).

The construction of what's normal and abnormal by the dominant group. In Chapter 3 we introduced the concept of social construction using the example of sex and gender. In the context of ability, there is a similar process of social construction. For example, while it is true that biological variance among humans exists, the *meanings* of particular biological differences are socially constructed. Consider this question if you wear glasses: At what point in the spectrum does your weak vision move from being perceived as a relatively insignificant biological variance that requires the socially accepted technology of eyeglasses, to being a significant variance (a disability) that requires your segregation from other children in schools and legal policies to protect you from discrimination?

Now take a moment to imagine what you consider a normal body. Perhaps you could sketch it out on a piece of paper. Try to describe that body in detail:

- What gender is that body?
- What race?
- What is its age?
- How tall is it?
- What does it weigh in relation to its height?

- Can that body walk? Can that body swim? How does it walk or swim? And for how long, or for what distance?
- Can it see? To what degree? Does it use technology to see (glasses, or intraocular implants)?
- To what extent can it hear? Does it use technology to hear?
- What emotions does that body have? Under what conditions does it show these emotions? How does its presumed gender impact what emotions it shows and under what conditions? Does its race impact what emotions you attribute to it? What about its age?

As you think about these questions, decide at what point this body would no longer be normal. Where in its range of "doing" and "being" and "feeling" does this body cross the line from being a "normal" body to being an "abnormal" or disabled body? If the body can do all of the above, but does them "differently" than most people, do you still consider the body normal? If not, why not?

If you are having trouble pinning this point down, it is because "normal" itself is socially constructed (Campbell, 2012). Normal is the line drawn around an arbitrary set of ideas a group determines as acceptable in a given place and time. For example, in the early part of the 20th century in many parts of the United States and Canada some people were categorized as "feeble-minded." This was a broad category that included many people considered "Other" including women who had children out of wedlock, vagrants, and immigrants. Those with this classification were in some cases forcibly (and in many cases without their knowledge and consent) sterilized to prevent them from passing on their feeble-mindedness (Grekul, Krahn, & Odynak, 2004; Kline, 2005). Today, a range of learning disabilities that are seen as normal (such as dyslexia) would have been included in the early-20th-century classification of abnormal (feeble-minded). Based on the socially constructed idea of what constituted normal, people's lived experiences become profoundly different.

As you can see, these constructions are significant, because depending on whether we fall into the normal or abnormal social category, very real privileges are either granted or denied. These privileges are embedded in *definitions* (at what point does a characteristic move from normal to abnormal?), *language* (classifications such as feeble-minded versus dyslexic), *structures* (the way cities and buildings are built), and *systems* of society (legal policies such as forced sterilization or educational segregation).

A powerful yet subtle way dominant group members have received the message that people with disabilities are not important is through the ways these groups have been segregated in major social institutions like schooling, housing, and the workplace. For example, in schools this segregation has been rationalized as necessary because were students with disabilities to be in the main classroom, "normal" students would be slowed down and limited. This rationalization conveys the powerful idea that the able-bodied have nothing to gain or learn from people with disabilities.

Consider the way classrooms are organized. A single teacher is expected to meet the needs of up to 40 students, often without supports such as classroom aides. This organization makes it virtually impossible to meet the needs of individual students. Therefore, the more alike and conforming students are, the easier it becomes to efficiently teach the group. Thus, with schooling organized in this way (out of the myriad ways it is possible to organize schooling), it becomes logical to remove children with disabilities from "regular" classrooms.

Even people who support mixed classes often do so in order to "help" children with disabilities, assuming that the flow of knowledge and benefit is always *from* the able-bodied *to* the disabled. This reveals one of the ironies of privilege: Because the dominant group does not see the minoritized group as valuable, the dominant group loses meaningful experiences and relationships. These rationalizations reinforce the idea that the "regular" classroom is a neutral space of equal opportunity, and that the students in this classroom are normal—obscuring the fact that schooling is constructed to accommodate the ways that certain children learn. Labels such as "regular," "normal," "gifted," and "special" shape the policies that social institutions (like schools and medicine) create that maintain this privilege and segregation.

Categories of special education referred to as nonjudgmental include children who are deaf or blind, or who have significant physical or mental disabilities and who come to school with their status identified by medical professionals. Unlike nonjudgmental categories, judgmental categories are based on an individual teacher's subjective assessments, such as "learning disabled" or "emotionally disturbed." Consider the subjective nature of the assessment to place students in Special Education versus Advanced Placement or Gifted Education. Figure 6.1 illustrates how a particular characteristic (such as activity level) can be interpreted in very different ways with profoundly different consequences.

In the chart, notice how being perceived as hyperactive is aligned with negative characteristics that are poorly tolerated by the school, whereas being perceived as energetic is aligned with positive characteristics that are welcomed by the school. These judgmental categories are consistently found to have overrepresentation of minoritized students—most

> 🖐 **STOP:** Many teachers believe that they evaluate each child as a unique individual and that their assessments are independent of race, class, and gender. However, as explained in Chapters 3 and 4, it is not possible to assess anyone outside of our preconceived and often unconscious beliefs about them based upon the groups that they and we belong to. This does not mean that it is impossible to make fair assessments, but that we must not deny that these group relations play a powerful role in what we "see."

Figure 6.1. Common Subjective Evaluations of Child Behavior

Negative and Abnormal	Positive and Normal
Hyperactive	Energetic
Impulsive	Spontaneous
Distractible	Creative
Daydreamer	Imaginative
Inattentive	Global thinker with a wide focus
Unpredictable	Flexible
Argumentative	Independent
Stubborn, irritable	Committed, sensitive
Aggressive	Assertive
Attention deficit disorder	Unique

Source: Thomas Armstrong as cited in Jawanza Kunjufu, *Keeping Black Boys Out of Special Education* (2005), p. 10.

significantly Black, Latino, and American Indian students (Adjei, 2016; Connor et. al., 2016; Gregory et. al., 2010)

Notice how one's preconceived attitudes toward the child shape which characteristics are attributed to him, and in turn, his schooling experiences and outcomes. Students of Color and Indigenous students are much more likely to be assessed by teachers as exhibiting problematic rather than desirable character traits (Gregory et. al., 2010; Harry, 2007; Harry & Klinger, 2006; Kunjufu, 2005). When you add the demographic of the teachers who make these assessments (the overwhelming majority of whom are White middle-class females) you can see how dominant culture determines what constitutes normal behavior.

The invisibility of privilege for the dominant group. Like the invisible current that is carrying us effortlessly forward, privilege is something we do not need to think about when we have it. Because those in dominant groups are not disadvantaged by the oppression, but in fact benefit from it, they find it fairly easy to dismiss the accounts of members of minoritized groups. Living lives that are segregated (in schools, neighborhoods, workplaces, and social circles), it's also easy to avoid seeing what minoritized group members experience. Further, we are not taught in schools and mainstream culture about the experiences of minoritized groups. This makes it difficult for dominant group members to see oppression, or to believe accounts of it happening to others. In addition to the structural barriers, there are psychological and social investments in not seeing oppression. To see and validate oppression requires that we question a system that benefits us where we are in dominant groups. These investments cause us to resist pressures to acknowledge oppression; where we are dominant, we generally don't like to have our privilege pointed out (and many of us actively deny having any benefits beyond those equally available to others). Thus simply naming privilege typically causes defensiveness and avoidance. This, of course, is another way that oppression stays in place: dominant group resistance to acknowledging it, and the social penalties meted to those who try to bring it up (Kimmel & Ferber, 2016).

The following are examples of ability privileges that we can take for granted on a daily basis if we are able-bodied:

- There are thousands of recreation leagues specifically set up for us and rarely, if ever, any for people with disabilities. When they are, they are often segregated from the "regular" events.
- We can choose courses by their academic appeal rather than by the building they might be located in.
- We do not have to make extensive travel plans just to get groceries, attend an event at a colleague's home, or go out to dinner with friends. We don't need to consider whether the building has ramps, handrails, or adequate lighting.
- We aren't labeled and segregated into "special" classes, schools, and buses.
- Our segregation isn't rationalized as necessary in order to avoid "slowing down" people with disabilities. The social paradigm that values competition, individualism, and speed over collaboration, patience, and diversity elevates able-bodied people.

Those of us who are defined as nondisabled will likely not recognize advantages as privileges at all but as simply normal aspects of life. We have been socialized into our position of dominance since birth and have internalized this position as natural. Now let's consider how the external and structural dimensions of privilege interact with internal and attitudinal elements.

Internal and Attitudinal Dimensions of Privilege

Imagine that you have lived your life in a small, gated community. You are surrounded by family and friends and overall live a happy and healthy life. One day the gates open and you are told that you must venture out and make your way in the larger society. You are excited about the adventure that awaits you and all that you will see and discover.

On the way into the nearest city you stop at a café for lunch and notice people staring at you and whispering. A child points at your head while her mother shushes her, and another child begins to cry and hide behind his mother's legs. Some people smile at you kindly and offer to help you sit down, while others turn away and ignore you. You ask for a menu and the waitress points it out on the wall behind you, and with an irritated sigh asks you if you need her to read it to you. You turn around and tell her no, you can see it just fine. When you turn your body, people look away in pity and disgust. As the waitress walks away, you notice that she has a third eye on the back of her head. You are shocked and quickly look around to realize that everyone in the café has an "extra" eye on the back of their heads. Feeling very uncomfortable, you rush through your meal and pay your check. When the waitress returns your change, you hold out your hand but she places it on the counter to avoid touching you.

As you enter the city, the same dynamics occur. Although you occasionally see other two-eyed people, they are usually in service positions, working with their heads down. You begin to feel shame and dread as throughout the day it becomes clear that the three-eyed people see you as abnormal and beneath them. A doctor approaches you and offers to "fix" you. He adds that although the technology to implant a third eye is expensive and dangerous, you might be a good candidate to participate in a university study he is directing on two-eyed people post-implants. You don't want a third eye; you have done just fine throughout your life and are not interested in becoming "normal" in their terms. You try to explain this to the doctor, but he insists that you would find more social acceptance, which would help you have a better quality of life. "Don't you want to be normal?" he asks. "We have the technology, why suffer unnec-essarily?"

You quickly leave the doctor and enter a sunglass store in the mall. Three teenagers are having fun trying on a range of trendy styles. Although the extra lens at the back isn't necessary for you, you can still wear them like everyone else does, wrapped fully around your head. You smile, excited by what you see, but as you pick up a stylish "trio," a saleswoman approaches, takes the glasses out of your hand, and offers you a choice between two "modified trios" while gently patting your arm.

The modified glasses are bulky and unattractive and you don't want them. The girls stop talking and watch your interaction with the saleswoman. You overhear one of them say, "Oh my god, can you imagine being born like that?" Then one of them calls out across the store, "What happened to you?" At this point you have had enough, so you tell her that nothing happened to you and that she is being rude. Shocked, she replies, "Whatever. I was just asking." And she says loudly to her friends, "Why are two-eyed people always so angry?" Her friends nod along in agreement. The saleswoman steps in and says, "Dear, maybe you should go," as one of the teens snaps a picture of the back of your head with her phone, "oh my god this is going to be my costume this Hallow-een!" Frustrated and near tears, you walk out. The last thing you hear is the saleswoman say, "What on earth was she doing in here anyway?"

To avoid further interactions, you decide to take in a play at the theater, looking forward to the relief of sitting in the darkness. As you purchase your ticket an usher hands you a white cane and tells you that you need the cane to get to your seat. You realize that although you don't actually need the cane, it does serve the purpose of alerting others to your difference. You sit down and try to read the program but it's written in a way that assumes a third eye; folded in order to be visible simultaneously to you and the person sitting in front of you. As you fumble with trying to figure out the sequence of the text, a three-eyed person sitting next to you glances over and speaking very loudly and slowly asks, "Do you need help?" Feeling insulted, you ignore her.

The play starts and you realize that it is a biographic drama. It takes place in a special community much like the one you grew up in. But although you loved your neighborhood, it is clear that from the perspective of the three-eyed people it is a sad and depressing place. The main actor is depicting a character who has lost his third eye in a tragic accident. The play tells the story of his struggle to come to terms with his "disfigurement." Once considered a handsome and talented young man with his life ahead of him, it is obvious to you that the three-eyed people now see him as ugly and his life as wasted. You begin to feel a sense of shame and sink lower in your seat, hoping others don't notice you only have two eyes. You see that the main actor is actually a three-eyed person concealing his third eye (you later learn that this actor wins an award for his "courageous and inspiring" portrayal of a two-eyed person).

When the play ends, you feel very self-conscious about what the three-eyed people who are the majority of the audience might be thinking about you, and quickly exit the theater. You walk home with your head down, feeling ugly, and begin to wonder if you are losing your mind.

While there is no "three-eyed society" that enacts its privileges in this way, we use this imaginary scenario to illustrate many very real dynamics minoritized groups must navigate every day. These dynamics include both the structural and institutional dimensions discussed earlier, as well as internal and attitudinal dimensions we will discuss below.

Privilege has the following invisible *internal and attitudinal* effects:

- The belief that your group has the right to its position
- The internalization of messages of your group's superiority
- The lack of humility that results from your limited knowledge of the minoritized group
- The invisibility of your privilege to you

Many educators use Peggy McIntosh's (1989) seminal "invisible knapsack" article to explain privilege. In this article, McIntosh lists 46 privileges she takes for granted on a daily basis because she is White. McIntosh's privilege inventory is useful for revealing the invisibility of White privilege for many White people and captures some of the important layers of internal and attitudinal effects of privilege. In the story of the three-eyed people above, we can see the following internal and attitudinal elements of privilege playing out:

- The privileged group feels comfortable invading the space of minoritized persons.
- The privileged group feels qualified to represent the experiences of minoritized persons.
- Members of the privileged group see themselves as superior and believe that the minoritized person could and should be "fixed" or otherwise assimilate to be like them.
- The privileged group prefers to live segregated from the minoritized group.

The belief that your group has the right to its position. Ideology is a powerful way to support the dominant group's position. There are several key interrelated ideologies that rationalize the concentration of dominant group members at the top of society and their right to rule.

One is the ideology of meritocracy. *Meritocracy* is the belief that people's achievements are based solely on their own efforts, abilities, or merits. Meritocracy posits that social positionality doesn't matter and that the son of a day-laborer has as much chance of "making it" as the son of Bill Gates or the daughter of Donald Trump, as long as they work hard. Canada and the United States are presented in dominant culture as meritocratic systems. From this perspective, those who do not succeed are simply not as capable or don't try as hard as those who do.

A second related ideology is that of *equal opportunity*. This is the idea that in today's world, people are no longer prejudiced, social injustice is in the past, and everyone has the same opportunities. In fact, many dominant group members believe that society has swung the needle past center to the opposite end and now unfairly privileges minoritized groups through "special" rights and programs that are denied dominant group members. From this perspective, there may occasionally be isolated cases of injustices, but these are explained away with the "bootstraps" myth—that anyone can pull themselves up by their bootstraps or improve their lot in life by working harder and having the right attitude.

A third related ideology supporting the dominant group's right to its position is *individualism*—the belief that we are each unique and outside the forces of socialization. Under individualism, group memberships are irrelevant and the social groups to which we belong don't provide us with any more or fewer benefits. The ideology of individualism explains gaps between dominant and minoritized groups (in education, health, income, and net worth) as the result of individual strength or weakness. Therefore, those at the top are there because they are the best, brightest, and hardest working.

A fourth related ideology is the ideology of *human nature*. This ideology rationalizes privilege as natural—"it's just human nature; *someone* has to be on top . . . "—and underpins ideas about civilized versus uncivilized societies. Through this ideology, some societies are seen as more "advanced" due to genetic superiority, cultural superiority (holding values and characteristics such as innovation and tenacity), and/or divine forces (such as Manifest Destiny or the Protestant work ethic). Because they are "advanced" societies, they often "help" less advanced societies. Concepts such as "First World versus Third World" illustrate how human societies are ranked and how these rankings are rationalized. Science and religion have historically been used to support this ideology. For example, science has been used to argue that it is biologically natural for women to be second to men, while religion has been used to argue that it is "God's will."

Ideologies such as "Someone has to be on top" further support these hierarchies—consider who is more likely to believe that someone has to be on top: those on the bottom or those on the top? Thus for scholars of critical social justice, because it is so difficult to separate ideas about nature from culture, the question moves from "Is this true?" to "Whom does this belief serve?"

With privilege rationalized through ideology, it follows that dominant groups are socialized to see their dominance as normal and/or earned.

The internalization of messages of superiority. In the story, it was clear that the three-eyed people believed that their bodies were better, more attractive, and more *normal* than yours. As was evident in the interactions, they set every aspect of what was considered normal in that society. These norms not only included the layout and organization of physical space, but also included *values* such as which kind of bodies were beautiful and preferable.

As members of the dominant group—in this case people defined as able-bodied—seeing how our privileges manifest can be extremely challenging because everything in our environment is constructed to enable us to take our privileges for granted. The story illustrates the following manifestations of internalized superiority:

- There is no value in the experiences of people with disabilities and nothing to gain or learn from their experiences. (The three-eyed people believed that it was better to be three-eyed, and wanted to "fix" you as a two-eyed person. Even though you told them you liked yourself the way you were, they felt entitled to tell you that it was better to be like them.)
- Able-bodied people are capable of understanding the experiences, representing, and speaking on behalf of people with disabilities. (The play's writers and producers were the ones to represent two-eyed people and believed that all a three-eyed person had to do was "pretend" to be two-eyed in order to understand and represent their experiences. This was reinforced

through the award granted to the actor by other three-eyed people, even though the script reinforced negative stereotypes.)

In ways such as these, those in dominant positions tend to see themselves as superior and tell stories that affirm and support that superiority. They tend to lack interest in the perspectives of the minoritized group except in limited and controlled situations such as writing and producing inspirational stories from the dominant perspective.

In an attempt to draw attention to the narrow "inspirational" stories that are often told by nondisabled people, essayist and blogger Haddayr Copley-Woods (2010) created "disability bingo" (Figure 6.2). This bingo card holds up a mirror for dominant culture to gain a rare glimpse of these stories through the eyes of people with disabilities.

An example of the "inspiration story" about people with disabilities was repeatedly told during the 2010 Olympic Games in Vancouver, British Columbia. The Canadian gold medal mogul skier Alexandre Bilodeau and his brother Frédéric, who has cerebral palsy, were prominently featured in stories about how Alexandre gets his "inspiration" from his big brother Frédéric. This story worked to make Alexandre appear heroic and even more talented and special than he already was as an Olympic-level athlete. The story also served to invest the crowd in his success; to root for Alexandre was to indirectly root for his brother Frédéric and in so doing demonstrate our sympathy for people with disabilities. The brother with cerebral palsy is only mentioned in order to further the story of the heroic Olympian brother. The "inspiration" we draw from this story reinforces the notion of the superiority of the able-bodied while denying Frédéric personhood; Frédéric becomes a prop to advance the story and privilege of Alexandre. This story of course does not stand alone; inspirational stories about people with disabilities are told and retold in mainstream culture in ways that uphold the superiority of those defined as normal.

Consider the idea of inspiration itself. Why are stories about people with disabilities so inspirational to able-bodied people? Notice how they can only be inspirational if the person is presented as overcoming the tragedy and suffering that the able-bodied believe to be inherent to having a disability. If we are telling a story of someone who cannot overcome their disability, then we draw our inspiration from their determination and courage to simply live. These narratives communicate and reinforce the idea that body diversity (anything beyond what is socially constructed as normal) is undesirable; a terrible and tragic medical condition that no one would ever choose and that, if possible, must at all costs be fixed. If the condition cannot be fixed, then it is perceived as a terrible waste of life. Thus the only way to "overcome" the condition is to "put a positive face on it" and struggle to be pleasant. If you have ever thought (or been reminded by others) how "fortunate" you were not to have a disability, consider what ideas about disabilities are being conveyed.

Figure 6.2. Disability Bingo

We hear so many annoying and unpleasant things as physically disabled people. Wouldn't it be nice if we could leap to our feet (or fall out of our chairs) and yell: 'BINGO!' This body of literature is so vast and rich, we decided to divide it into categories for easy reference:

General Annoying Ignorance	Smug Superiority/ Condescension	Astoundingly Stupid Advice	More Annoying Ignorance	Outraged Hatred
You're too young to have that problem/use that mobility device/ need those painkillers!	Must be nice not to have to walk everywhere/work!	My [acquaintance] had that! She used [panpipes/pesto/ aromatherapy/reiki/ satanic chants] and is better now!	What's wrong with you? Why are you wearing/using those?	Being fat isn't a disability!
You don't look/act disabled!	Well, I just don't *do* sick.	Maybe if you'd exercise more, you'd get better!	Your spouse/ parent/ roommate must be a SAINT!	These parking spaces are for old people!
Are you sure you have [condition]? Do you really need that [mobility device/hearing aid/service dog]?	[Talking v-e-r-y s-l-o-w-l-y]	**Free Space** **YOU'RE SO BRAVE!**	Everyone has SOME sort of disability!	If you really had X then there's no way you'd be able to do Y.
But you speak/ walk/write/ think so well!	Careful you don't get a speeding ticket on that scooter! Heh, heh, heh.	If you'd stop being so negative/gave it over to God, you'd be cured!	How do you have SEX?	People with [your disease] are a burden and the reason the government had to raise taxes.
I should totally get my pet a vest like that; then I could take him with me everywhere!	I wish I could sit down all the time!	You don't really have to take those medications. Big Pharma has just convinced you that you do.	Oh yeah; I have [totally unrelated thing], so I know how hard it is!	By using [mobility device], you're just letting the illness win!

Source: haddayr.livejournal.com/604179.html

These discourses of overcoming disability obscure the nature of disability itself. Disability isn't a condition external to a person that can be discarded with a cure and left behind. People with disabilities must navigate structures of privilege, definitions of normalcy, and the internalized superiority of the able-bodied every day. Their development is profoundly shaped by this navigation. Thus disability is a central (although certainly not the only) part of the experience and identity of a person with a disability. Many people with disabilities embrace them because it gives them an outsider's vantage point and generates innovative perspectives, insights, and opportunities.

In addition to how the inspiration story positions the person with disabilities, notice what the story of inspiration does for the storyteller, for example, when we glorify people who are "willing" to work with special needs kids. For able-bodied people, the telling and retelling of the inspiration story affirms *our* goodness, benevolence, and superiority. Unfortunately, this sense of superiority results in an arrogance and ignorance that limits our understanding of ourselves and others.

The lack of humility that results from your limited view of others. The dominant group, while the least likely to understand oppression and the most likely to be invested in holding it in place, is the group in the position to write the rules. Thus the rules will continue to benefit them. In addition, the minoritized group is rarely at the table in any numbers significant enough to challenge the dominant group or provide another perspective, even when the intentions of the rules are to prevent oppression. One of the outcomes of unearned privilege—arrogance— causes the dominant group to feel capable of representing the interests of the minoritized group (if they consider them at all), regardless of whether they have consulted with them. In fact, the dominant group members may be seen as more legitimate to represent minoritized group interests since they will see themselves as "objective" and not furthering a "special interest agenda."

In Chapter 3's discussion of socialization, we introduced the concept of code switching, explaining how our relationships to others are so deeply internalized that we shift effortlessly back and forth between them. For example, we know that when we are talking to our supervisor we need a level of deference that is not necessary when we are talking to our friends. We may also reveal secrets to a significant other that we would never share with coworkers. Adding the dimension of social power, we can think about internalized dominance as the default mode for engaging with the minoritized group. Because we have internalized our position in relation to theirs, we automatically interact with them from a position of unconscious superiority. We are seldom aware of this, because the messages of superiority have been planted and reinforced since birth. Further, because we have been taught that it is wrong to treat others differently, we would likely deny our sense of superiority.

Yet research shows that dominant-group interactions with minoritized groups are based in a sense of internalized superiority and are different from interactions with other dominant group members (Bonilla-Silva, 2006; Myers, 2003; Picca & Feagin, 2007). Again and again, studies have shown that *actual* behavior toward minoritized groups does not line up with dominant group beliefs about these interactions—recall the resume study described in Chapter 3 (Dovidio, Glick, & Rudman, 2005; Greenwald & Krieger, 2006). Our lack of awareness or denial of our behavior does not lessen the reality of its impact. In fact, our unawareness and denial makes it more likely that we will continue.

The invisibility of privilege for the dominant group member. While many of the dynamics discussed above make privilege invisible to the dominant group, there is also a phenomenon that scholars describe as "sanctioned not-knowing" or "willful ignorance" (Dei, Karumanchery, & Karumanchery-Luik, 2004). These terms attempt to describe dynamics that allow dominant group members to remain ignorant of the overwhelming evidence of injustice in society. While many dominant group members claim that they simply don't know about the minoritized group, invoking a sense of innocence, the information is easily available. Thus we use the phrase "willful ignorance" because minoritized groups have always tried to get dominant groups to see and understand their experiences, but dominant group members often aggressively resist this information. These forms of denial and resistance include:

- Demanding more data to prove the injustice ("When were these statistics published? I think things have changed in the last 10 years.")
- Feeling qualified, without any study of the issue, to argue with people who experience the oppression and with experts in the field ("I disagree that disability is socially constructed.")
- Giving counter examples or exceptions to the rule ("But Roosevelt had a disability and he was president!")
- Channel switching ("The true oppression is class. If you eliminate classism all other oppressions will disappear.")
- Intimidation ("You might advance more if you were a team player.")
- Defensiveness ("Are you calling me ableist? I have an aunt with a disability!")
- Negating research and explaining away injustice by giving personal and anecdotal stories ("There was a kid in a wheelchair in our class. Everybody loved him and no one even noticed his wheelchair.")
- Emotional fragility ("It hurts my feelings that you think I would say something ableist.")

All the dominant ideologies in society support willful ignorance. The ideologies of meritocracy, equal opportunity, individualism, and human nature we described above play a powerful role in denying the current of privilege and insisting that society is just.

Perhaps the most subtle yet powerful way we resist knowing is by simply being uninterested. Internalized superiority makes us indifferent to learning about the minoritized group because we don't see them as valuable. If we did see them as valuable, we would seek them out. For example, we might not know much about what it means to be rich and famous, but many of us spend a lot of time reading about their lives because they are important to us.

Common Dominant Group Misconceptions About Privilege

As you read through these common misconceptions, it might be helpful to identify a group that you are dominant in and through which you experience privilege. Apply the dynamics discussed here to your experience as a member of that group.

"If we haven't personally discriminated, we are not benefitting." Some dominant group members can admit that the minoritized group is oppressed, but still have a limited view of oppression. We don't realize that we are looking at the minoritized group from a specific position—one that is elevated. Instead, we see ourselves as *neutral*, perhaps recognizing that they are below us, but seeing ourselves as on level ground. It follows that if we could just pull them up to where we are, their lot would improve. What we don't recognize is that their oppression *lifts us up*; because the minoritized group has *less*, we necessarily have *more*. The concept of privilege challenges this perceived-neutral reference point by revealing that the dominant group is actually elevated by virtue of the oppression of the minoritized group. Language helps illustrate this point: While we refer to the minoritized group as *underprivileged* or *disadvantaged*, we rarely talk about the dominant group as *overprivileged* or *overadvantaged*.

"If we can't feel our social and institutional power, we don't have it." Dominant group members do not have to feel powerful in order to have privilege. The social and institutional power and privilege of dominant groups is so normalized that it is outside of conscious awareness. Yet we often expect that power is something that one can feel, rather than something one takes for granted. For example, in the case of race privilege, a struggle in one aspect of a White person's life often becomes confused with a lack of racial privilege. In discussions on race we often hear White working-class men protest that they don't have any social power. They work long and grueling hours, often in jobs in which they have no long-term security, and come home feeling beaten and quite disempowered. These men often cannot relate to the concept of holding social power. The key to recognizing group-level power is recognizing *normalcy*—what can be taken for granted. These men are indeed struggling against classism, but they are not struggling against racism. A man of Color in the same job would be dealing with both classism and racism. Indeed, men (and women) of Color have traditionally been kept out of these jobs. Thus, our own sense of power is not necessarily aligned with how others perceive or respond to us, nor our relationship to social and institutional networks.

"If a minoritized person is in charge, there is no oppression." In our work we are often asked questions such as, "But our dean is a woman so how can there

be sexism in our department?" In thinking about numbers, there is an important distinction between *rank* and *status* (Nieto et al., 2010). *Rank* refers to social membership (such as race, class, gender, sexual orientation, ability, age), and thus rank is not temporary and impacts all aspects of one's life. *Status* refers to a temporary position/job and is contextual (e.g., the infamous story of Oprah Winfrey, one of the richest women in the world, unable to hail a cab once outside her workplace). Your dean may be a woman but she will have to enact male norms and values to keep her position and will still deal with unaware sexism from the men she supervises.

A Latino manager, while holding status over a White person he supervises, will still have to deal with the racism of his employees. Research shows that women and peoples of Color in positions of leadership are scrutinized more closely and judged more harshly than White men (Elsass & Graves, 1997). Peoples of Color are often assumed to be the recipients of special programs rather than to have earned their positions, and are often perceived as being biased, having special interests, and being "troublemakers" (Bonilla-Silva, 2006; Calliste, 1996; Duncan, 2014). Conversely, one of the privileges of being in the dominant group is that you are perceived to be "just human" and thus neutral and unbiased in your viewpoint.

"If we are oppressed in one social group membership, we can't be privileged in another." Remember that we occupy multiple social groups. One may be oppressed as a female but elevated as White; oppressed as a person with a disability but elevated as male; and so on. Consider the oppression of sexism. While all women experience sexism, they experience it differently based on its interaction with their other social group identities.

The experiences of a woman will vary greatly if she is heterosexual or a lesbian. Further, imagine this woman is heterosexual and has a disability. Perhaps she is living with a disability and is Muslim; or living with a disability and is Asian, Muslim, and a nonnative English speaker. In these ways, her experiences are determined not simply by her gender, but also by her ability status and racial, religious, and sexual identity. Thus we can be oppressed in one axis of life and still experience privilege in another. Intersectional analysis requires that we consider how these various social group identities interact with one another.

Forms of oppression can overlap and compound the experience of minoritized groups. Notice how in the examples below, adapted from the work of Zeus Leonardo (2004, 2009), racism intersects with ableism to produce the following manifestations of oppression:

- Women of Color, Indigenous women, and women with disabilities have been forcibly sterilized, denying them agency over their own bodies.

- Intelligence testing and eugenics (selective breeding of humans) construct the idea of the genetic inferiority of Blacks, Latinos, and Indigenous peoples.
- Beliefs that Asian-heritage people are smarter than other groups of Color sets up a competitive hierarchy and reinforces racist concepts of intelligence as genetic.

The life and work of Leroy Moore (Figure 6.3) illustrate these intersections of oppression.

Dynamics of privilege are deeply embedded into our socialization and thus into our psyches. Ending a system of privilege is not as simple as identifying their external manifestations and "stopping them" or "giving them away." We may be able to do this with some types of privileges, such as changing the way we design buildings in order to make them more accessible, or challenging our assumptions about who is more or less likely to engage in criminal activity (i.e., reduce racial

Figure 6.3. Leroy Moore Jr. (b. 1967)

Writer and activist Leroy Moore lectures throughout the United States and Canada, as well as other parts of the world, on topics including the intersections of disability, race, and sexuality, as well as police brutality against people with disabilities. He has written extensively on the history of Black artists and musicians with disabilities in popular culture. Moore was the founder of Disability Advocates of Minorities Organization and a member of the U.S. National Minorities with Disabilities Coalition. He is a regular contributor to Poor Magazine, a webzine for community activism. He is also the cofounder of an arts performance series in San Francisco called *Sins Invalid: An Unshamed Claim to Beauty in the Face of Invisibility*. The project serves as a dialogue space where artists with disabilities examine and challenge normative conceptions of beauty and sexuality. Moore was also a founding member of the disability radio collective, Pushing Limits at KPFA 94.1 FM in Berkeley, CA and is the founder of Krip-Hop Nation, an international project bringing together and disseminating the work of hip-hop artists from around the world. Moore is currently writing a book about Krip-Hop Nation and, in collaboration with Emmitt Thrower, working on a film documentary about police brutality against people with disabilities that will complement the Krip-Hop mixtape CD on the same issue.

Source: https://disabilityrightnow.wordpress.com/2012/05/14/interview-with-leroy-moore-2/

profiling). But many aspects of our privilege are intertwined into our very identities and personalities—how we see ourselves in relation to those around us and thus how we interact with them.

Returning to our opening vignette concerning the prime minister and her cabinet, we can see some of these deeply internalized manifestations. The men assume that it is women whose movements will be restricted. They also assume it is their right to walk freely wherever and whenever they choose. They take offence at the suggestion that their rights should be restricted, even though it is their group that is causing the problem. They appear to be unaware that women must monitor and restrict their movements on a daily basis. Ironically, women as a group must do this monitoring because of the patterns of men as a group. In this situation, it isn't as simple as suggesting that the men "give away" their privilege to women so that women can move more freely. There are many complex dynamics involved that make this not only challenging, but also highly unlikely. The very idea of men giving up their privilege is foreign to them, even though it makes sense—or is rational—that it should be *their* movements that are restricted under these conditions, not the women's. Due to internalized dominance, we can be confident that they will vigorously resist the prime minister's proposal. The prime minister also now risks being seen as seeking "special rights" for women and of having a biased perspective. In other words, she now becomes a *woman* prime minister who is no longer seen as representing everyone or playing by the rules. Deep-level ideological, institutional, and behavioral shifts would need to occur in order to challenge the male cabinet members' privileges.

Discussion Questions

1. The authors argue that privilege is not the product of luck, happenstance, or natural occurrence. If it is not these things, then what is it?
2. What are the "external and structural" dimensions of ableism? Identify some specific examples beyond those the authors provide. What are the "internal and attitudinal" dimensions of ableism? Identify some specific examples.
3. Identify the external/structural and internal/attitudinal dimensions of another form of oppression (such as sexism, heterosexism, classism, or racism).

Extension Activities

1. Identify an aspect of privilege that makes you uncomfortable to think about. Write a short letter to yourself explaining why you are uncomfortable thinking about this privilege.
2. a. Review the Disability Bingo card (Figure 6.2). Working with other members of a minoritized group that you belong to, create a bingo card of the assumptions that the dominant group has about your group (if you don't

belong to any minoritized group, explore the attitudes and assumptions you have been taught about people with disabilities).

b. For homework, watch a movie, television show, or commercials on mainstream TV and, focusing on the representation of the group you chose, record how many of the bingo squares you can mark.

c. Back in the classroom, share your findings from your homework. What patterns do you notice? Were there any groups that were virtually (or perhaps totally) invisible? If so, how is that also significant?

3. Research the writing, poetry, and performance art of Leroy Moore, Jr. (see Figure 6.3). Write an essay that examines how his work illustrates the concept of intersectionality.

Patterns to Practice Seeing:

1. Practice identifying the physical accessibility of your work or school structure (the external dimensions of ability privilege).

2. How many people who have clearly identifiable physical or cognitive disabilities (and who are not family members) have come to your home? If few or none, why do you think that is?

CHAPTER 7

Understanding the Invisibility of Oppression Through Sexism

"I believe women are equal but I am not a feminist"

This chapter traces a specific form of oppression—sexism—in order to illustrate how our ideas, views, and opinions are shaped by the interlocking and ongoing social messages circulating in popular culture. We describe the ways in which such messages serve as barriers to seeing oppression and as such are central to how oppression is normalized.

Vocabulary to practice using: feminism; postfeminism; commodification; internalized oppression; misogyny; androcentrism; patriarchy

---

Imagine: A prominent politician is running for office. He has been married 3 times and has 5 children by 2 different women. He owns several Las Vegas nightclubs that are famous for their servers who work while wearing lingerie. This politician is on record for making several sexist comments about women, including his own daughters. He has run on a platform that would deny women access to all forms of reproductive healthcare, including birth control. Just before the election a recording emerges that shows him bragging about having extramarital affairs and sexually assaulting women. When his behavior is made public and critiqued, several women you know say that they don't think it was very nice behavior but he was only joking. And besides, these women add, it's only the radical feminists who are complaining. They don't see why feminists are making such a big deal about it. The politician goes on to win the election, with a majority of women voting for him. Within the first week in office, he removes all mention of women's rights, civil rights, and LGBT rights from the official state website, and ends global funding for women's health.

Our socialization shapes our below-the-surface ideas about groups of people. These ideas are the result of myriad institutional forces. Among the most powerful forces are media and popular culture. In this chapter we examine a specific form of oppression—sexism—in order to surface how our ideas, views, and opinions are the product of interlocking and ongoing social messages. These messages are central to how oppression is normalized.

Today, women have the right to vote and a multitude of other rights afforded to them by law, and many women in the United States and Canada would argue that women's oppression is a thing of the past. However, sexism is a cogent example of how oppression adapts over time and how the cultural "water" is difficult to see while we are swimming in it.

What Is an Institution?

The term *institution* refers to a large-scale and established set of laws, customs, practices, and organizations that govern the political or social life of a people. Institutions make and enforce a society's rules and norms. Examples of institutions include marriage and family, religion, schooling, military, prisons, government, law, mass media, and corporations.

From a critical theory perspective, institutions serve as primary socializing forces in society. Institutions are the systems that guide our practices in daily life. For example, consider again how schools regulate students. Schools establish the hours of attendance, decide what will be studied and how, define good and bad behavior and then reward students for good behavior and punish them for bad, determine which holidays will be celebrated and how, establish dress codes, define play, establish the norms and language with which to speak to authority, and so on. Thus there is more going on within schools than intentional instruction of subject matter.

Institutions produce, circulate, and maintain the dominant culture's norms, values, definitions, language, policies, and ideologies—and do so in ways that are above as well as below the surface of the cultural water. Institutions are directly connected to (and reflective of) larger dynamics (interests, power relations, fears) of a given society. The overarching ideology that has shaped all institutions is *patriarchy*. We might think of patriarchy as the macro-level belief system from which sexism (the oppression of women) flows. Patriarchy is the belief in the inherent superiority of men and the creation of institutions based on that belief. Examples of patriarchal ideology worldwide are: a male god; the father as the head of the household; males as authority in all social realms such as law, government, religion and culture; women as inherently inferior to men and the property of men.

> 📖 **Patriarchy:** The belief in the inherent superiority of men and male norms and the organization of society based on this belief.

To think critically about institutions and how patriarchy (and other forms of oppression) is embedded within them requires us to move beyond our personal experiences and see the big picture; we must consider the interlocking outcomes institutions produce collectively and the impact of these outcomes in society.

An Example: Sexism Today

A key challenge in understanding current manifestations of oppression is that they are often much easier to see in the past than in the present. For example, it is easy for most people to accept that denying women the right to vote, enslaving Blacks, or forcing Indigenous children to attend residential schools are all examples of oppression. Because our attention is directed to isolated events from the past, rather than the overall picture, current patterns of oppression become harder for us to see. We are led to believe that once women got the right to vote (or enslaved people were freed, or residential schools closed), the issue of oppression was over. What is important to understand about oppression is that it can adapt and change over time, while still maintaining inequitable outcomes overall.

Let's trace a specific example of oppression today: sexism. The following statistics demonstrate the importance of addressing overall outcomes in order to understand current manifestations of sexism.

In the global context:

- Women are working as commercial sex workers; working in sweatshop factories sewing garments, peeling shrimp, weaving carpets, picking cotton, mining minerals, harvesting rice, and working in households as domestic care workers. They are bonded by debt that is almost impossible to pay off and must do this menial, degrading, and debilitating labor for long hours with no rights or protections (U.S. Department of State, 2010).
- Assault and violence based on trafficking (the illegal trade in human beings that constitutes a modern form of slavery) of women and girls for forced labor and sex is widespread (Watts & Zimmerman, 2002; World Health Organization, 2009).
- 4.5 million of the estimated 21 million people in forced labor are victims of sexual exploitation, 98% of them are women and girls (United Nations, 2017).
- In 2012, one in two women killed worldwide was killed by their partner or family (Unnited Nations, 2017).
- In the 1994 Rwandan genocide, it is estimated that up to 500,000 women were raped during a 100-day period (Surf Survivors Fund, n.d.).
- In 1992 Croatian and Bosnian women were subjected to rape and gang rape by soldiers in rape/death camps (Allen, 1996).

While war rape is considered a crime against humanity and trafficking affects women in developing nations at higher rates than women in the United States or Canada, violent crimes and other forms of exploitation against women are not restricted to developing nations. Sexism occurs in U.S. and Canadian women's lives in these ways:

- One in four women in the United States has experienced domestic violence, and one in three women has been a victim of rape (Center for Disease Control, 2017).
- The number of American troops killed in Afghanistan and Iraq between 2001 and 2012 was 6,488. The number of American women who were murdered by current or ex male partners during that time was 11,766. (HOPE, n.d.).
- A woman is beaten every 9 seconds in the United States (National Coalition Against Domestic Violence, 2015).
- Less than 10% of sexual assaults in Canada are reported to the police (Statistics Canada, 2006b); despite the rate of self-reported sexual assaults remaining relatively stable, the percentage of offenses that were reported to the police has dropped from about 12% in 2009 to 5% in 2014 (Canadian Women's Foundation, 2016).
- Fifty-one percent of Canadian women report having experienced at least one incident of physical or sexual violence; four out of five female undergraduates at Canadian universities have been victims of violence in a dating relationship; and 83% of women with disabilities will be sexually assaulted during their lifetime (Sexual Assault Centre of Hamilton Ontario, n.d.).
- In the United States, an estimated 10 million women are victims of physical assault by an intimate partner each year (National Coalition Against Domestic Violence, 2015).
- On average a woman is killed by her intimate partner every 6 days in Canada (BC Society of Transition Houses, 2016).
- On average 3 women are killed every day in the United States. (National Network to End Domestic Violence, 2012).

What these statistics reveal is not only that rape, sexual assault, and violence against women (perpetrated primarily by men) occurs at extraordinary rates in Canada and the United States, but that many of us are unaware of the severity and pervasiveness of this violence. In addition to direct experiences of gender violence, there are indirect ways that many of us support violence against women and girls. For example, Canada and the United States are primary consumers of clothing, accessories, and household goods produced by sweatshop labor.

What Makes Sexism Difficult to See?

Given the extent of violence against women globally as well as locally, how are so many of us able to deny its existence? Why does mainstream culture position women's oppressions as a problem of marginalized societies (developing nations or people living in poverty) rather than as a pervasive system that affects all women throughout the world, mediated by their additional social positions (of race, class, sexuality, and other identities)? In order to understand how the pervasiveness of violence against women, and violence against women of Color, poor women, trans women, and women with disabilities in particular, becomes so normalized as to be virtually invisible, one must practice seeing the interconnections between socialization, institutions, and culture.

There are several reasons why sexism is difficult to see. First, the way that dominant culture focuses on individuals obscures group-level patterns. If we view oppression as isolated events (such as suffrage or reproductive rights), or as an extreme example of violence against a single woman, the broader patterns become obscured. It is harder to see everyday and ongoing sexism when placed alongside the sensationalized examples (e.g., a woman whose nose is chopped off to "restore honor," or a woman locked away in a basement for years and forced to bear children by her father/abuser). When we define oppression solely as individual acts that individual bad people do, we conceal the everyday ways that social institutions organize and hold sexism in place. Further, there is a silence that surrounds most individual cases, which helps keep gender violence hidden.

Second, corporate-produced popular culture has become a more pervasive institution in our lives through multiple points of entry such as advertising, sponsored curriculum in schools, and mass media. For example, corporate-produced toys amplify rigid gender roles, socializing girls into femininity (nurturing, caring, beauty play) and boys into masculinity (aggressive, violent, physical play). Walk through any major toy store and peruse the aisles and you will see that rather than definitions of masculinity and femininity expanding and stretching, these definitions have become increasingly narrow and rigid. Male musculature in toys and media representations has become more exaggerated, the emotional range has become more limited—usually to some variation of rage—and violent play for boys has become more realistic through video games (Morrison & Halton, 2009). At the same time, girls' toys and imagery have become more passive as girls' play is focused primarily on self-grooming, friendship, and performing domestic duties.

As corporate culture represents masculinity as dominance, disconnection from feelings, invulnerability, and immunity from emotional attachment, it simultaneously represents femininity as passive, pleasing, and above all else attractive to boys. In this way, sexism is naturalized very early on in children's popular culture.

At the same time, corporate-produced advertising promotes the idea of individualism and free choice. According to corporate culture, it is through their products (and the lifestyles advertisers associate with them) that we can demonstrate our uniqueness and freedom of choice. The sexism is thus sold to us and continually reinforced, while at the same time it is denied.

Third, the sexism in our everyday lives is obscured through the ideology of the "West" as civilized and liberated, in contrast to places that are uncivilized and backward, such as the "East." For example, "The Muslim Woman" is an archetypal oppressed woman, standing in stark contrast to our own perceived liberation in the United States and Canada (places that are presumed to be free of Muslim women). Indeed, many of our female students frequently deny that sexism is a socializing force in their own lives and support this denial by giving the example of the Muslim woman as the woman who is *truly* oppressed (Sensoy & DiAngelo, 2006). When our students look to the Muslim woman in this way, they see the opposite of themselves. Think about the following list and consider which side is associated with "Western" women and which side is stereotypically associated with Muslim women:

Modern/Primitive
Active/Passive
Individual/Group
Industrious/Idle
Pretty/Ugly
Open/Covered
Free/Restricted

Notice that although one can be both a Muslim woman *and* a Western woman, the binary view positions these identities as opposites and therefore prevents us from seeing the complex and intersecting nature of identity. Because we have not been taught to see the complexity of social identity, without further study we can only understand forms of social oppression such as sexism through the most simplistic explanations. These simplistic explanations cannot account for the ways that other social positions such as race and class also determine women's experiences under sexism. Thus these binaries also reinforce racism, classism, and other forms of oppressions.

At the same time that corporate interests are amplifying rather than reducing rigid gender roles, we are socialized to believe that in the United States and Canada, we are liberated and free; the way we "do gender" just seems normal, even healthy, and certainly better than the way *they* do it (for example, we can wear whatever body-revealing clothes we choose from chain stores in the local mall where our heavily marketed brand choices are believed to demonstrate our individuality, while *they* "have to" wear clothes that cover their bodies and all look the same). While our attention is continually drawn to examples of sexism that occur "over there"—in non-White, non-Western contexts—examples of sexism "over here" are usually situated in the past. Together, these dynamics hide the patterns and outcomes of sexism that surround us all. Let's examine a few contemporary locations in which patterns of sexism are normalized.

Discourses of Sexism in Advertising

Many people cite sports as now open to women, and a strong emphasis on sports often begins in schools. But what is emphasized between boys and girls varies. There is often a lack of support for girls sports in school, and even when there is funding for girls, the broader culture reinforces the idea that girls' sports are not as valuable since girls in sports don't "go" anywhere in terms of professional leagues. The results of games between women's teams are not announced daily on local and national television as they are for men's teams (men's teams of course are not identified as "men's" teams at all, but just as "teams").

Girls and women in sports are not taken seriously in the mainstream culture, except in contexts such as the diet/fitness industry or as male-oriented entertainment such as the Legends Football League (formerly known as the Lingerie Football League). While society's interest in women athletes increases during the Olympics, the final matches that end the Games (and most other competitions, such as the U.S. Open or Wimbledon) are between men.

Once girls who are highly interested in sports reach puberty, a new pressure to establish their heterosexuality (by demonstrating their interest in boys and by remaining feminine) emerges. One of the clearest recent examples of establishing the heterosexuality and gender normativity of female athletes through advertising was illustrated with Canadian ice hockey player Hayley Wickenheiser, a four-time Olympic medalist and seven-time World championship medalist. As an athlete, Wickenheiser has logged an impressive resume of accomplishments. However, the stereotype of women hockey players not being feminine follows Wickenheiser, as it does all female players. Despite their strength and skill at their sport, their lack of traditional femininity is problematic.

After the 2010 Olympic Games Wickenheiser was featured in ads for Betty Crocker. In these ads the audience sees Hayley in a domestic setting; she sits with her husband and son around the kitchen table eating Hamburger Helper. Hayley tells us that just like us, she's a busy mum and the last thing she wants is to come home and spend a lot of time in the kitchen making dinner for her family.

What's powerful about these ads is how quickly they reinforce important ideas about the social construction of gender in relation to the institution of marriage and family. Hayley is separated from her athleticism as the viewer is explicitly asked to identify with her as "a mum just like you," presented in a typical nuclear family. Her heterosexuality is confirmed, along with her commitment to her traditional family responsibilities (for example, that she will do the cooking for her husband and son is taken for granted). Regardless that she is an athlete at the pinnacle of athletic accomplishment, as a woman, she is still expected to come home and put dinner on the table for her family.

The rates at which women's hockey is funded are relevant to her participation in a campaign for a product that any health-conscious athlete is unlikely to consume. The ten highest paid professional male hockey player salaries are 10–14 million U.S. dollars per season (not including bonuses that players are usually awarded when they enter the play-offs). The Canadian Women's Hockey League (established in 2007) and the first U.S. Women's Hockey League (established in 2015) draw some of the greatest Olympic-level athletes from the United States and Canada. Yet the players in the leagues (such as Hayley Wickenheiser) receive no league salary, and while their travel costs and ice time are covered, they pay for their own equipment (Canadian Press, 2010). Were Hayley male, she would have received the top contracts that the most skilled male players receive. Thus many women athletes must depend on endorsements and contracts with European leagues and other sources to fund their sport.

Female athletes often endure media representations that position them in demeaning domestic or sexualized ways. For example, Olympic medalist trap-shooter Corey Cogdell, Olympic gold medalist Katie Ledecky, and three-time Olympic gold medal swimmer Katinka Hosszu are athletes whose accomplishments were presented in media in relation to their male partners. Also, gendered/sexual comments about female athletes' bodies are common in media. Gold medal gymnast Gabby Douglas was criticized for her hair, many athletes are referred to as "girls," and references to the "great bikini bodies" of beach volleyball players are all too common. 2016 Olympic gold medal gymnast Simone Biles represents another cogent example of media and advertising in particular stripping women athletes of power and repositioning them in traditional (sexist and domestic) gendered roles. A 2016 Tide campaign featuring Biles called "Small But Powerful" starts with a focus on her extraordinary strength, and ends with her doing laundry. The connection is that the laundry detergent is powerful just like she is. Yet the juxtaposition of her athleticism at the start of the commercial and putting laundry in the washing machine in the latter half is striking. It is relevant to note that the association between Black women and domestic work is also reinforced. How many male athletes have you seen in ads focused on domestic labor? What might the impact be of this pervasive curriculum that repeatedly reminds us that women athletes must also be domestic, maternal, sexy, and accountable to men?

While kids may spend 6 hours a day for 180 days per year in school receiving instruction, they interact with media every day, in some cases up to 11 hours a day (Strasburger et. al., 2013). A 2010 study by the Kaiser Family Institute reports that youth between the ages of 8–18 spend approximately 7.5 hours per day, 7 days a week with media (Rideout, Foehr, & Roberts, 2010). Youth aged 8 to 12 spend 6 hours a day, while teens spend up to 9 hours on average streaming online media like videos and music (Marshall & Sensoy, 2016). A 2015 Pew Research Center study reports that 88% of American teens have a mobile phone, 56% of teens go online several times a day, and 24% report being online "almost constantly." According to the Campaign for a Commercial-Free Childhood, "Children ages 2–11 see at least 25,000 advertisements a year on TV alone, a figure that does not include product placements within shows. They are also targeted with advertising on the Internet, cell phones, mp3 players, video games, school buses, and even in school" (n.d., p. 2; see also Federal Trade Commission, 2007). Most of teens' activity online is facilitated by smartphones, where they access multiple social media platforms—Facebook, Instagram, Snapchat, Twitter (PEW, 2015). These platforms go hand in hand with carefully curated advertising activities.

There is no doubt that kids are plugged in. Yet when discussing the power of advertising with our students, we often hear, "I don't pay any attention to the ads. They don't affect me at all." Advertising is a multibillion-dollar industry based on copious research. There are no accidents in ads—every aspect of an ad is designed to affect us, even if we only glance at it for a moment. This is important because one of the ways that media and popular culture work to perpetuate sexism and androcentrism is by normalizing particular kinds of people and relationships. Over and over, as we see *these* kinds of women and girls (and not others) playing out certain scripts of behavior (and not others), those roles and relations become normal (and ideal) to us.

Virtually everything in advertising is gendered, furthering the strict division between men and women and their roles in society and shaping our seemingly neutral and personal consumer "choices." Food is a cogent example of gender divisions reinforced through marketing. According to advertisers, women drink iced tea and eat yogurt, salads, chocolate, and cake, while men drink beer and eat pizza, hamburgers, bacon, and other red meat. Even smell is gendered. While there is no biological difference in hair between women and men, we cannot use the same shampoo. What makes a shampoo masculine or feminine? Smell. The smell of fruit or flowers is for women, while smells associated with the rugged outdoors, such as pine and musk, are for men.

Alcohol and cigarettes are another example of gendering in

STOP: While White people as the dominant racial group do emulate peoples of Color, the terms under which they do so are not the same. White people don't seek to emulate peoples of Color in the halls of power; White emulation is typically confined to the realm of entertainment in order to attain some temporary social capital of coolness. This is an isolated pattern that treats racialization as something that can be taken on and off at whim. For example, Miley Cyrus twerking with Black dancers and coopting reductive caricatures of Blackness, then claiming that she was over hip-hop.

advertising. Marlboro, Winston, and Camel cigarettes are top-selling brands. Their iconic ad campaigns are heavily geared toward men, often depicting very tough and masculine men riding horses or driving pickup trucks. Yet women as well as men smoke these brands. On the other hand, Virginia Slims are heavily marketed to women. Because of this, men will not typically smoke them. Remember that a cigarette is a cigarette. It is its *association* with women that prevents men from consuming the product.

This association and its impact on our behavior indicate the direction of power. The minoritized group can emulate the dominant group because in doing so they are emulating the higher status group and thus gain status; but the dominant group does not emulate the minoritized group because they are emulating the lower status group and thus lose status. This is why women wear pants as well as dresses, but men do not wear dresses as well as pants (there has been a small resurgence of kilts for men in alternative subculture, but these kilts are acceptable because they are masculinized by their association with ancestry and battle). Men who order cosmopolitans or other fruity drinks risk ridicule (because fruit is gendered female). This is an illustration of how powerful gender roles, unequal power, and marketing are in shaping our everyday choices.

Discourses of Sexism in Movies

Because we all share the same socialization through the wider culture, familiar stock characters and plots are an effective way to quickly communicate an emotion, story element, or plot tension. For example, if a director wants to convey ideas about a "studious female," he can quickly signal this idea by visually coding the character as someone who wears glasses, has brown hair, and dresses conservatively.

Conversely, in a slasher film, we know from the start which females will be murdered (all but one) and which won't (only one will survive). The women who will be murdered are sexually promiscuous and often unintelligent and thus "deserve" to die. This is quickly signaled through cues in dress, behavior, and music. The audience, because it has seen these signifiers repeatedly, immediately understands the character types. This process normalizes these outcomes for women and what they deserve. What women deserve is always tied to their relationships to men, whether she will be killed by a man if she is bad, or get the man if she is good. Further, because the women who die in slasher films are highly sexualized, the violence toward them is also sexualized. The repetitiveness of these story lines makes these roles and outcomes for women normal and

> **Signifier:** A sign or symbol that conveys specific cultural meaning. Signifiers connect to larger discourses that work together to construct that meaning.

unremarkable, while reinforcing these concepts under the surface of our conscious awareness.

Another typical character and plot sequence is in the subgenre of romance movies (often called "chick flicks"). The script usually follows the fairy-tale story line: The main character is a young woman who is a selfless caretaker (*Me Before You, The Wedding Planner*) or ultra career-oriented (*27 Dresses, The Proposal, How to Lose a Guy in 10 Days, The Boss, The Intern*) or she is too involved in her work/ school to realize how wonderful she is "inside and out" and doesn't "fix herself up" or "accept herself for how special she is" (*Miss Congeniality, My Big Fat Greek Wedding, The Holiday, Bridget Jones's Diary, Love Actually, La La Land*). Perhaps it is *she* who does not realize that he is really a prince in beast's clothing, a beast that she will tame with her love or risk her life trying: (*Beauty and the Beast, Fifty Shades of Grey, King Kong*). She is often encouraged by her friends (or sister or gay best friend) to get out more, try something new, take a chance, and/or fix her hair and makeup. Despite her career success, family commitments, and fulfilling friendships, this state of being without Prince Charming is presented as problematic. She is not as beautiful, desirable, or fulfilled as she could be were she to also have that perfect man in her life. When she meets Prince Charming through a serendipitous encounter, she often does not realize that he is "the one." He must break her coma in order to complete her life. After Prince Charming breaks her coma, she becomes more beautiful, which is signaled to the audience through improvements in hair, makeup, clothes, and softer lighting.

Mainstream movies, as well as many reality makeover shows, normalize the idea that it is important for women to transcend their race and class status and realign with traditional notions of femininity. Prince Charming facilitates her transformation, as through him, she acquires access to an improved life, self-esteem, and often a better wardrobe. These movies reinforce the ideology that women are fundamentally incomplete without a man. This man brings not only personal fulfillment and definition, but also increased social status through heterosexual marriage and a middle- or upper-class consumer lifestyle.

Just as we might find ourselves laughing at a racist joke, we might find ourselves enjoying a film that reproduces sexism. Indeed, it's likely that due to how normalized these narratives are, we won't see them as sexist at all. Yet the more a narrative appeals to us (especially if we are women), the more important it is for us to be able to think critically about it so that we can resist its effects. Recall the concept of internalized oppression and that minoritized groups often collude with dominant ideology. Thus, no socially constructed text can or should be off-limits to a critical analysis, regardless of how popular or enjoyable it is.

Discourses of Sexism in Music Videos

If we add music videos to this popular-culture landscape, we can see that media is so extraordinarily consistent in its rigid gender divisions that it is virtually impossible to escape sexist messages. Our concerns here are not with sex per se, nor with a return to prudish mores, but with the relentless gender-based narratives of domination and subordination in popular culture. We are also concerned with the increasing sexualization of girls at earlier ages and the near total reduction of female value to their bodies. The messages conveyed to girls are that their value depends solely on how attractive they are to men and how well they can please them.

Although music videos as we know them are relatively recent phenomena (MTV debuted in 1981 and MuchMusic in 1984), they are among the most powerful media for normalizing sexism. What dominant culture may view to be transgressive in music videos are actually very traditional representations of women performing classic porn tropes as defined by men. For example, Fergie's "M.I.L.F.$" video sexualizing mothers and breastfeeding, Katy Perry's "I Kissed a Girl," Britney Spears's "If U Seek Amy" (F-U-C-K me). Or videos by Madonna, Lady Gaga, Miley Cyrus, Ariana Grande, and Nicki Minaj (among countless others) crawling on their hands and knees—sometimes literally with leashes around their necks. Virtually all of these videos are written and directed by men.

Scholars such as Diane Levin and Jean Kilbourne (2008), Gail Dines (2010), Sut Jhally (2007, 2009), Chyng Sun and Miguel Picker (2008), and Robert Jensen (2007) have offered compelling evidence that the line has been blurred between popular and porn culture, and this blurring is most evident in music videos. Through music videos the narratives of pornography have merged into the everyday worlds of young people. It is not uncommon for female porn stars to appear in music videos (and in mainstream movies; Academy Award winning director Steven Soderbergh cast porn star Sasha Gray in one of his films), and porn directors such as Gregory Dark direct music videos for artists such as Britney Spears. Pole dancing and lap dancing classes are offered at many sports clubs and bridal showers. It is now common for young women to remove all of their pubic hair (giving them a prepubescent look) and expect to have and enjoy anal sex. These practices were not mainstream just 20 years ago, but have now been normalized through the widespread circulation of Internet pornography.

Pornography increasingly amplifies the most violent aspects of the rigid gender divisions between men and women. The physical brutalization and emotional degradation of women in porn, particularly in gonzo (one of the biggest moneymaking genres of online porn, which depicts painful penetration, gang rape, and men slapping, choking, and gagging women while they penetrate them orally, anally, and vaginally) has become more normalized as men become desensitized and need ever more intense images to feel stimulated (Dines, 2010; Jensen, 2007; DeKeseredy, 2015).

To some, it may seem an exaggeration to connect pornography to music videos and popular culture. However, consider that within a few decades, pornography has moved from an underground business with ties to organized crime, to a huge corporate industry (DeKeseredy, 2015). The worldwide porn industry is estimated to be worth 96 billion dollars (Dines, 2010), and as many as 10,000 new sites are added every week (DeKeseredy & Schwartz, 2013). In the United States and Canada, the sites Pornhub and Livejasmin rank just after the most visited websites such as Google, Facebook, and YouTube; and have more visitors in Canada than CBC, Pinterest, and Craigslist, and more visitors in the United States than the *New York Times,* Paypal, Zillow, and Yelp (Alexa, 2017). Many of us regularly receive unsolicited pornographic spam in our workplace and other email accounts. In addition, consider that the largest consumers of online pornography are children between the ages of 12 and 17. In fact, many porn websites target children by using the names of popular characters from kid culture, such as Pokémon, on their websites. These techniques trick children into early exposure (Gomez, 2007).

Porn is ubiquitous in popular culture and an increasing presence in young people's lives. In addition to the misogyny (hatred of women) in gonzo porn, the racist discourses are extreme and unparalleled in their degradation of peoples of Color. Yet pornography is simultaneously everywhere and nowhere, as few people talk openly about their porn consumption. It is critical that we set aside whatever discomfort about or attachment to porn we may personally feel, and think deeply about the power of porn to shape our sexuality and normalize misogyny, racism, and classism.

The representation of men as dominant, aggressive, and in control of women's bodies depends upon the representation of women as submissive, pleasing, and available for every aspect of *men's* desire. If the narratives of pornography were to acknowledge women as human beings with thoughts, feelings, and desires of their own rather than as "suffering sluts" and "stupid whores" (Dines, 2010, pp. xx–xxi), the viewer could not tolerate the pain, physical damage, and humiliation inflicted upon women that are a basic feature of gonzo porn (Dines, 2010; Jensen, 2007; Sun & Picker, 2008). Yet over time, even as we are looking directly at men brutalizing women, the ideology of sexism rationalizes it as a natural outcome of biological roles, personal choice, and mutual desire.

In many music videos, the characters and plots are predictable and include the obligatory cheerleaders, schoolgirls, strippers, and prostitutes. Peep shows, sex clubs, and sex parties are primary settings, and money is often being thrown on women's seminude bodies. Women of Color fare especially poorly in music videos, as Black women are most likely to be portrayed as whores and reduced to their "booties" and Asian and Latina women are virtually absent unless specifically named by their race, reduced to caricatures, and fetishized.

Told over and over, these clichés construct an ideal female who is always available for and seeking sex with any, every, and multiple partners; who wants to be watched, touched by strangers, and objectified; who enjoys humiliation and abuse; and who has no real power, other than the illusory and temporary power of sexual attractiveness. It is impossible to ignore the parallels between music videos and mainstream pornography. Through repetition, the rigid gender roles presented in movies, videos, pornography, and ads, come to seem normal and natural and make it difficult to conceptualize any other reality. As elements of porn cross over into the mainstream, our sexuality is ever more rigidly defined and we become less free, not more.

We may see these videos as a matter of choice—the women choose to perform in them and we can choose to watch them or not. But if the most popular mainstream pop stars, such as Miley Cyrus, Nicki Minaj, Fergie, Lady Gaga, Rihanna, and Katy Perry can choose the storylines of their music videos, why do they all choose the same stories? And at what cost could they make different choices, in an industry dominated by men? As for our choice to watch them or not, we would first have to be able to avoid them, which is difficult given how ubiquitous they are. We may intentionally watch and enjoy them, but insist that we don't take them seriously. Perhaps we should, for what does it mean to *not* take seriously (or be unaware of) how corporate culture has co-opted hip-hop, stripped it of its critique of racism and classism, and sold it back to us filled with misogyny and the worst possible stereotypes about Black people and urban life? How might oppressive forces depend on our not taking these dynamics seriously?

> ✋ **STOP:** While a few pop superstars such as Beyoncé have been able to push back somewhat against the tropes of racism and sexism in their work, consider that for the bulk of her 20 year career beginning in the 1990s, Beyoncé has had to stay within a narrow script of characters, costumes, and storylines. We might ask, then, under what conditions and to what extent can she truly choose to challenge and critique racism and sexism and remain popular and economically successful on mainstream terms?

But on a deeper level, we *are* influenced by these images. No one is outside of socialization, and marketers spend billions on research to find ever more effective techniques for infiltrating our subconscious. Money spent on advertising to children alone was estimated at over $15 billion annually in the early 2000s (Linn, 2004) and corporations now spend $17 billion annually marketing to children, a significant increase from what was $100 million in the 1980s (Crane & Kazmi, 2010). The next time you are sitting in a classroom or conference room, look around. How different are the choices that you have made in dress, hairstyle, accessories, and lifestyle from those around you? Where do you shop and what brands do you chose? How different are these locations and brands from those chosen by your peers? The insistence that the women of music videos or porn can just chose not to participate, or that we can just chose not to watch them, or if we do watch them that we can just choose to be unaffected by them, is naïve.

The life and work of Rachel Lloyd (Figure 7.1) illustrates the impact of prostitution on the lives of women and girls, as well as the possibility to challenge it.

Of course sexism doesn't stand in isolation from other forms of oppression. Women are not *just* women with one shared experience under sexism. Our race, class, ability status and sexuality profoundly shape how we will experience our

Figure 7.1. Rachel Lloyd (b. 1975)

Lloyd is the founder and executive director of Girls Educational and Mentoring Services (GEMS). She is an activist, international speaker, and nationally recognized expert on child sex trafficking in the United States. She played a foundational role in the passage of the 2010 Safe Harbor Act for Sexually Exploited Youth, which puts into effect protections from prosecution for youth victims of sexual exploitation.

Lloyd's organization serves young women and girls who have experienced commercial sexual exploitation. Her advocacy is important because she examines the ways in which misogyny and violence are normalized in popular culture. She has won countless awards for her activism and is featured in the 2007 documentary *Very Young Girls*.

Source: www.gems-girls.org/about/our-team/our-founder

gender under patriarchy. Still, the gains women have made thus far have been fought for long and hard and can be revoked at any time. In 2017 men control all major institutions, as they have since the founding of our countries:

> 📖 *The Equal Rights Amendment (ERA) in full: Section 1.* Equality of rights under the law shall not be denied or abridged by the United States or by any state on account of sex. [The ERA has not passed.]

- Fortune 500 CEOs: 98% male
- The 10 richest Americans: 100% male
- Forty-five U.S. presidents: 100% male
- Forty-five U.S. vice presidents: 100% male
- U.S. Congress: 81% male
- U.S. mayors: 82% male
- U.S. governors: 92% male
- The 10 richest Canadians: 100% male
- Twenty-two elected Canadian prime ministers: 100% male
- Canadian House of Commons: 74% male
- Canadian provincial premiers: 77% male
- Canadian mayors: 82% male

These numbers illustrate that, by definition, oppression is a one-way historical imbalance of legal and institutional power; there is no reverse sexism or any other form of oppression. If men as a group chose to deny women's civil rights, *they could*; if women as a group wanted to deny men their civil rights, they *could not*.

📖 *Feminism:* The belief that women are equal to men. The advocacy for the social, economic, and political equality of all sexes.

Returning to the vignette that opens this chapter, consider the platform our candidate ran on. This platform—as well as his success running on it—illustrates how tenuous women's gains are and how critical it is that we not take them for granted. It also illustrates that both groups internalize dominant ideology, while dominant ideology only serves one group's interests. This is demonstrated in the fact that the majority of men (as well as women) also voted for this candidate.

Feminism is defined as the advocacy of women's rights, based on the idea that men and women are equal. Whose interests does it serve to represent feminism in false, reductive, and dismissive forms, so that many women (as well as men) distance themselves from it?

Discussion Questions

1. According to the authors, oppression is difficult to see. Discuss some of the reasons why this is so.
2. Pick a social group and describe how that group is represented in advertising, music videos, movies, magazines, and wider popular culture. As an extension activity, you might collect some data on how that group is represented in various institutions besides media (remember, a group's absence is also significant).
3. The authors argue that there are three reasons why sexism is difficult to see: the focus on individuals rather than patterns, the influence of corporate culture, and the ideology of *civilized* versus *uncivilized* people in the world. Explain in your own words what each of these are and how they work.

Extension Activities

1. The authors argue that one of the most common patterns in dominant culture that makes oppression difficult to see is the focus on individual people or issues, rather than on broader patterns. Identify a well-known individual from a minoritized group who has been held up as "making it" and generate a list of the ways in which oppression (organized at the group level) is obscured by mainstream representations of that individual. What does focusing on a single person prevent us from seeing?
2. Spend an evening recording information contained in commercials depicting the "average family." What is the composition of the average family? What do

they do? What kinds of activities does each member of the family engage in? Record all the places you have seen this "average family" in mainstream culture. How do they communicate to us what is normal in terms of race, class, gender, ability, and sexuality? How does their presence function as a kind of "looking-glass self"?

3. Watch the documentary film *Very Young Girls* (2007) by David Schisgall and Nina Alvarez, an exposé on the sex trafficking of adolescent girls (www.gems-girls.org). Imagine that you are a journalist investigating this issue. Research at least two other anti-sex-trafficking activists/organizations in addition to Rachel Lloyd and GEMS (see Figure 7.1). Based on what you learn, convey the issue to the broader public or your peers, in ways such as (but not limited to) the following: a poster, stencil art, article, graph, or short public service announcement video (3–5 minutes long).

Patterns to Practice Seeing

1. Think about all of the most popular television shows about friendship between women.
   - What race and class are most of the women?
   - What activities organize these women's days?
   - What seems to be the most important aspect of life to them?
2. How often do you hear women speak up publically against sexism? How often do you hear men speak up publically against sexism? What response do they most often receive when they do speak up? How do these responses differ based on the gender of the person speaking up? Identify examples of the range of responses, with silence on one end and violence on the other.

CHAPTER 8

Understanding the Structural Nature of Oppression Through Racism

"I was really lucky. I grew up in a good neighborhood and went to good schools. There were no problems with racism, I didn't learn anything negative about different races. My family taught me that everyone is equal."

This chapter traces a specific form of oppression—racism—in depth. Racism within the U.S. and Canadian contexts is defined as White/settler racial and cultural prejudice and discrimination, supported intentionally or unintentionally by institutional power and authority, and used to the advantage of Whites and the disadvantage of peoples of Color. We illustrate aspects of racism through an examination of economic, political, social, and cultural structures, actions, and beliefs. We revisit the concept of intersectionality and describe how building an in-depth understanding of racism allows an entry point into building an in-depth understanding of other forms of oppression.

Vocabulary to practice using: racism; structural; institutional; peoples of Color

---

In this chapter we examine racism. One note before we begin: Race is a deeply complex sociopolitical system whose boundaries shift and adapt over time. As such, "White" and "peoples of Color" are not discrete categories, and within these groupings are other levels of complexity and difference based on the various roles assigned by dominant society at various times. For example, Asians and Blacks, while both identified as peoples of Color, have very different experiences under racism based on the roles dominant society assigns to each of these groups, as do Indigenous and multiracial peoples. When we use the term "peoples of Color," we realize that not everyone would accept this term because (a) it conflates very complex dynamics among and between groups and (b) does not deal adequately with the experiences of Indigenous and multiracial peoples. However, at the introductory level, we use this terminology because it is most widely understood as capturing the overall dynamics of White-settler dominance over Indigenous groups and groups of Color, and people perceived as belonging to those groups. The term "peoples" is used (rather than "people") to signal the heterogeneity of groups' experiences under this umbrella term. These terms indicate the two broad, socially recognized divisions of the racial hierarchy in the United States and Canada. Thus, when we use the terms *White* and *peoples of Color*, we are speaking in general terms about dynamics that occur at the group level and are pervasive throughout U.S. and Canadian societies. When we use the pronouns "we" and "us," we are speaking specifically as White authors about ourselves and other White people.

Racism is among the most charged issues in society and is challenging to discuss for many reasons: pervasive miseducation about what racism is and how it works; a lack of productive language with which to discuss racism; institutional and economic interests in upholding racism; ideologies such as individualism and colorblindness; and an emotional attachment to commonsense opinions that protect (rather than expand) our worldviews. In order to meet these challenges, we offer the following reminders:

- A strong opinion is not the same as informed knowledge.
- There is a difference between agreement and understanding: When discussing complex institutional dynamics such as racism, consider that "I don't agree" may actually mean "I don't understand."
- We have a deep interest in denying those forms of oppression which benefit us.
- We may also have an interest in denying forms of oppression that harm us. For example, peoples of Color can deny the existence of racism and even support its structures. However, this still benefits Whites at the group level, not peoples of Color.
- Racism goes beyond individual intentions to collective group patterns.
- We don't have to be aware of oppression in order for it to exist.
- Our racial position (whether we are perceived as White, a person of Color, Indigenous, or multiracial) will greatly affect our ability to see racism. For example if we swim against the current of racial privilege, it's often easier to recognize, while harder to recognize if we swim with it.
- Putting our effort into protecting rather than expanding our current worldview prevents our intellectual and emotional growth.

Many of the dynamics of racism that we explain here will be familiar to peoples of Color. However, they may find this discussion useful in that it provides language and a theoretical framework for everyday experiences that often go unacknowledged by dominant culture.

What Is Race?

In order to understand racism, we first need to address our ideas about race itself. Many of us believe that race is biological; in other words, that there are distinct genetic differences between races that account for differences in traits such as sexuality, athleticism, or mathematical ability. This idea of *race as biology* makes it easy to believe that many of the divisions we see in society are natural. But race, like gender and disability, is socially constructed (Brzuzy, 1997; López, 2000; Weber, 2010). The differences we see with our eyes, such as hair texture and eye color or shape, are superficial and emerged over time as humans adapted to geography (Cavalli-Sforza, Menozzi, & Piazza, 1994). However, *race as a social idea* has profound significance and impacts every aspect of our lives. This impact includes where we are most likely to live, which schools we will attend, who our friends and partners will be, what careers we will have, and even how long we can expect to live (Adelman, 2003; Johnson & Shapiro, 2003).

Race as we commonly understand it is a relatively modern concept (Gossett, 1997). Humans have not been here long enough to evolve into separate species and we are, in fact, among the most genetically similar of species on Earth. External characteristics we attribute to race, such as skin color, are not a reliable indicator of internal variation between any two people (Cooper, Kaufman, & Ward, 2003). To challenge deep-seated ideas about racial difference and genetics, we need to understand the early social investment in race science that was used to organize society and its resources along racial lines.

A Brief History of the Social Construction of Race in the United States

Ancient societies did not divide people into racial categories, although other categories of organization (such as religious affiliation or class status) were common. When the United States was formed, freedom and equality—regardless of religion or class status—were radical new ideas. At the same time, the United States' economy was based on the enslavement of African peoples and the displacement and genocide of Indigenous North American peoples. There were enormous economic interests in justifying these practices. To reconcile the tension between the noble ideology of equality and the cruel reality of genocide and enslavement, Thomas Jefferson (who owned hundreds of enslaved Africans) and others turned to science. Jefferson suggested that there were natural differences between the races and set science on the path to find them (Jefferson, 1787/2002). These social and political interests shaped race science (for example, in the early to mid-1800s, skulls were measured in an attempt to prove the existence of a natural racial hierarchy). In less than a century these studies enabled Jefferson's suggestion of racial difference to become commonly accepted scientific fact (Stepan, 1982).

But while race has no biological foundation, it has developed as a social idea with very real consequences. In the late 1600s the term *White* first appeared in colonial law. By 1790 people were asked to claim their race on the census, and by 1825 the degree of blood determined who would be classified as "Indian." In the late 1800s through the early 20th century, as waves of immigrants entered the United States, the idea of Whiteness became more and more concrete (Gossett, 1997; Ignatiev, 1995; Jacobson, 1998).

While slavery was abolished overall in 1865, Whiteness remained profoundly important as legal racist exclusion and violence continued. To gain citizenship and other rights, one had to be legally classified as White. Individuals seeking these rights began to challenge their classifications and petitioned the courts to be re-classified as White. These legal challenges put the courts in the position to decide who was White and who was not. In fact, in 1923 the court stated that Whiteness was based on the common understanding of the White man. In other words, people already seen as White got to decide who was White (Tehranian, 2000).

While they may have initially been divided in terms of ethnic or class status, over time European immigrants were united in Whiteness. For example, early Irish, Italian, and Jewish immigrants were not considered White, but they "became" White as they assimilated into the dominant culture (Brodkin, 1998; Ignatiev, 1995; Jacobson, 1998; Roediger, 1999). Reflecting on the social and economic advantages of Whiteness, critical race scholar Cheryl Harris (1993) coined the phrase "Whiteness as property." This phrase captures the reality that being perceived as White carries more than a mere racial classification. It is a social and institutional status and identity imbued with legal, political, economic, and social rights and privileges that are denied to others.

A Brief History of the Social Construction of Race in Canada

Like the United States, Canada is a nation that was built on the genocide and forced removal of Indigenous peoples who had been living on the territory for several thousands of years before the arrival of Europeans (Dickason, 2002; Thobani, 2007). The Indigenous peoples of Canada (also referred to as Aboriginal) were living in all regions of the territory when first contact occurred in the 15th century, and had very well-developed social, political, and economic structures. Today, Canada recognizes three main groups of Indigenous peoples: First Nations, Inuit, and Métis. In the 2006 Census, one million people self-identified as Aboriginal—approximately 4% of Canada's total population (Statistics Canada, 2006a).

There was a very complex relationship between French and English colonial powers and the various Indigenous communities during the process of colonization. In some cases the colonizers forced relocation and even genocide, while in other cases colonizers pursued strategies to coexist. These strategies included "civilizing" processes whereby the government and religious organizations set out to reform the "savage Indian" and help him assimilate into colonial society (Milloy, 2000). A major part of this strategy was the Gradual Civilization Act of 1857, and one of its mechanisms was the system of Residential Schools (Haig-Brown, 1998; Hare, 2007). The mission of these schools was primarily to "civilize" Indigenous children. By the late 1800s, attendance in residential schools for Indigenous children aged 7–15 was compulsory. These children were forcibly removed from their homes, taken to residential schools, forbidden (and punished) for speaking their native languages, forced to convert to Christianity, and prevented from seeing their families for long periods; in many cases they were physically, sexually, and emotionally abused. The mortality rate at some schools was over 50% (Milloy, 1999). Most of the schools were closed by the 1960s, but the last school didn't close until 1996. The psychic trauma is still a part of the Indigenous community's collective memory and has resulted in a generational gap within Indigenous communities. Scholars who study the history and legacy of residential schools contend that this trauma is deeply connected to the higher rates of alcoholism, drug abuse, and suicide among Indigenous people (Haskell & Randall, 2009; Kirmayer & Valaskakis, 2009).

The race science being conducted and disseminated in the United States was adopted into government programs and policies in Canada as well. Blacks and Indigenous people were enslaved (Winks, 1971/1997), Chinese workers were excluded from citizenship (Li, 1988; Mar, 2010), and extremist hate groups have long flourished in Canada (Lund, 2006). But since the 1970s one of the key strategies for managing racial diversity has been the policy of multiculturalism. The "melting pot" ideology of the United States was not useful in Canada, in part because it pressures the so-called two founding, colonizing nations (France and England) to assimilate. It would have meant an end to official bilingualism, on which Quebec would not compromise. The ongoing challenges to sustain the Canadian federation (and prevent Quebec from seceding) required an ideology that represented Canada as a tolerant, pluralistic, multicultural society. For these reasons, the "mosaic" (rather than "melting pot") became the dominant image used to describe Canadian racial and ethnic diversity (Joshee, 1995, 2004). In 1985 the Government passed the Act for the Preservation and Enhancement of Multiculturalism in Canada. These policies promote the idea that all groups are positioned equally in Canadian society (the colonizer nations of England and France and their respective languages, people of Aboriginal heritage, and the multitude of immigrant communities in the nation) while leaving structural inequality unaddressed.

What Is Racism?

Racism is a form of oppression in which one racial group dominates over others. In the United States and Canada, Whites are the dominant group and peoples of Color are the minoritized group; therefore, racism here is White racial and cultural prejudice and discrimination, supported intentionally or unintentionally by institutional power and authority, used to the advantage of Whites and the disadvantage of peoples of Color (Hilliard, 1992). In other nations the dominant and minoritized racial groups will not be the same because of the difference in their social and political histories. From here forward, we will be speaking of racism only as it plays out in the United States and Canada.

> ✋ **STOP:** Remember, we are addressing racism at the group, not individual, level. At the group level, all of us navigate the current of dominant culture. In the United States and Canada, if we are White, we swim *with* that current, and if we are a person of Color, we must swim *against* it. While this is the racial reality at the group level, how we respond individually may vary.

Racism is not fluid in that it does not move back and forth, one day benefiting Whites and another day (or even era) benefiting peoples of Color. The direction of power between Whites and peoples of Color is historic, traditional, normalized, and deeply embedded in the fabric of U.S. and Canadian societies (Henry & Tator, 2006; James, 2007; Wise, 2005). The critical element that differentiates *racism* from *racial prejudice* and *discrimination* is the historical accumulation and ongoing use of institutional power and authority that supports discriminatory behaviors in systemic and far-reaching ways. Peoples of Color may hold prejudices and discriminate against Whites, but do not have the social and institutional power backing their prejudice and discrimination that transforms it into racism; the impact of their prejudice on Whites is temporary and contextual. Peoples of Color may also hold prejudices and discriminate against their own and other groups of Color, but the impact of their prejudice and discrimination ultimately serves to hold them down and in this way, reinforces the system of racism and serves White interests. From a critical social justice perspective, the term *racism* refers to this system of collective social and institutional White power and privilege.

Two Key Challenges to Understanding Racism

Dominant society teaches us that racism consists of individual acts of meanness committed by a few bad people. The people who commit these acts are considered racists; the rest of us are not racist. These ideas construct racism as an individual binary: racist/not-racist (Trepagnier, 2010). As we have discussed, a binary is an either/or construct that positions a social dynamic into two distinct and mutually exclusive categories. As with the gender binary, virtually all people know how to fill in the two sides of the race binary: If you *are* a racist, the discourse goes, you are ignorant, prejudiced, mean-spirited, and most likely old, southern, and drive a pickup truck (working class). If you are *not* a racist, you are nice, well-intentioned, open-minded, progressive, and "don't have a prejudiced bone in your body." Most of us understand, at this moment in our cultural history, which is the right side of this binary to be on. But these categories are false, for all people hold prejudices, especially across racial lines in a society deeply divided by race.

> 📖 *Racism:* White racial and cultural prejudice and discrimination, supported by institutional power and authority, used to the advantage of Whites and the disadvantage of peoples of Color. Racism encompasses economic, political, social, and institutional actions and beliefs that systematize and perpetuate an unequal distribution of privileges, resources, and power between Whites and peoples of Color.

So the first problem with the binary is that it is a false division. It reinforces the idea that racism only occurs in specific incidences, and is only done by specific (bad) people. Of course, racism can certainly manifest as individual acts of meanness, ignorance, and violence. However, the focus on individual *incidents*, rather than on racism as an all-encompassing *system*, prevents the personal, interpersonal, cultural, historical, and structural analysis that is necessary in order to challenge it.

The second problem with the binary concerns the impact of such a worldview on our actions. If, as a White person, I conceptualize racism as a binary and I see myself on the "not racist" side, what further action is required of me? No action is required at all, *because I am not a racist*. Therefore racism is not my problem; it doesn't concern me and there is nothing further I need to do. This guarantees that as a member of the dominant group, I will not build my skills in thinking critically about racism, or use my position to challenge racial inequality. Further, if I conceptualize racism as an either/or proposition, then any suggestion that I have racist thoughts or feelings places me on the wrong side of the binary. As a result, all of my energy will go to denying and negating this possibility rather than to trying to understand what these thoughts and feelings are and how they are manifesting. If you are White and have ever been challenged to look at an aspect of yourself related to racism—perhaps you told a joke or made an assumption that someone pointed out to you was racially problematic—it is common to feel very defensive. This defensiveness reveals the binary that informs our understanding of racism; we interpret the feedback to mean that we have done something bad and are thus being told that we are bad people. This binary, which is the foundation of how Whites conceptualize racism (Trepagnier, 2010), and the defensiveness it triggers are primary obstacles preventing us from moving forward in our understanding.

As a person of Color, you may also be invested in denying racism for a range of complex reasons including these: You have also been socialized to see racism in binary terms; You have been socialized to see peoples of Color as "just as racist" as Whites; Denying racism helps you to cope with its overwhelming dynamics; You have had some measure of success in mainstream society and rationalize that members of minoritized racial groups just need to work harder; You have an immigrant experience that is different from that of some other racial groups; You do not carry the weight of internalized racial oppression because you have not grown up in the U.S. or Canadian contexts; Whites are more comfortable with your racial group, with the shade of your skin, social class expression, or other aspects of your identity. Yet there are costs for this denial, including a disconnection from one's cultural roots and separation from other minoritized racial groups. Ultimately, this denial supports the dominant group.

The racist/not-racist binary illustrates the role that ideology plays in holding oppression in place, and the ideology of individualism in particular. Individualism is a storyline or narrative that creates, communicates, reproduces, and reinforces the concept that each of us is a unique individual and that our group memberships, such as our race, class, or gender are not important or relevant to our opportunities. This narrative causes a problematic tension because the legitimacy of our institutions depends upon the concept that all citizens are equal. At the same time, we each occupy distinct race, gender, class, and other positions that profoundly shape our life chances in ways that are not natural, voluntary, or random; opportunity is not equally distributed across race, class, and gender (Flax, 1998). Individualism helps manage this tension by claiming that there are no intrinsic barriers to individual success, and that failure is not a consequence of social structures but of individual character. According to the ideology of individualism, race is irrelevant. Specifically, individualism obscures racism because it does the following things (DiAngelo, 2016):

- Denies the significance of race and the advantages of being White
- Hides the collective accumulation of wealth over generations
- Denies the historical context of our current positions
- Prevents a macro analysis of the institutions and structures of social life
- Denies collective socialization and the power of dominant culture (such as media, education, and religion) to shape our perspectives and ideology
- Maintains a false sense of colorblindness
- Reproduces the myth of meritocracy, the idea that success is the result of hard work alone

Let us be clear—we are not arguing against individualism *in general*. Rather, we are arguing that White insistence on individualism *in regard to race* prevents cross-racial understanding and denies the salience of race and racism in White people's lives. Further, being viewed as an individual is a privilege only available to the dominant group. In other words, peoples of Color are almost always seen as "having a race" and described in racial terms (e.g., "a *Black* man," "an *Aboriginal* director"), whereas Whites are rarely defined by race (e.g., "a man," "a director"), thereby allowing Whites to move through society as "just people," while peoples of Color are seen as part of a racial group (Dyer, 1997; DiAngelo, 2016). This dynamic also allows Whites to see themselves as objective and peoples of Color as having "special" or biased interests and agendas.

Of course to see oneself as an individual is a very different dynamic for peoples of Color. While for White people insisting that one is an individual is often a strategy for *resisting* acknowledging that their race has meaning, for peoples of Color it can be a strategy for *coping* with always being seen in racial terms. Since peoples of Color are denied individuality by dominant society, individualism can actually be a way to challenge racism and an important counter to the relentless imposition of racial identity on them. Because the social and institutional positions are not the same between Whites and peoples of Color, the dynamics of how ideologies are used are not the same.

Thus to challenge a particular form of oppression requires different tasks based on one's position. If we fall into the dominant group, one of our tasks is to look past our sense of ourselves as individuals and examine our group history and socialization. If we fall into the minoritized group, one of our tasks is to claim individual complexity. That is, to challenge the way in which society has focused solely on our minoritized identity and denied us a sense of individuality.

Racism Today

Contrary to the opinions of many Whites, we are not living in a postracial society. Racial disparity between Whites and peoples of Color exists in every institution across society. Here we give brief examples of how racism plays out within a few social institutions.

Health. According to the UN ranking of the standard of living of the world's nations (the Human Development Index or HDI), Indigenous people in Canada and the United States have a lower HDI score when compared to the general population (Mikkonen & Raphael, 2010):

🤚 **STOP:** While they may be difficult to see and thus are often denied, racial disparities and their effects on overall quality of life have been extensively documented by a wide range of agencies, including: federal (such as Statistics Canada, U.S. Census Bureau, United Nations), university (such as UCLA Civil Rights Project, Metropolis Project), and nonprofit (such as Canadian Centre for Policy Alternatives, Canadian Anti-Racism Education and Research Society, NAACP, Anti-Defamation League).

- U.S. general population HDI: ranks 7th internationally
- Canadian general population HDI: ranks 8th internationally
- U.S. American Indian/Alaska Native population HDI: ranks 31st internationally
- Canadian Aboriginal population HDI: ranks 33rd internationally

In 2015 the average life expectancy for a U.S. citizen was 79.3 years, and for a Canadian citizen was 82.2 years, which are both higher than the average global life expectancy of 71.4 (WHO, 2016). While Canada overall ranks 13 of 38 OECD nations, the U.S. ranks 26 of 38 nations for life expectancy (Organization for Economic Cooperation and Development, 2015).

At birth, the life expectancy in the United States is as follows (Arias, Heron, & Xu, 2012):

White males—76.7   Black males—72.3
White females—81.4   Black females—78.4

Economy. In the United States in 2014, the median household income was $53,657 (DeNavas-Walt & Proctor, 2015), broken down as:

- Black household—$35,398
- Hispanic (any race) household—$42,491
- White (not Hispanic) household—$60,256
- Asian household—$74,297

The 2014 poverty rate in the United States was 14.8% (46.7 million people in poverty). The 2014 rate was 2.3% higher than the 2007 rate (DeNavas-Walt & Proctor, 2015). By race:

- Non-Hispanic Whites—10.1%
- Asians—12%
- Hispanics—23.6%
- Blacks—26.2%

Racialized Canadians are at greater risk of living in poverty. The 2006 Canada Census (the last stats available) show the overall poverty rate in Canada was 11% but 22% for racialized persons, and 9% for non-racialized persons (Government of Canada, 2013).

For every dollar earned by a non-racialized man, a racialized woman in Canada will earn 55.6 cents (Block & Galabuzi, 2011).

Criminal justice. When broken down by race and gender, incarceration rates in the United States are as follows (Mauer & King, 2007; Sakala, 2014):

- White (non-Hispanic) men: 64% of U.S. population, 39% of incarcerated population—450 per 100,000
- Hispanic men: 16% of U.S. population, 19% of incarcerated population—831 per 100,000
- Black men: 13% of U.S. population, 40% of incarcerated population—2,306 per 100,000

In Canada, the 2014 federal incarceration rate was 54 per 100,000 (Statistics Canada, 2015a). Aboriginal people account for a disproportionate percentage of the prison population. They make up approximate 3% of the national adult population, Adult Aboriginal people made up 26% of correctional admissions with Aboriginal females accounting for a higher proportion of female admissions (36%) than Aboriginal males for male admissions (25%) (Statistics Canada, 2015a). This gap is more pronounced for Aboriginal youth, who accounted for 41% of corrections admissions while representing 7% of the youth population. Aboriginal girls accounted for 53% of female youth admitted to corrections, where Aboriginal male youth accounted for 38% of males admitted (Statistics Canada, 2015b).

These disparities are an important reminder about the role of theory in explaining data. Readers may recall from the discussion in Chapter 2 that theory is the way we make sense of what we see. Reflect for a moment on how you explain racial disparities. This is an important exercise because our explanations reveal our meaning-making frameworks and thus are a great entry point into deeper racial self-knowledge. We can explain these statistics with cultural deficit theory (in other words, there is something wrong with the culture of communities of Color that results in these disparities). However, cultural deficit theory blames peoples of Color for their struggles within a racist society while obscuring larger structural barriers. Cultural deficit theory also exempts dominant culture from the need to play any role in the eradication of racism.

If we consider historical, institutional, and cultural racism, the explanation looks very different. Many incarcerated peoples of Color have attended underfunded and deteriorating schools, have had poor access to health care, have historically been denied mortgages and other wealth-building programs, and have received inequitable treatment in every other major institution that would have given them and their children an equal starting point in life (Alexander, 2010). These are examples of institutional racism, not a personal lack of responsibility or a cultural flaw.

The way that we explain (or theorize) a problem determines how we respond to the problem. If we perceive the problem as one of a violent and criminal people, we might build more prisons and create more sophisticated mechanisms to monitor them. And in fact, although crime has actually *decreased* over the last 30 years, this is the view we have taken, and in response the United States has built more and more prisons and incarcerated more and more peoples of Color, so that the United States now has the highest number of people incarcerated in the world, and the vast majority of them are Black and Latino, a rate that is way out of proportion with their numbers in the wider population (Alexander, 2010). But if we perceive the problem as one of structural racism, we might change the way we fund schools, ensure that every family has affordable access to health care and social services, work to decrease racial profiling, and change the policies that allow wealth to be ever more concentrated into fewer hands.

Both Canada and the United States are nations that were built on the labor of peoples of Color: the labor of Indigenous peoples who were enslaved, served in military capacities, and helped early colonizers navigate the land; the labor of enslaved Africans who fueled high-value agricultural industries such as cotton, tobacco, sugar, and coffee; the labor of Chinese and Japanese workers who did the backbreaking work of building the railways that formed the major transportation portals for the early period of the nation state. All of this labor was given for very little if any financial remuneration, authority, or ownership of the national infrastructure and wealth that was built on it.

While we might acknowledge that these were unfair practices of the past, consider the division of labor along race lines in the United States and in Canada today. Who are the people picking the fruit we buy, cleaning our homes, hotels, and workplaces, providing at-home child care or elder care, and sewing the clothes that come to our local department and box store at remarkably cheap prices? Backbreaking, low-wage, low-reward work is still performed primarily by peoples of Color (Marable, Ness & Wilson, 2006; Schoenfish-Keita & Johnson, 2010; Sharma, 2002).

There have been some protections put in place to guard against the most blatant and intentional manifestations of racism from the past, but racism still operates in new and modified ways. Colorblind racism is a cogent example of this adaptation. This is the belief that pretending that we don't notice race will end (or has already ended) racism. This idea comes out of the civil rights movement of the 1960s and Martin Luther King's "I Have a Dream" speech. King's speech symbolized a turning point in the adaptation of racism in dominant culture. Before the period leading up to his speech, many White people felt quite comfortable to admit to their racial prejudices and sense of racial superiority. But once the civil rights movement took root and civil rights legislation was passed, there was a significant change in mainstream culture; it was no longer as acceptable for White people to admit to racial prejudice.

White racism didn't disappear, of course; Whites just became somewhat more careful in public space (Picca & Feagin, 2007). Seizing on one part of King's speech—that one day he might be judged by the content of his character and not the color of his skin—dominant culture began promoting the idea of "colorblindness" as a remedy for racism. King's speech was given at a march for economic justice—the March on Washington for Jobs and Freedom—and he was there to advocate for the elimination of poverty, but few people today know what his cause was fully about (Bonilla-Silva, 2006).

While colorblindness sounds good in theory, in practice it is highly problematic. We *do* see the race of other people, and that race has meaning for us. Everyone receives racist messages that circulate in society; they are all around us. While some of these messages are blatant (racist jokes, for example), we must understand that most of the messages we receive are subtler and are often invisible, especially to Whites. Drawing on what we discussed in Chapter 3 on socialization, we know that while we learn very early about race, much of what we learn is below the level of our conscious awareness (as with the iceberg) and colorblind ideology makes it difficult for us to address these unconscious beliefs. While the idea started out as a well-intended strategy for interrupting racism, in practice it has served to deny the reality of racism and thus hold it in place.

To get a sense of what might be below the surface of our conscious racial awareness, try the following thought experiment:

At what point in your life were you aware that people from racial groups other than your own existed (most peoples of Color recall a sense of "always having been" aware, while most White people recall being aware by at least age 5). If you were aware of the existence of people from racial groups other than your own, where did they live? If they did not live in your neighborhood, what kind of neighborhood did they live in? Were their neighborhoods considered "good" or "bad"? What images did you associate with these other neighborhoods? What about sights and smells? What kind of activities did you think went on there? Where did your ideas come from? Were you encouraged to visit their neighborhoods? Or were you discouraged from visiting their neighborhoods? If you attended a school considered "good," what made it good? Conversely, what made a school "bad"? Who went to "bad" schools? If the schools in your area were racially segregated, were their schools considered equal to, better, or worse than yours? Why didn't you attend school together? If this is because you lived in different neighborhoods, why did you live in different neighborhoods? If you were told by your parents and teachers that "all people are equal regardless of the color of

> ✓ **PERSPECTIVE CHECK:** If some of these questions do not apply to the cultural context you grew up in, try the following: Adjust the questions to capture how you learned about racial difference, for example how you saw people from racial groups residing outside of your nation state or perhaps people from ethnic groups different from your own residing within your nation state. Use socioeconomic class to think through the questions, for example, how did class differences shape where you lived and how you learned your "place" in society? Consider the impact of Whiteness as a global phenomenon. What did you learn it meant to be White? What did you learn it meant to be a member of a racial group that is not White?

their skin," yet you lived separately from people who had a different skin color, what message did that contradiction send? If you lived and went to school in racial segregation you had to make sense of this incongruity. In other words, what does it mean to say that all people are equal but live separately from them? Our lived separation is a more powerful message than our words of inclusion because the separation is manifested in *action,* while inclusion is not.

Dynamics of White Racial Superiority

If we are White we receive constant messages that we are better and more important than peoples of Color, regardless of our personal intentions or beliefs (Fine, 1997). These messages operate on multiple levels and are conveyed in a range of ways, for example: our centrality in history textbooks and other historical representations; our centrality in media and advertising; our teachers, role models, heroes, and heroines all reflecting *us*; everyday discussions about "good" neighborhoods and schools and the racial makeup of these favored locations; popular TV shows centered around friendship circles that are all White, even when they take place in racially diverse cities such as New York (*Friends, Seinfeld, Sex and the City, Gossip Girl; Girls*); religious iconography that depicts Adam and Eve, other key Christian figures, and even God as White; newscasters referring to any crime than occurs in a White neighborhood as "shocking"; and the lack of a sense of loss about the absence of peoples of Color in most White people's lives. These are examples of implicit (indirect) rather than explicit (direct) messages, all telling us that it's better to be White. Although we can attempt to notice and block out each one, they come at us collectively and so relentlessly that this is virtually impossible to do. While we may explicitly reject the notion that we are inherently better than peoples of Color, we cannot avoid internalizing the message of White superiority below the surface of our consciousness because it is ubiquitous in mainstream culture.

Let's look a little more closely at the increase in racial segregation as an example. Whites are the racial group that lives the most racially segregated lives (Johnson & Shapiro, 2003), and Whites are most likely to be in the economic position to choose this segregation (rather than have it imposed on them). In the United States we are actually returning to pre-integration levels of racial segregation; schools and neighborhoods are becoming *more* racially separated, not less (Frankenberg, Lee, & Orfield, 2003). In fact, racial segregation is often what defines schools and neighborhoods as "good" for Whites; we come to understand that a "good school" or "good neighborhood" is often coded language for "White," while "urban" is code for "not-White" and therefore less desirable (Johnson & Shapiro, 2003; Watson, 2011). At the same time, although we prefer segregation, most Whites profess to be colorblind and claim that race does not matter (Bonilla-Silva, 2006). Even when Whites live in physical proximity to peoples of Color (and this is exceptional outside of a lower-class urban neighborhood), segregation is occurring on many other levels in the culture (and often in the school itself), including images in media and information in schools. Because Whites choose to live primarily segregated lives within a White dominated society, we receive little or no authentic information about racism and are thus unprepared to think about it critically.

> 🖐 **STOP:** Not all our messages are as *implicit* (under the surface) as de facto segregation. We are also surrounded by friends and family who make direct comments and jokes about people of other races.

Stereotypical media representations compound the impact of racial segregation on our limited understanding of peoples of Color. Most people understand that movies have a profound effect on our ideas about the world. Concepts of masculinity and femininity, sexuality, desire, adventure, romance, family, love, and conflict are all conveyed to us through the stories told in films. Anyone who is around children—even as young as 2—will see the power of movies to shape children's interests, fantasies, and play. Now consider that the vast majority of all mainstream films are written and directed by White men, most often from the middle and upper classes. In fact, the top 25 highest grossing films of all time worldwide were all directed by men (with one woman as co-director for *Frozen*) and all White (with one man of Color director for *Furious 7*) (Box Office Mojo, 2017). Of the top 100 films worldwide, 99 were directed wholly by men. Of these top 100 films, 95 were directed by White people. Because of the racial segregation that is ubiquitous throughout society, these men are very unlikely to have gone to school with, lived nearby, been taught by, or been employed by or with peoples of Color. Therefore they are very unlikely to have meaningful or egalitarian cross-racial relationships. Yet these men are society's "cultural authors"; their dreams, their desires, their conceptions of "the other" become ours. Consider the implications of this very privileged and homogenous group essentially telling all of our stories.

The life and work of Jay Silverheels (Figure 8.1) illustrates the challenges peoples of Color have dealing with racism in Hollywood.

Because we all share the same socialization through the wider culture (the frames in our glasses metaphor) familiar images are an effective way to quickly communicate a storyline. For example, consider a director making a film about a White teacher who is courageous enough to teach in an "inner-city" school and, in so doing, teaches the children valuable lessons that it is assumed they wouldn't otherwise receive. The director will very likely pan the camera down a street to show houses and apartments in disrepair, graffiti, and groups of Blacks, Latinos, or Southeast Asians hanging out on street corners. The audience, because it has seen this association many times before, immediately knows that we are in a dangerous

Figure 8.1. Jay Silverheels (1919–1980)

Silverheels was an elite athlete competing in high-level wrestling, lacrosse, and boxing events, playing on Canada's national lacrosse team before he developed an interest in acting. Like many Indigenous actors, early in his career he was credited in bit parts simply as "Indian." But many of us remember him in the role that made him famous, playing the Lone Ranger's companion, Tonto. Silverheels himself recognized the difficulty of portraying a character that was described by some as the Uncle Tom of Indigenous peoples. However, with this role Silverheels would be the first Native American actor to star in a leading role on a television show.

Like many minoritized actors, Silverheels found it difficult to break out of the stereotypical characters he was asked to play. He was also an activist for improving the portrayal of Native American peoples in media. He was very aware of the problems of Hollywood's representation of Indigenous peoples but felt that working Indigenous actors could influence the films and shows in which they appeared. In 1966 he helped found the Indian Actors Workshop to offer free classes to aspiring Native American actors to work in film, theater, and television.

Source: www.poorwilliam.net/pix/silverheels-jay.jpg

---

neighborhood, and the context has been set. Over and over, White male directors depict peoples of Color and their neighborhoods in narrow, limited, and stereotypical ways. Not having many (if any) cross-racial friendships, most Whites come to rely on these images for their understanding of peoples of Color, reinforcing the idea of a positive "us" versus a negative "them."

In addition to a wide range of film roles, Whites see their own images reflected back in virtually any situation or location deemed valuable in dominant society (e.g., academia, politics, management, art events, popular magazines, the Academy Awards). Indeed, it is a rare event for most Whites to experience a sense of *not* belonging racially, and these situations are usually temporary and easily avoidable. Thus racial belonging and "rightness" become deeply internalized and taken for granted.

A key dynamic of the relationship between dominant and minoritized groups is to name the minoritized group as different, while the dominant group remains unnamed. For example, when we say "American" we do not mean "any and all-Americans," we mean White Americans but are not naming White because it is assumed unless otherwise noted. Just as when we say "soccer game" we do not mean "any and all-soccer game," we mean men's soccer game but are not naming men because it is already assumed unless otherwise noted. We would have to make the point that it was a Chinese American or women's soccer game that we are referring to. We are comfortable with this pattern because we are socialized to name the minoritized groups (*Chinese* American, *women's* soccer) and assign a universal neutrality to dominant groups.

This naming/not-naming dynamic sets race up as something *they* have, not *us*. Whites tend to see race only when peoples of Color are present, but see all-White spaces as neutral and nonracial. Because racial segregation for most Whites is normal and unremarkable, we rarely, if ever, have to think about race and racism. Conversely, peoples of Color must always bear the mark of race as they move about their daily lives. The psychic burden that peoples of Color must carry to get through a day is often exhausting, while Whites are freed from carrying this racial burden. Race becomes something for peoples of Color to think about—it is what happens to them. This allows Whites much more energy to devote to other issues and prevents us from developing the stamina to sustain attention on an issue as charged and uncomfortable for us as race.

Dynamics of Internalized Racial Oppression

All of the messages that White people receive about their value, both explicitly and implicitly, are also received by peoples of Color (Mullaly, 2002; Tatum, 1997). In other words, peoples of Color are also told, in myriad ways, that to be White is better than to be a person of Color. And similar to the mixed messages that White parents send to their children by saying that everyone is equal while simultaneously living in segregation, children of Color also get mixed messages. Their parents may tell them that they are good, strong, and beautiful, but the society around them is still conveying that they are of lesser value.

Internalized racial oppression occurs when a person of Color, consciously and subconsciously, accepts the negative representation or invisibility of peoples of Color in media, education, medicine, science, and all other aspects of society. Over time, the person comes to believe that they are less valuable and may act this out through self-defeating behaviors and sometimes by distancing themselves from others of their own or other non-White racial groups. Although there are important differences in how various racialized groups experience internalized racial oppression, groups of Color are collectively shaped by the following:

- Historical violence and the ongoing threat of violence
- Destruction, colonization, dilution, and exoticization of their cultures
- Division, separation, and isolation from one another and from dominant culture
- Forced changes in behaviors to ensure psychological and physical safety and to gain access to resources

- Having individual behaviors redefined as group norms
- Denied individuality and held up as representative of (or occasionally as exceptions to) their group
- Being blamed for the effects of long-term oppression by the dominant group, and having the effects of that oppression used to rationalize further oppression

The internalization of and adaptation to dominant culture's messages can cause a kind of self-defeating cycle. Carter Woodson, writing in 1933, powerfully captures the dynamics of internalized racial oppression when he writes:

> If you can control a man's thinking, you don't have to worry about his actions. If you can determine what a man thinks, you do not have worry about what he will do. If you can make a man believe that he is inferior, you don't have to compel him to seek an inferior status, he will do so without being told, and if you can make a man believe that he is justly an outcast, you don't have to order him to the back door, he will go to the back door on his own, and if there is no back door, the very nature of the man will demand that you build one. (p. xiii)

Woodson is speaking to one of the more profound and painful dynamics of oppression; once people believe that they deserve their position in society, external force is not needed. As can be seen in several important studies discussed below, this internalization occurs at a very early age. It is important to note, however, that peoples of Color have always resisted internalized racial oppression, but this resistance has costs and can be very dangerous; resistance has historically been used to further rationalize violence against peoples of Color.

Claude Steele's (1997) work on stereotype threat demonstrates the impact of internalized racial oppression. *Stereotype threat* refers to a concern that you will be evaluated negatively due to stereotypes about your racial group, and that concern causes you to perform poorly, thereby reinforcing the stereotype. Because there is a powerful stereotype in mainstream culture that Blacks are less intelligent than Whites and other racial groups, Steele and his colleagues examined the effects of this stereotype on test performance. They found that the mere threat of the stereotype can diminish the performance of Black students. Their research shows that when Black students are told that their racial group tends to do poorly on a test, they score lower when taking that test. When the stereotype is not raised, they perform better.

In light of Steele's work, consider how much attention is given in schools to the so-called achievement gap and other disparities in outcome between Whites and some groups of Color (Black, Latino, and Indigenous students in particular), and how often these disparities are formally and informally explained as a function of genetics or inferior cultural morals that do not value education. Concerns and assumptions about their abilities constantly surround students of Color. It is important to remember that these stereotypes are not just "in their heads"; Whites do hold these stereotypes and they do affect the way Whites evaluate peoples of Color (Bertrand & Mullainathan, 2004; Picca & Feagin, 2007). White teachers, for example, who comprise over 90% of K–12 teachers (Picower, 2009), are in a particularly powerful position to evaluate students of Color. Thus, Steele's research captures the relationship between internalized oppression and internalized superiority.

Another powerful illustration of internalized racial oppression was demonstrated through the work of psychologists Kenneth Clark and Mamie Clark (1950). The Clarks used dolls to study children's attitudes about race. The Clarks testified as expert witnesses in *Briggs v. Elliott,* one of the cases connected to the 1954 *Brown v. Board of Education* case in the United States, which ruled that enforced racial segregation in schools was illegal. The Clarks found that Black children often preferred to play with White dolls over Black dolls and that when asked to fill in a human figure with the color of their own skin, they frequently chose a shade lighter than their skin actually was. Black children also described the White doll as good and pretty, but the Black doll as bad and ugly. The Clarks offered their results as evidence that the children had internalized racism. Chief Justice Earl Warren delivered the opinion of the Court: "To separate [some children] from others of similar age and qualifications solely because of their race generates a feeling of inferiority as to their status in the community that may affect their hearts and minds in a way unlikely ever to be undone" (*Brown v. Board of Education,* 1954). This is an important quote to remember as we watch schools in the United States return to pre-civil-rights-era levels of racial segregation.

In 2005 Kiri Davis, an African American teen, repeated the Clarks' experiment to see what had changed in Black children's attitudes over the past 50 years. In her documentary film *A Girl Like Me,* 15 out of the 21 children she interviewed (or 71%) preferred the White dolls for the same reasons as children cited in the 1940s; the White doll was "good" and the Black doll was "bad." While many people believe that children are innocent and unaware of racial messages, research has shown that children of all races and as young as 3 have internalized the societal message that White is superior to Black (Doyle & Aboud, 1995; VanAusdale & Feagin, 2001). The effect of this on White children is internalized racial superiority; the effect on children of Color is internalized racial inferiority. Internalized racial inferiority has devastating impacts on all aspects of a person's life.

This brief discussion of some of the dynamics of internalized racial oppression is not meant to blame the victim for the effects of racism. Rather, it is meant to briefly highlight the damaging effects of White racism and White supremacy on peoples of Color.

Racism and Intersectionality

While we have discussed racism in general terms, our other social group memberships, such as class, gender, sexuality, and ability greatly affect how we will experience race. For example, one of the key limitations of Second Wave Feminism was that the movement addressed women as though they were a cohesive group and assumed they had shared experiences and interests. Actually, the women we think of as at the forefront of the women's movement of the 1960s were White middle-class women (Frankenberg, 1993; Moraga & Anzaldúa, 1981). In many key areas, their interests were not the same as other groups of women. For example, while White middle-class women may have been eager to break their domestic confinement and enter the workplace, women of Color had long been in the workplace. Women of Color's interests may have been better served by fighting for the economic and social conditions that would allow them to stay home to raise their children without being seen as lazy or bad mothers.

Intersectionality is the term scholars use to acknowledge the reality that we simultaneously occupy both oppressed and privileged positions and that these positions intersect in complex ways (Collins, 2000; Crenshaw, 1995). For example, poor Whites, while oppressed through classism, are also elevated by race privilege, so that to be poor and Asian, for example, is not the same experience as being poor and White. Further, because of sexism, to be a poor White female will create barriers that a poor White male will not face due to gender privilege. However, while the poor White female *will* have to deal with sexism, she will not have to deal with the racism that a poor Asian female will face. Indeed, race privilege will help a poor White female cope with poverty, for example, when looking for work or navigating social services such as welfare and health care. Facing oppression in one area of social life does not "cancel out" your privilege in another; these identities will be more or less salient in different situations. The challenge is to identify how our identities play out in shifting social contexts.

We return now to the student quote that opened this chapter: "I was really lucky. I grew up in a good neighborhood and went to good schools There were no problems with racism. I didn't learn anything about different races. My family taught me that everyone is equal." This quote is a powerful illustration of how White people make sense of race and the invisibility of racism to us.

First, the term "good neighborhood" is usually code for "predominately White." To believe that one learned nothing about racism and that there were "no problems" with racism in a White enviroment positions Whites as outside of race; Whites are "just human," with no racial experience of their own. Race becomes what peoples of Color have. If peoples of Color are not present, race is not present. Further, if peoples of Color are not present, not only is race absent, so is that terrible thing: *racism*. Ironically, this positions racism as something peoples of Color bring to Whites, rather than a system that Whites control and impose on peoples of Color. To place race and racism on peoples of Color and to see race and racism as absent in an all-White space is to construct Whiteness as neutral and innocent. We need to ask ourselves why a neighborhood is seen as good if it's segregated.

Second, a predominately White neighborhood is not the product of luck, a natural preference to be with one's "own," or a fluke; all-White neighborhoods are the end result of centuries of racist policies, practices, and attitudes that have systematically denied peoples of Color entrance into White neighborhoods (Conley, 1999). In the past this was done legally. Today this is accomplished through mechanisms such as discrimination in lending, real estate practices that steer homebuyers into specific neighborhoods, funding roads but not public transportation that could make suburbs more accessible, and White flight. All-White neighborhoods and schools don't just happen.

Contrary to her claims, this student learned quite a bit about race in her White neighborhood and schools. As we noted earlier, there is a contradiction in saying to our children, "Everyone is the same," while raising them in all-White spaces. Conveying to our children that living in a White neighborhood makes them lucky, rather than conveying to them that they have lost something valuable by not having cross-racial relationships, is to teach them a great deal about race.

Discussion Questions

1. The authors argue that racism is more than the acts of individual bad people. What, then, is racism? What is problematic about reducing racism to simply the bad things some people think and do?
2. The authors argue that to have grown up in racially segregated communities is to learn a great deal about race. How? What kinds of things do we learn?
3. What is intersectionality? Choose a few of your other social group memberships (class, gender, sexuality, religion) and describe how they influence how you experience race.

Extension Activities

1. Watch the film *Reel Injun* (C. Bainbridge, D. Ravida, C. Fon, L. Ludwick, & E. Webb, Producers; N. Diamond, Director; Montreal, Canada: Rezolution Pictures, 2009. Available at www.reelinjunthemovie.com). Read *The Lone Ranger and Tonto Fistfight in Heaven* by S. Alexie (New York: Grove Press, 2005). Write an essay about how Hollywood has shaped how you think about Indigenous people. At what cost do Indigenous people play roles that are written for them by White people? (See Figure 8.1 for information on Jay Silverheels.)
2. a. Track racism today in the context of schooling. Identify a grade level (elementary, secondary, postsecondary) and an organizational level (district, province, state, or federal) and collect data on the following dimensions of schooling and race:

    » Demographics of the student, teaching, and staff populations
    » Information about the content of the curriculum (textbooks used
      and year of publication, key figures studied, literature read)
    » School calendar and other events (holidays, celebrations, days off)
    » Funding levels and sources
  b. Compare your findings with another school in a different socioeconomic
     context (e.g., the race and gender demographics of school tracks, such as
     special and gifted in the K–12 context, or disciplines in higher education;
     teacher credentials and length of tenure at the school).
  c. Write a letter to the school district outlining your findings. Draw on the
     ideas from this chapter and other readings that analyze racism in educa-
     tion.

Patterns to Practice Seeing

1. Think about the primary places you live, work/learn, and take leisure. How
   racially diverse are these environments? Where there is racial diversity, which
   groups are most represented? Which groups are least represented? Do people
   tend to have close relationships across groups?
2. How racially diverse are the people in leadership positions in your environment? How informed and concerned do they seem to be about racial inequity?
   How is this concern or lack thereof conveyed? What have been the outcomes of
   any concern they might have expressed?

CHAPTER 9

Understanding the Global Organization of Racism Through White Supremacy

"Why can't we all just be human? Isn't it this focus on race that divides us?"

This chapter continues the examination of racism by identifying a few of the ways in which racism adapts to and co-opts efforts to challenge it. We contrast multicultural education and antiracist education, introduce Whiteness and White supremacy, and end by addressing common misconceptions about racism.

Vocabulary to practice using: whiteness; white supremacy; colonialism; antiracism

As with other forms of oppression, one of the most tenacious elements of racism is its ability to adapt to and co-opt efforts to challenge it. Consider the example of multicultural education. Multicultural education is an educational approach that has taken root over the last several decades. Proponents of multicultural education recognize that schools are not set up to meet the needs of minoritized groups. While there are variations in approaches to multicultural education, Banks and Banks (1995) define it as:

> a field of study . . . whose major aim is to create equal educational opportunities for students from diverse racial, ethnic, social-class, and cultural groups. One of its important goals is to help all students to acquire the knowledge, attitudes, and skills needed to function effectively in a pluralistic democratic society and to interact, negotiate, and communicate with peoples from diverse groups in order to create a civic and moral community that works for the common good. (p. xi)

However, although it started as a movement to challenge the dominant norms, definitions, practices, and polices in education, multicultural education today all too often manifests simply as "celebrating diversity." This celebration of diversity is often done through activities such as sharing food from different cultures and celebrating holidays such as Hanukkah and Kwanza along with the traditional celebration of Christmas. Yet this approach does not acknowledge the history and politics of difference. In practice, this approach to multicultural education is the ideology of individualism applied to each unique ethnic group in a school. Celebrating diversity is important, but because it tends to occur without a study of power, this celebration actually reinforces structural inequality by obscuring unequal power between groups. This allows us to appear as though we are progressive and racially inclusive without actually addressing oppression. Contrast celebrating diversity as it is commonly practiced in schools with the Banks and Banks definition above. Clearly, much complexity is missing from the former practices.

Unlike mainstream forms of multicultural education, antiracist education focuses on the inequitable distribution of power, and racial power in particular. Antiracist education deliberately goes beyond the celebrating approach common to most multicultural programs. Instead, it centers the analysis on the social, cultural, and institutional power that so profoundly shape the meaning and outcome of racial difference. Antiracist education recognizes racism as embedded in all aspects of society and the socialization process; no one who is born into and raised in Western culture can escape being socialized to participate in racist relations. Antiracist education seeks to interrupt these relations by educating people to identify, name, and challenge the norms, patterns, traditions, ideologies, structures, and institutions that keep racism in place. A key aspect of this education process is to raise the consciousness of White people about what racism is and how it works. To accomplish this, we must challenge the dominant conceptualization of racism as individual acts that only some bad individuals do, rather than as a system in which we are all implicated. Using a structural definition of racism allows us to explore our own relationship to racism as a system and to move beyond isolated incidents and/or intentions.

What is Whiteness?

Critical scholars define *racism* as a systemic relationship of unequal power between White people and peoples of Color. *Whiteness* refers to the specific dimensions of racism that elevates White people over all peoples of Color. Basic rights, resources, and experiences that are assumed to be shared by all, are actually only available to White people. Although many

> **STOP:** Racism is about a relationship of unequal *power*. As we recall from Chapter 5, relationships of unequal power do not flip back and forth; they are deeply and historically embedded in one direction.

White people feel that being White has no meaning, this feeling is unique to White people and is a key part of what it means to be White; to see one's race as having no meaning is a privilege only Whites are afforded. To claim to be "just human" and thus outside of race is one of the most powerful and pervasive manifestations of Whiteness.

People of Color, among them W. E. B. Du Bois and James Baldwin, wrote about Whiteness as early as 1900. These writers urged White people to stop studying racial Others and turn their attention onto themselves to explore what it means to be White in a society that is so divided by race. Finally, by the 1990s, White scholars began to rise to this challenge. These scholars examine the cultural, historical, and sociological aspects of being White and how they are tied to power and privilege.

White power and privilege is termed *White supremacy*. When we use the term *White supremacy*, we do not mean it in its lay usage to indicate extreme hate groups such as the Ku Klux Klan or the dozens of others like it. Rather, we use the term to capture the pervasiveness, magnitude, and normalcy of White privilege, dominance, and assumed superiority.

STOP: When we use the term *White supremacy*, we are not referring to extreme hate groups or "bad racists." We use the term to capture the all-encompassing dimensions of White privilege, dominance, and assumed superiority in mainstream society.

The life and activism of Fred Korematsu (Figure 9.1) illustrate the power of institutional racism.

White Supremacy in the Global Context

Although commonsense understandings about social power often have us thinking in terms of numbers, as we have argued, power is not dependent on numbers but on *position*. In other words, power is dependent on what position a group holds and their ability to affect other groups from that position. Through movies and mass media, corporate culture and advertising, and Christian missionary work, White supremacy is able to circulate in the global context. In addition to specific political practices, policies, and military control, White supremacy is also a powerful ideology that promotes the idea of Whiteness as the ideal for humanity.

Consider how White supremacy (invisible and universalized White cultural practices and structural privileges) circulates globally in each of these instances:

- European (most notably English, French, and Spanish) discovery myths of Africa, Middle East, North/Central/South Americas

Figure 9.1. Fred Korematsu (1919–2005)

Fred Korematsu was one of the many U.S.- and Canadian-born citizens of Japanese descent who were identified for relocation and internment during World War II. After being denied entry to serve in the U.S. military, Korematsu worked as a welder. In 1942, Roosevelt signed the executive order authorizing the detention and relocation to holding camps of Americans of Japanese heritage. Korematsu refused detainment. His case was the first to challenge the constitutionality of the federal government's internment of Japanese Americans. He was convicted in 1944 when the U.S. Supreme Court decided that the Japanese American incarceration was justified due to military necessity and was not motivated by racism.

In 1983 his conviction was overturned, and in addressing the court, Mr. Korematsu said, "According to the Supreme Court decision regarding my case, being an American citizen was not enough. They say you have to look like one, otherwise they say you can't tell a difference between a loyal and a disloyal American. I thought that this decision was wrong and I still feel that way. As long as my record stands in federal court, any American citizen can be held in prison or concentration camps without a trial or a hearing. That is if they look like the enemy of our country. Therefore, I would like to see the government admit that they were wrong and do something about it so this will never happen again to any American citizen of any race, creed, or color."

Throughout his life, Korematsu continued his social justice work on behalf of others. He received numerous awards for his advocacy, including the U.S. Presidential Medal of Freedom in 1998.

Source: www.peoplesworld.org/calif-assembly-honors-japanese-american-civil-liberties-fighter/

- Colonizing geographical territories (and renaming them in colonial languages, and in relation to colonial powers—New York, New Brunswick)
- Redrawing or establishing borders in colonized territories according to the interests of colonial powers
- Colonial impositions of language onto Indigenous peoples
- The promotion of a consumer lifestyle and the values of consumption, profit, and competition, and the peoples most often exploited in the production of consumed goods
- The exploitation of global labor for increasing Western corporations' profits, and primarily for the West's consumption
- Environmental polluting, extraction of resources, and ravaging of countries in the global south (and rural or non-White dominant areas of Canada and the United States)

- Multinational corporations increasing profits for shareholders through practices such as those listed above, resulting in the concentration of wealth into fewer and fewer (White) hands
- Christian missionary work that endeavors to bring Christianity to "Third World" and Indigenous peoples and simultaneously brings White supremacy

> ✋ **STOP:** Remember, *White supremacy* does not refer to individual White people per se and their individual intentions, but to a political-economic social order based on the historical and current accumulation of structural power that privileges White people as a group.

Let's take one of the examples above to map out how White supremacy plays out: the partitioning of territories in accordance to Colonial/White Western powers' interests.

> ✋ **STOP:** Notice if you feel disinterested in history other than that of your own nation-state, and believe that this history is irrelevant to you. In the global context, Whiteness reduces our cultural tolerance for (and thus understanding of) alternative historical accounts. Understanding these alternative accounts is necessary for challenging White supremacy.

World War I brought an end to what was then known as the Ottoman Empire. The allies divided the territories of the Ottoman Empire primarily into the British and French mandates (contracts to govern). The British mandate included Mesopotamia—what is known today as Iraq and Palestine, and the French mandate included what is known today as Lebanon, Syria, and Jordan. The relevance of this history of British and French rule is that the dynamics of the partitioning and creation of these territories set in motion a whole series of political struggles, debates, and tensions that continue today. And of course British and French interests were not simply to be a stabilizing force; they included political, economic, and ideological investments in how these territories were divided and governed.

Now consider a very simplified historical overview of how these divisions played out in the example of Iraq. Almost overnight, the people of Iraq were governed by a foreign power who had no real knowledge or understanding of their culture, history, or ethnic relations. Britain imposed a monarchy and rule by class elites that did not take the various ethnic and cultural dynamics of the territory into consideration. Many of the ethnic groups within Iraq (such as the Shiites and the Kurds) rose up in resistance and attempted to gain their independence. But Britain, which was dependent on oil from Iraq, suppressed these attempts and the monarchic power structure lasted for much of the 20th century, until it was overthrown by the national army in 1958. In many ways, the Baath party (which Saddam Hussein eventually took over) was tied to this struggle for independence from colonial rule.

One of the ways in which White supremacy circulates is by obscuring, negating, rewriting, or reducing to folklore the histories of colonized peoples (who are almost always peoples of Color). When there is a gap in historical knowledge and perspective, that gap is filled by the dominant discourse (story) of how things came to be, or why a certain region or people are violent and seemingly endlessly at war. White supremacy circulates in how we explain these conditions, for example, that some cultures are uncivilized (in contrast to the White West) or lack a civilizing religion (in contrast to the Christianity of the White West) or are genetically predisposed to violence (in contrast to White people of the West). All of these explanations hide White complicity in establishing the conditions of violence we see outside the West. They rationalize the need for "civilized" people to take control, bring order, and properly use and distribute the resources of the territory, while simultaneously reinforcing White culture as superior.

Common White Misconceptions about Racism

We have worked to address many of the common misconceptions about racism. However, given their tenacity, we end by revisiting many of the most common arguments we hear. Regardless of intentions, these arguments (some seemingly innocent and others seemingly progressive) serve dominant interests and ultimately function to protect rather than to challenge racism. In this way they can be conceptualized as ideologies of White supremacy.

"Why can't we all just be human? Isn't it this focus on race that divides us?" In Chapter 8 we discussed the discourse of individualism and how it functions to obscure the reality of racism and White privilege. While individualism asks, "Why can't we all just be different?" the "just human" discourse asks, "Why can't we all just be the same (after all, everyone's blood is red under the skin)?" Remember that a key dimension of White socialization is a sense of oneself as existing outside of race. Of course on the biological level we *are* all humans, but when applied to the social level, insisting that we just see each other as human has similar effects as individualism. Once again the significance of race and the advantages of being White are denied. Further, this discourse assumes that Whites and peoples of Color have the same reality, the same experiences in the same context, and that the same doors are open. Whites invoke these seemingly contradictory discourses— we are either all unique or we are all the same—interchangeably. Both discourses

deny White privilege and the significance of race. Further, on the cultural level, being an individual or being a human outside of a racial group is a social position only afforded to White people. Someday, if and when racism is overcome, this discourse will make sense, but to pretend that day has already arrived is a form of willful ignorance that works to deny the reality of racism.

As for the claim that focusing on race divides us, evidence shows that we are already divided by race on every measure of demographics and outcomes. We would argue that it is the refusal to take an honest account of the power of race as a social construct that keeps us divided.

"I have a friend who is a person of Color, which shows that I'm not racist." First, keep in mind that we are not defining racism as something that only some people are, but as a system that impacts everyone. All Whites who swim in the cultural water of Canada and the United States are socialized into psychological, institutional, and economic investments in upholding the racial system that privileges them. This socialization is not something we had a choice about nor is it something we can avoid. At the same time, this does not mean that we can't challenge our socialization and work to overcome it, although this takes a lifetime of commitment. Having peoples of Color in your life is of profound importance but does not in and of itself end White supremacy in the wider culture that shapes you, them, and your relationship.

Friendships alone are not enough to overcome all of our socialization; Whites still experience White privilege and maintain institutional control. Having a friend of Color does not, in and of itself, mean that you are educated about the complexities of racism, that you have worked to address your internalized dominance, or that you consistently treat your friend with cross-racial sensitivity and awareness. In addition, how much knowledge you have about the history of your friend's racial group and your receptivity to hearing about their personal experiences of racism will also impact the depth of your relationship.

"I went to school with a lot of people of Color. In fact, I was the minority at my school." What seems like a racially diverse environment for Whites does not always appear diverse for peoples of Color. But if you are White and went to school with a lot of peoples of Color, you probably grew up in an urban environment, and possibly urban poor. Even so, most schools with a racially diverse student population are still segregated *within* the school, mirroring the racial segregation of wider society. In addition, as you progress through life, upward mobility will often move you away from these schools, neighborhoods, and friends. We often find that White people who had a lot of childhood friends of Color rarely keep them because our schools, workplaces, and other environments channel us in separate directions. This illustrates the power of White solidarity to trump early cross-racial friendships.

Some Whites experience being a minority when they travel to another country. These experiences are important because they can provide some understanding of what peoples of Color experience here in Canada and the United States. However, being a minority in these contexts is not the same, because for most Whites, this is a temporary situation. While you can experience prejudice and can be discriminated against as a White person in the minority—and that is of course hurtful—it is *not* racism. First, to be in the minority as a White person is usually a situation Whites have chosen to be in and can easily escape. Second, in the larger society we are still affirmed as more valuable than peoples of Color and we receive White privilege.

In the context of another country, keep in mind that most of the countries in which a White person would be a minority have a history of being colonized by White people and of being forced to defer to Whites. Further, our movies and media have been exported globally and Whiteness has worldwide currency. For example, blepharoplasty, a surgical technique to make the eyes appear more "Caucasian," is the most popular cosmetic surgery in Asia and the third most frequently requested procedure among Asian Americans (Motapharthi, 2010); light skin is advertised in countries such as India as the most beautiful, and skin-lightening cream is a huge industry around the world (Li, Min, Belk, Kimura, & Bahl, 2008). While Whites might feel like outsiders when traveling in non-White countries, they are still elevated in myriad ways.

"People of Color are too sensitive. They play the race card." "Playing the race card" is a common accusation Whites make when peoples of Color bring up racism. To accuse a person of Color of playing the race card is to assert that the person's claim of racism is false. This is insulting to peoples of Color because it suggests that they are dishonest and that they lie about racism. This expression also reveals the lack of knowledge Whites have about racism and our arrogance that we could understand it better than peoples of Color.

Because of the factors we have discussed, there is much about racism that most Whites simply don't understand. Yet in our racial arrogance, we don't hesitate to debate the knowledge of people who have lived or studied these issues for many years. We feel free to dismiss these informed perspectives rather than to acknowledge that they are unfamiliar to us, reflect further on them, or seek more knowledge. Because of our social, economic, and political power within a White supremacist culture, Whites are in the position to legitimize peoples of Color's assertions of racism. Yet we are the least likely to see, understand, or be invested in validating those assertions, and the least likely to be honest about their consequences.

Because most Whites construct racism as specific acts that individuals either do or don't do, we think we can simply look at a specific incident and decide if "it" happened. But racism is infused in every part of society and in our perspectives. It is reinforced every day in countless and often subliminal ways. Our inability to think with complexity about racism, as well as our investment in it, makes Whites the least qualified to assess its manifestations. Our investment in denying racism also ensures that we will most often determine that "it" did *not* happen. The very concept of a race card at all, in a society so deeply divided by race, is a cogent example of White denial. Ironically, it's not much of a card to play since raising racism rarely gets peoples of Color anywhere with Whites. Very few Whites believe that structural racism is real or have the humility to engage with peoples of Color about it in an open and thoughtful way.

"This is just political correctness." Charges of political correctness often surface when Whites are being challenged to acknowledge racism. Like other terms that originate as a challenge to unequal power, the concept of political correctness has been co-opted by dominant interests. Political correctness originated as a term to describe language, ideas, policies, and behavior that seek to minimize social and institutional oppression. Now, it has come to mean cultural sensitivity that has been brought to absurd levels. As soon as the term political correctness surfaces, discussion ends, for no one wants to be accused of being "PC." Take for example the word *feminism*, which is simply the idea that women should have equal status and opportunity, but has now become a derogatory term with insulting variations such as "femi-nazi." Consider how conservative pundits have managed to take the idea of equality for women and equate it with Nazism, and how such absurd perversions of the term have been so normalized that many young women today don't want to be associated with feminism. We might reflect on whose interests it serves to position political correctness as something to be avoided.

"People of Color are just as racist as we are. In fact, now there is reverse racism and White people can't get into college or get good jobs." If you define racism as racial prejudice, then yes, anyone across any race can have just as much racial prejudice as anyone else. But racism is not merely racial prejudice. Racism is racial prejudice backed by institutional power. Only Whites have the power to infuse and enforce their prejudices throughout the culture and transform it into racism. If you understand what racism is, then you understand that there is no such thing as reverse racism. The term reverse racism implies that power relations move back and forth, one day benefiting one group and the next day the other. But as we can see from the founding of Canada and the United States to the present time, White power and privilege remain deeply rooted and intact.

For example, while the United States has elected a biracial President, and this is very significant, focusing our attention on isolated exceptions allows us to deny the significance of the rules themselves and whom they serve. The vast majority of

CEOs, Fortune 500 executives, managers, professors, doctors, lawyers, scientists, and other prestigious positions of leadership and decision making are Whites. While Whites are the majority of people in the United States and in Canada, their overrepresentation in leadership does not match their numbers in society.

Programs such as Affirmative Action in the United States and Employment Equity in Canada are often cited as examples of reverse racism or special privileges that peoples of Color and Indigenous peoples have over Whites. These programs were developed in order to redress the reality and pervasiveness of White discrimination against peoples of Color. Still, commonsense understanding of these programs is very limited; for example, no employer is required to hire an unqualified person of Color, but they *are* required to be able to articulate why they didn't hire a *qualified* person of Color.

Federal protections are important because although many Whites claim they would "hire the best person for the job," they do not understand that because of the constant messages that peoples of Color are inferior, who we *perceive* as the best person for the job will likely be someone White. According to Pager (2007), White men with a criminal record are slightly more likely to be called back for a job interview than Black men with no criminal record, even when they are equally qualified. In addition to unconscious preference for White applicants, another way racism manifests in the workplace is through the concept of "fit." This is the tendency to prefer people whose cultural style matches the workplace culture. Unfortunately, the culture of the workplace, unless owned by peoples of Color, will likely be White. This plays out in industries such as fashion, wherein there is a very specific and limited ideal of female beauty (such as narrow noses and slim hips), and in schooling when teacher candidates are evaluated based on whether the staff will be able to relate to them.

Although women were not originally included in Affirmative Action, White women have numerically been the program's greatest beneficiaries. While Affirmative Action and other programs have made an impact on increasing the numbers of underrepresented groups in employment, these programs have not come close to reaching their goals. Still, states such as California and Washington have ended Affirmative Action, and the Supreme Court ruled that giving points based on race could not be used in college admissions.

When thinking about programs such as Affirmative Action, it's important to remember the dynamics of race. Because Whites are seen as "just people" rather than as *White* people, when they are hired it is assumed to be because they are qualified. When peoples of Color are hired (regardless of whether an employment equity program had anything to do with their hire), Whites often assume that they were hired due to a special program. This assumption reveals that Whites see peoples of Color as *inherently* unqualified; we have difficulty imagining they could have gotten the job on their qualifications alone. Further, this assumption reveals the sense of entitlement Whites have to all desirable positions ("they got *my* place in law school" or "they got *my* job"). This also suggests that we are not quite as colorblind as we often claim.

"Racism is a thing of the past. Besides, I didn't own slaves; I wasn't around when Indians were put in residential schools." Many White people are woefully uninformed when it comes to the continuing presence of racism. Seeing ourselves as individuals, with no connection to our nations' pasts, erases history and hides the way in which wealth and social capital have accumulated over generations and benefit us as a group today. Canada and the United States were founded on the exploits of slavery as well as genocide, and racism did not end when slavery or the residential school systems ended (Zinn, 1980/2010). Legal and institutional exclusion of peoples of Color, in addition to illegal acts ranging from lynching to racial profiling, continue today. Racist acts of terrorism and the state-sanctioned killing of peoples of Color, such as the executions of Vincent Chin (1982), Dudley George (1995), James Byrd (1998), Amadou Diallo (1999), Kendra James (2003), Kathryn Johnston (2006), Trayvon Martin (2012), Andy Lopez (2013), Sammy Yatim (2013), Michael Brown (2014), Tamir Rice (2014), Akai Gurley (2014), Tanisha Anderson (2014), Eric Garner (2014), Freddie Gray (2015), Andrew Loku (2015), Walter Scott (2015), Jacqueline Salyers (2016), Alton Sterling (2016), Philando Castille (2016), Terence Crutcher (2017), Jose Nieves (2017), Charleena Lyles (2017), and countless others are commonplace.

Peoples of Color were denied Federal Housing Act (FHA) loans as recently as the 1950s. These loans allowed a generation of Whites to attain middle-class status through home ownership. Home ownership is critical in the United States because it is the means by which the average person builds and passes down wealth, providing the starting point for the next generation. Peoples of Color were systematically denied this opportunity and today the average White family has eight times the wealth of the average Black or Latino family (Federal Reserve Board, 2007). Excluding peoples of Color from the mechanisms of society that allow wealth building continues today through illegal but common practices such as higher mortgage rates, more difficulty getting loans, real estate agents steering them away from "good" neighborhoods, discrimination in hiring, and unequal school funding.

Racial group membership is consistently traced to inequitable outcomes on every indicator of quality of life and these outcomes are well documented and predictable (Hughes & Thomas, 1998; Williams, 1999). Limiting our analysis to the *micro* or individual level prevents a macro or big picture understanding. At the micro level ("*I* didn't own slaves"), we cannot assess and address the macro dimensions of society that help hold racism in place, such as practices, policies, norms, rules, laws, traditions, and regulations. For example, in the United States peoples of Color have been formally—and now informally—prevented from participating in government wealth-building programs that benefit White Americans.

Consider, for example, the ways in which schools are funded through the property tax base of the community in which they are situated. Given the fact that youth of Color disproportionately live in poor communities and their families rent rather than own, youth of Color are penalized through this policy, which ensures that poor communities will have inferior schools. In turn, this practice ensures that middle- and upper-class students, who are more likely to be White, will get a superior education and have less competition in the future workplace—an example of institutional racism and White privilege (Kozol, 1991).

In light of all the possible creative options for funding schools to ensure that every child has equal access to quality education, the current acceptance of the status quo is an example of institutional racism. Other examples of institutional racism that serve to reinforce the ways in which schools reproduce inequality include: mandatory culturally biased testing; ability tracking; a primarily White teaching force with the power to determine which students belong in which tracks; cultural definitions of intelligence, what constitutes it, and how it is measured; and standards of what constitutes good behavior as determined by White teachers and administration. Rather than serving as the great equalizer, schools function in actual practice to reproduce racial inequality. Insisting that we could not have benefited from racism because we personally didn't own slaves is extremely superficial and hides the reality of White advantage at every level of our past and present society.

Discussion Questions

1. What are the key differences between multicultural education and antiracist education? Discuss each of these differences and provide examples for each.
2. What is Whiteness? The authors claim that Whiteness is organized globally. How?
3. What do the authors mean when they use the term *White supremacy*? How does White supremacy manifest in institutions?

Extension Activities

1. Discuss some of the common misconceptions about racism. How would you counter these misconceptions from an antiracist perspective? In pairs or small groups, practice articulating your counter arguments.
2. Watch the film *Of Civil Wrongs and Rights: The Fred Korematsu Story* (Fournier et al., 2000) (korematsuinstitute.org/). (See Figure 9.1 for information on Korematsu.) Next, conduct further research into Japanese internment in WWII, or conduct research on another minoritized racial group who has challenged

legalized racism. Write an essay using these cases to illustrate how racism and White supremacy work, and their connections to the global circulation of Whiteness.

Patterns to Practice Seeing

1. Learn the history of the place names in your local community. Which have colonial roots and which have Indigeneous roots?
2. How is Whiteness exported globally in various domains? Consider industries such as technology, entertainment, education, beauty, sports and health industries.

CHAPTER 10

Understanding Intersectionality Through Classism

"Nowadays, it's White men who are the victims."

This chapter examines class oppression. We explain current economic relations of power, address concepts such as capitalism and socialism, wealth and income, as well as provide common class vernacular. The chapter also addresses the concept of intersectionality as an important theoretical development for understanding the multidimensional nature of oppression. We identify elements of class privilege, name common misconceptions about class mobility, and speak back to dominant classist narratives.

Vocabulary to practice using: classism; class vernacular; capitalism; social capital; net worth; intersectional/ality; meritocracy

Mr. Rich White and Mr. Poor White Strike a Bargain†

Once upon a time there was Mr. Rich White, whose forefathers had become rich by exploiting the land and labor of others. Mr. Rich White realized that in order to stay rich, he had to maintain control over his workers. But how? He looked around and his eyes fell upon the Black man. He snapped his fingers, "I've got it!" he whispered. He called Mr. Poor White to his office and said, "I've been thinking a lot about you and me and how hard it is for us to keep our factory competitive and growing so we can make enough money. To keep the business going the way I want it to go, making big profit off of little capital so I can keep you on the job, I have to keep my wages low, you can see that. It's good for me and essential for you too, for any job is better than no job at all. And whatever is causing the troubles with our economy isn't my fault or your fault, but the fault

---

† This parable is adapted from Lillian Smith's "Mr Rich White and Mr Poor White strike a bargain" in her book *Killers of the Dream* (1949).

of those coming here and taking your jobs and acting all uppity like they've been here all along. The thing we can't forget is that whatever our differences the color of our skin makes us kin. We are made in God's image and He intends us to lead. We are the chosen and we can't let others, like the Black man, push us out of our place. And when I say 'Black man' I'm not discriminating because I also mean the Latino man, whose job is to pick our crops, and the Asian man, who builds our railroads, and the Indigenous man, whose land we will take and use properly (*he just wastes the land, lettin' it sit there*). As for the woman, everybody already knows that the Bible ordained her place as secondary to ours, that's just nature. Men must always rule over and take care of the women.

"The way I see it, there are 2 jobs that need doing. Somebody has got to tend to making the money, to jobs, credit, prices, hours, the politicians, and so on (*and you are too low class to do that or else you'd be rich like I am*), and somebody has got to tend to the Black man—keep him in his place. So how about I boss the money and you boss the Black man. Don't worry about what I do, but here's what you do: Anything to show you are the boss you can do (*as long as you don't touch my business*). You can decide where he will live, what schools he will go to and what books his children will read. If science scares you, remember that you don't have to accept it—this is God's country and a free one at that. If you get restless when you don't have a job or your children are sick, just remember your lot is a damn sight better than the Black man's. If you need to let off some steam and rough some up now and then, go right ahead. I will make sure the law overlooks it (*but don't expect to see me in the crowd*).

"Now, if some other Mr. Poor Whites are fool enough to forget that they are White men, I'm willing to put up plenty of money to keep the politicians talking, and I don't mind supporting a demagogue or two. Of course I'll ensure the media keeps everyone distracted. Long as you keep the Black man out of your unions, we'll give you the pick of whatever jobs there are and if things get too tight you can take over his jobs too, 'cause remember, any job is better than no job at all. If you keep your end of the bargain, I will make sure that you're always better off, even if only slightly, than the Black man."

And Mr. Rich White and Mr. Poor White thought they'd made a good bargain. Of course Mr. Poor White didn't really have much choice, but no matter how hard things got for him, at least he would always be better off than the Black man. It was hard at first for Mr. Poor White's labor to keep being exploited by Mr. Rich White, but gettin' to be the boss of someone else started to feel good and helped him hold up his end. Because the Black man reminded Mr. Poor White about what he'd done, he hated and feared him. And that hatred and fear helped Mr. Poor White continue with the bargain. It never occurred to Mr. Poor White that the Black man could help him raise his wages and make the business work fairly for both of them.

As time passed, Mr. and Ms. Middle Class White also had a role in the bargain. They became the lawyers, social workers, teachers, professors, doctors, judges, managers, advertisers, journalists, and celebrities—the mediators of the agreement. They settled disputes, administered policies, taught the children, and tended to the social services Mr. Poor White and the Black man would need, all while keeping everyone entertained. But sometimes Mr. and Ms. Middle Class White felt bad about their role in the bargain. "This can't go on," they'd say. They were worried about freedom and democracy, which many of them still believed in. They called their worry "multiculturalism" or "diversity" or "the achievement gap" or "social justice." They wore t-shirts and safety pins to show their worries. But in truth they were more worried about getting the best for their children, securing their property values, and maintaining their position between Mr. Rich White and Mr. Poor White. They feared what integration would mean for that position. And it was certainly better to be Mr. and Ms. Middle Class White than Mr. Poor White or the Black man. In the end, despite their worries, they always decided that segregation was best. After all, wasn't it just human nature to prefer to live near your own? Segregation enabled them not to see the methods used to keep the Black man away from their neighborhoods and their jobs; and not to feel as badly about the bargain. But they knew not to say aloud what they didn't want to see or feel. Mr. Rich White knew what was in their hearts, and smiled.

What Is Class?

As with all forms of social division, social class is a human construct. The division of labor that characterizes class did not emerge until the Neolithic era, approximately 8,000–10,000 years ago (Little, 2016; Rueschemeyer, 1986). This period of human history was marked by agricultural advancement and land settlements by human population, prior to which many human communities were nomadic hunter–gatherers. This era is sometimes described as the *agricultural revolution*, and resulted not only in settlements of land, but in the organized, systematic production of crops that could be harvested, shared, traded, and sold to others. Where once resources might have been scarce or difficult to gather, they were now more plentiful, and the outcome of increasingly managed processes.

According to the foundational social class theorist Karl Marx, this

> 🖐 **STOP:** Remember, in the same way that terms such as "feminism" have been reduced to simplistic caricatures (e.g. "femi-nazis"), so has the terminology of Marxism and Socialism. In recent years, activist movements have returned some legitimacy to this terminology. In thinking about language as political, we want to ask ourselves how our perceptions are shaped by the terms we use and who those perceptions serve.

era of collective agricultural output created the initial divisions of labor that form the basis of class division: those who own the land (whom he called the *bourgeoisie*) and those who owned their labor (whom he called the *proletariat*). Class division today might arguably be drawn back to these same binary groups: those who own the resources of a society and create the rules of exchange and ownership, and those who trade their bodies (their minds and hands) to work, and whose opportunity for work *depends on* the increase of capital, which the bourgeois control.

> **STOP:** Remember, oppression is less about numbers and more about inequity in historical, ideological, cultural, and institutional *control*. The wealthiest people are a numerical minority yet wield an extreme amount of power in social institutions.

An example of owner control is the fight for minimum wage. When workers organize to raise the minimum wage, they are told by the owners that the prices of goods must then be increased, hours cut, or people laid off. What is rarely questioned is why the owners cannot tolerate making slightly less profit. For example, in 2012 the average CEO in the United States was paid 354 times what the average worker in their corporation earned (354:1), and 774 times what full-time minimum wage workers made (AFL-CIO, 2013). Chief executives took home, on average $11.7 million annually in 2012, while the average employee earned $35,293. In Canada the gap is 206 times wider (206:1). These are the highest gaps between workers and owners in human history. Illustrating how astronomically this gap has widened, in 1968 the gap between workers and CEOs was 20:1. When workers ask for a living wage and owners threaten to take their jobs away or lament how raising wages will "hurt the economy," the effect is to shift our focus away from the owners and back onto the workers, who are essentially being blamed for income inequality, as Figure 10.1 satirizes.

When owners threaten to take away workers' livelihoods, workers back off, for as Mr. Rich White warns, *any job is better than no job at all*. Sometimes owners pacify workers by insisting on "trickle-down economics," which is the claim that cutting taxes and increasing benefits for the richest will improve the standard of living for everyone else. The basic idea is that the more money those at the very top make, the more money will trickle down to the bottom. The claim is that in order to ensure that owners make more money, they need to be less regulated and less taxed than workers are, and this will result in more jobs being created, higher wages for the average worker, and an overall upturn in the economy. However, data from the past 50 years strongly refutes the argument that cutting taxes for the richest will improve the economic standing of the lower and middle classes (OXFAM, 2017; United for a Fair Economy, 2003).

Data compiled by the American Federation of Labor (AFL-CIO, 2012) from the

Figure 10.1. The Boss

Source: soc331.files.wordpress.com/2012/02/420748_183792161725872_129370207168068_2
59071_2121981741_n1.jpg

Organization for Economic Cooperation and Development shows the ratio between average workers' and their CEO's annual pay (in U.S. dollars) (see Figure 10.2).

Until the mid-1990s, income polarization in Canada and the United States remained relatively stable (Hulchanski & Murdie, 2013). However since then, the gap between the richest and poorest has widened immensely. In other words, the rich got richer, the poor got poorer. Here are some examples:

Figure 10.2. Ratio of CEO to Worker Compensation

	Average CEO compensation	Average worker compensation	Ratio
Norway	$ 2,551,420	$ 43,990	58 to 1
The Netherlands	$ 3,576,156	$ 47,056	76 to 1
United Kingdom	$ 3,758,412	$ 44,743	84 to 1
Germany	$ 5,912,781	$ 40,223	147 to 1
Canada	$ 8,704,118	$ 42,253	206 to 1
United States	$ 12,259,894	$ 34,645	354 to 1

- Since 2015, the richest 1% has owned more wealth than the rest of the planet (OXFAM, 2017).
- Eight men own the same amount of wealth as the poorest half of the world (OXFAM, 2017).
- Over the next 20 years, 500 people will hand over $2.1 trillion to their heirs—a sum larger than the GDP[‡] of India, a country of 1.3 billion people (OXFAM, 2017).
- The incomes of the poorest 10% of people increased by less than $3 a year between 1988 and 2011, while the incomes of the richest 1% increased 182 times as much (OXFAM, 2017).
- In Bloomberg's daily ranking of the world's 500 richest people, the world's wealthiest 3 people (Bill Gates, Warren Buffet, and Jeff Bezos), all White American men, have total net worths of 85, 79, and 73 billion U.S. dollars, respectively (Bloomberg, 2017). By comparison the 2015 GDP of Sri Lanka was $82 billion, Luxembourg was $58 billion, and Iceland $16 billion (World Bank, 2017).
- The world's 10 richest people are all men. Nine of ten are White men (Bloomberg, 2017).
- Had growth been good for the poor between 1990 and 2010, 700 million more people, most of them women, would not be living in poverty today (OXFAM, 2017).
- In 2015/16, the world's 10 biggest corporations together had revenue greater than that of the government revenues of 180 countries combined (OXFAM, 2017).
- Estimates are that 21 million people (mostly women and girls of Color) are forced laborers, generating an estimated $150 billion in annual profits for corporations (OXFAM, 2017).

---

‡. Gross Domestic Product is typically used as an indicator of a nation's economy and measures the value of all goods and services in a given period.

- Canada and the United States have among the widest gaps between the rich and poor (OECD, 2015).
- In Canada, between 1976–2010, the top 20% of income earners had their income rise by 29%, while the bottom 20% had their income fall by 23% (Rajotte, 2013).
- In the United States, over the last 30 years the growth in the incomes of the bottom 50% has been zero, whereas incomes of the top 1% have grown 300% (OXFAM, 2017).

When we think about what class positions we hold, we might initially focus solely on *economics*—that is, being rich or being poor; in other words, how much money each of us has or earns. This is an important element for understanding social class, and income distribution is among the most available statistic collected. However, income is not the only element that forms our class positions. Class is also (and perhaps primarily) about political power: the ability to influence policy, control capital, and shape institutional structures.

For example, the ruler of a nation state might draw a relatively modest income: the prime minister of Canada's salary is 170,000 Canadian dollars, while the U.S. president's salary is 400,000 U.S. dollars (Parliament of Canada, 2017; U.S. House of Representatives, 2017). These are likely salaries that few of us will ever see. However, this is not the primary source of their power; there are people earning much higher incomes. Yet both of these men have a great deal of political power that lies in their ability to influence social and institutional policy. Very few among us will ever have access to this kind of political power.

Global activist movements such as Occupy have made the 1% more visible, helping to uncover the relationship between economics and political influence. Thus, thinking about class requires that we consider together issues of *income* and issues of *power*.

Class refers to relative social rank in terms of income, wealth, status, and/or power. *Classism* is the systematic oppression of poor and working people by those who control necessary resources (jobs, wages, education, housing, food, services, medicine, cultural definitions, and so on). Classism is held in place by a system of beliefs

📖 **OCCUPY (Also Occupy Wall Street, Occupy Movement):** The Occupy movement is an international sociopolitical movement against social and income inequality and the lack of real democracy (full participation by all and representation for all) around the world; its primary goal being to advance social and economic justice and new forms of democracy.

Class: The system of relative social rank as measured in terms of income, wealth, status, and/or power.

that ranks people according to economic status, "breeding," job, and level
of education. Discourses of classism
present upper-class people as naturally smarter and more articulate than
lower-class people. Upper-class people
define what's normal, acceptable, and
intelligent. Their ideas, values, and
culture form the canon of what is con-

> 📖 **Classism:** The institutional, cul-
> tural, and individual set of practices
> that assign differential value to peo-
> ple according to their socioeconom-
> ic status (SES). Classism ensures
> inequality between classes.

sidered "high class" culture (think opera, golf, literature), as compared to "low class"
or "popular" culture (think WWE, county fairs, reality television).

Common Class Vernacular

While there are no universal rules about what makes someone poor versus working class versus middle class, there are some common trends in the usage of class
terminology that are important to understand. For example, in political discourse
we frequently hear politicians talking about protecting the *middle class*, and activists refer to the *1%* or the *99%* and wanting to help *the poor*. But what do these
terms mean?

As discussed above, *classism* captures the overall dominance of the owning
class over all other classes. As with all forms of oppression, classism exists on binary terms (in this case, rich versus poor). Yet actual measures of class are often tied
to measures of income distribution, which is a spectrum (DeNavas-Walt & Ber-
nadette, 2015; Metzgar 2003; Skuterud, Frenette, & Poon 2004). These measures
of income distribution are complex, but overall refer to average family incomes in
a given geographical context, as well as the gap between those at the very top and
bottom of the range.

While these official class measures are typically organized around income distribution and shape what constitutes the middle class (often also called, *average income* families), class is a more complicated landscape than the average, the highest,
and lowest on the spectrum. Depending on the framework being used, there are
anywhere from two, to twelve, to dozens of class groupings you may have heard of.
At the same time, dominant culture provides only a handful of class categories to
fit ourselves into. The categories made available to us through language are sometimes referred to as *class vernacular* (Metzgar, 2010).

In Canada and the United States there are typically three broad class categories in our class vernacular: the *owning* class (the rich), the *middle* class (the
middle), and the *working* class (the poor). What this class vernacular reveals is
that:

- Class positions are relational. The boundaries between these categories can shift; a family designated as working class in the 1950s might be designated as low income in the 2000s.
- Class positions are fluid. Much like gender existing as a spectrum (rather than a binary with two sides), some scholarship defines class as a spectrum. This allows us to include additional groups in order to acknowledge different lived experiences.

For our purposes, we will focus on the following four class groups. These capture the broad groups in Canada and the United States that are recognizable and in line with income distribution information and social signifiers. They are:

The owning class: Those who inherit wealth and who are not dependent on work for income. They can live on the interests of their holdings. The owning class is sometimes referred to as the ruling class. Although the ruling class might have a lot of wealth and not much actual income, they have a great deal of political power and ability to influence government.

The middle class: Those who must use their bodies (hands and minds) to work for income; who have some advanced education beyond high school. Sometimes these are described as white-collar workers, indicating office work (primarily mind-work). Generally middle-class people are able to own their homes and expect their children will go to college.

The working class: Those who must use their bodies (hands and minds) to work for income; who have typically high school education and possibly some trade schooling. Sometimes these are described as blue-collar or pink-collar workers, indicating physical jobs (primarily body-work) such as policing, trade labor (plumbing, carpentry), secretarial, and food services. They may only be able to rent rather than purchase a home and are often unable to help their children go to college.

The poor: Those who must rely on assistance (such as welfare or other government benefits); possibly chronic or intermittent joblessness/ homelessness. They may also be minimum-wage workers who fall under the federal poverty line (sometimes called the *working poor*). Some scholars (e.g., Metzgar, 2010; Zweig, 2000) argue that the poor are not a class per se, but a *condition*. The condition of poverty is more likely to impact the working class than the middle or owning classes because the working class have less of a safety net. (We have chosen to keep this category in our class vernacular list because it is a recognizable social discourse especially in media and has a particular function in the oppression of working people.)

Capitalism is the name given to the economic system by which resources and means of production and profits are privately held (e.g., by corporations and shareholders), as opposed to jointly or publicly held. In contrast, *socialism* is the name given to the economic system by which resources are jointly held and profits shared (Anyon, 2011). According to Marx's conception of capitalism, capitalism cannot function without inherent inequality built into its system. In other words, in order to maximize profits the owning class must continuously exploit the labor of workers (make them work more for less, and sell the outcome of their labor for more than they pay for it), and workers must in turn compete with one another for fewer and fewer resources and benefits (Anyon, 2011). Whoever is willing to work for the least wages, benefits, and conditions is the most desirable worker for the corporation. And the more efficient the workers, the more their job security is at risk (if we can get 5 people to do the work that 10 people were doing last year, then company profits increase, and those 5 workers will be more desirable employees to the corporation). Thus, under capitalism, the interests of owners to maximize profits are in tension with the interests of workers to have fair wages, benefits, and a share of the product of their labor, as Figure 10.3 satirizes.

> 📖 **WEALTH vs. INCOME:** *Wealth* refers to the value of a family's assets (e.g., land or stocks) that can increase in value over time. *Income* refers to the specific amount of money coming into a family's home over a period of time (e.g., salary). This income can be added to assets, or used for needs (e.g., housing and transportation).

> 📖 **Sweatshops:** Sweatshops are factories and other manufacturing facilities where workers work long hours under poor conditions and for very low wages. They are characterized as settings where labor laws do not exist or are not enforced. Sweatshops produce many different goods from toys, shoes, clothing, and furniture to high-tech assembly line items.

The need to make ever more owner/shareholder profit and deny workers' rights has played a fundamental role in the current economic conditions in the United States and Canada (and of course elsewhere in the world). Increasing profits have driven the export of jobs and manufacturing to poorer countries where workers can be paid pennies per day and do not have rights (including the right to take a break). These factories are called *sweatshops*.

Minimal pay, forced overtime, and poor and dangerous health and safety conditions are commonplace in sweatshops employed by companies including Mattel, Disney, and Victoria's Secret (Jankowski, 2016). Victoria's Secret employs Bangladeshi and Sri Lankan women who reportedly are expected to sew one bikini every 3 minutes, for which they are paid $0.04 cents (the bikinis sell for $14); they work 15 hours per day, and receive only

Figure 10.3. Pyramid of Capitalist System, 1911

Source: en.wikipedia.org/wiki/Pyramid_of_Capitalist_System

one day off every 3 months (Jankowski, 2016).

As workers strategize and use
their (limited) resources to pressure
corporations for more equitable conditions (via collective action, union-
ization, work slow-downs), the owners strategize and use their abundant
resources to stop them (e.g., union
busting, dividing workers from each
other via bonuses and privileges to a
select few, controlling the message via
networks of power such as government and media, threatening to fire
workers and hire workers who will
work for less, and lobbying politicians
to deregulate).

✓ **PERSPECTIVE CHECK:** Remember: If workers' rights are re-
spected, sweatshops could actually
help poor countries. For example,
in Honduras, the average clothing
sweatshop worker earns 13 U.S.
dollars per day, and yet 44% of the
country's population lives on less
than 2 dollars per day. Look for fair-
trade labeled products. Fair-trade
labels ensure higher salaries and
better working conditions as well
as higher social and environmental
standards.

Class Socialization

Class is about money and power, but it is also about culture. Different class
groups have different cultural norms and patterns associated with them. So how
do we each learn our class positions as well as the class positions of others? Or,
because class is also a form of our cultural identity, we might ask how we learn
to perform our class and to read and understand the class performance of others? There are two key sites where a majority of this learning occurs: school and
media.

School and class messages. Scholars have explained how mass public schooling is about more than subject-matter education; it is also about ideological socialization (Apple, 1993). In Chapter 2, we reviewed Jean Anyon's study comparing
schoolchildren from working-, middle-, and affluent-class schools, and learned
how children are schooled to conceptualize knowledge and their relationship to
it, based in part on the school curriculum they receive. As the histories of both
Canada and the United States show, the requirement for mass schooling has always been about more than education. Through both required attendance (e.g.,
via a system of residential schooling) as well as denied attendance (e.g., females,
and racialized children), mass schooling has been in large part a project of mass
socialization. In fact, compulsory mass schooling is a relatively new social idea
in Western nation states (Ballantine & Spade, 2008). The architects of the compulsory mass schooling that started in the mid-19th century wanted to educate
children into a common curricula (a common language, national history, and set

of values) in order to become productive citizens of the nation state (Tyack, 1976). Thus we may rightly ask, whose language, history, and values were the framework into which all children were required to fit? Those who created, implemented, and monitored compulsory attendance in mass public schooling, or those who were forced to attend them?

Media and class messages. Media is another primary institution socializing us about what it means to be owning class, middle class, and working class (Leistyna, 2009). Two key elements of this institution in relation to class messaging are the consolidation of media ownership (control by fewer and fewer entities and therefore more homogeneous messaging) and the class representations that circulate through media. In other words, who is in the position to control the messages, what are those messages, and how do they serve the interests of those who control them?

Media consolidation is an issue around the globe. As multinational corporations have bought up other companies, there are fewer and fewer corporations owning more and more of the news and entertainment that we consume. As of 2012, 90% of media outlets (print, radio, TV, Internet) were owned by six corporations (Van Esler, 2016). These are:

- Comcast (NBC, MSNBC, Universal Pictures, Dreamworks, Hulu)
- Walt Disney (Disney theme parks, Disney Channels, ESPN, Marvel, Touchstone)
- NewsCorp (Fox News, National Geographic, Wall Street Journal, Harper-Collins)
- Viacom (BET, MTV, CMT, Spike, Paramount Pictures, Ratemyprofessors. com)
- Time Warner (CNN, HBO, DC Comics)
- CBS (MTV, Simon & Schuster, VH1)

Once we understand that media consolidation necessarily limits the range of perspectives available to us, we need to examine how media represents class. To do so, try a brief thought experiment:

As you read your favorite magazines and gossip blogs, read reviews of films you plan to see, watch videos of your favorite pop songs, concerts, and endorsements from superstars, consider how those forms of representation are classed. For example, consider work. What work is presented? Who is doing what kinds of work (paid work as well as unpaid work) and how do they seem to feel about it?

How are speech and accents classed? Which accents and speech patterns are considered "low class"? Which are "sophisticated" or "romantic" or "threatening"?

Who wears business suits and who wears other uniforms? How do people move? How are various movements classed? How do race and gender inform how we understand class embodiment?

How is food classed? Who eats organic? What does farm-to-table mean? What about alcohol? Which beers are "high class" and which are associated with "low class"? What kind of leisure activities do the various classes engage in? Who goes to the symphony? Who sky dives? Who goes to monster truck shows and watches the WWE?

All of these cues are telling us what it means to be working, middle, or owning class. Now consider what class the people who generate these images—the writers and directors—most likely occupy. In other words, who is in the position to represent class? While media messages may not deliberately set out to teach about class, how the various class groups are represented (or absent altogether) is a critical part of our class socialization.

Common Misconceptions About Class

"We live in a classless society where anyone can make it." From very early on in school we are taught that anyone can make it if they try, and that the West is the land of opportunity. We are told Rags to Riches stories (from Cinderella to Sam Walton) and that we live in a classless society. The myth of the American Dream is so powerful that research shows the vast majority of Americans (over 70%) overestimate class mobility and believe that personal motivation is more important to mobility than the state of the economy or the economic circumstances they are born into (Kraus & Tan, 2015; Wyatt-Nichol, 2016). In addition to strictly economic reasons for class immobility such as net worth, class immobility is also influenced by class culture. The cultural norms we are socialized into relate to the class we are born into, and this ensures that we will be most comfortable in and surround ourselves with people who share our class culture. The schools we go to, the neighborhoods we live in, the jobs we aspire to, all reinforce our class positions and who surrounds us. While some people will change class, they will be the exception rather than the rule. The Rags to Riches story so beloved and repeated in Hollywood is unlikely in real life. Only 6% of children born to parents with income at the very bottom rise to the very top (Isaacs, 2007). Consider the 10 richest people in the United States in 2016 (Forbes, 2016), most if not all of whom were already born into the upper classes (also notice that they are all White men). Now imagine their children. What schools will they go to? Whose children will they be surrounded by? What opportunities will

> 📖 **Social Mobility:** The idea that one can move from one class position to another.

they have? Are they likely to mingle with your children? It is highly unlikely that we will interact across these vast class differences.

"A rich person can become poor as easily as a poor person can become rich." Because we tend to think of class strictly in terms of how much money we have, we assume that a rich person who loses everything will end up in the same boat as a poor person. But in reality, a rich person does not lose everything when they lose their money. They will still have an internalized sense of entitlement, contacts with other wealthy people they can call upon and network with, knowledge of systems and how to navigate them, and the language and norms of the upper class that will open doors for them. In other words, they do not lose their *cultural capital*. Further, they have much more time before they use up all of their material capital—real estate, antiques, artwork, cars, boats, jewelry—known as *net worth*.

> 📖 **Net worth:** All of your assets combined together. When you subtract your debt from what you own, you have your net worth.

"Education is the key to getting ahead." While certainly there are more opportunities open to people with more education, education itself is also stratified. As discussed in Chapter 2, the kind of education we receive is based on the kind of school we go to (public or private), where it is located, and how it is funded. Within the school are different tracks that offer different kinds of knowledge intended to prepare us for different kinds of careers. If we graduate from K–12 public schools and go on to college, we again enter a system that is stratified. Consider the difference between a 2-year college with a focus on the trades and a student population from the local community, and an Ivy League university with wealthy students from all over the world, many of them *legacy* (i.e., students whose parents also attended and therefore were automatically accepted). Whether you have to work while in college and still graduate with a massive amount of debt or have everything paid for by your family will also impact the outcome of your education. Which doors your education opens is greatly impacted by the status of the school you go to. So while education clearly makes a difference in terms of life opportunities, schooling is a stratified political structure that very predictably and efficiently reproduces rather than eliminates class hierarchies.

"Sports and sports scholarships offer minorities a way out." The idea that sports are a way out of poverty for poor youth of Color is deeply cherished and continually reinforced in films and televison. Yet this is an extremely rare possibility. Consider the following: How many openings on professional teams are actually available? Take basketball as an example. There are 5 positions on a team, with 7 extra players, for a total of 12 players. There are 11 players on a football team. Base-ball is played with 9 players. The degree of exceptionality required to make it onto the field for these teams is very high. The possibility of women making it through sports is even more limited, given that their teams do not have the visibility or bring in the kind of wealth that men's teams do. It is also relevant that for the few who do succeed through sports, their run is limited. The average age of retirement for a football player is 35, and they often suffer from lifelong debilitating injuries.

The people who really get rich from sports are the owners. In 2016, 28 of 30 U.S. men's professional basketball team owners were White; 31 of 32 men's pro football team owners were White, 32 of 33 men's pro baseball team owners were White. Of the 95 people who owned these teams, 4 were White women (*New York Times,* 2016). Of the 30 National Hockey League owners, only one is not White. While a poor boy from the projects or his small town making it big in sports is a romantic idea reinforced through countless movies, that dream comes true for an extremely rare number of men of Color. It is important to notice how the physical bodies of men of Color are seen as potentially valuable and thus worthy of scholarship supports (in this case in the service of our entertainment) but not their minds. This is a key signifier of class position. The lower your class status, the more your body is seen as exploitable. Think about who decides to go to war and who actually does the fighting, who owns the coal mines and who does the min-ing, who writes the laws and who is on the street enforcing them. Most of the latter are not the upper class. Manual labor literally means working *with your hands*. We also have to ask ourselves what it means to see sports as a way out of poverty for young men of Color but not other fields such as law, medicine, or teaching.

"Class is the true oppression. If we eliminate classism we will eliminate rac-ism." The point of the opening parable is that class and race are deeply intertwined. Even if Mr. Rich White stopped exploiting Mr. Poor White we would still be left with racism. Peoples of Color who occupy the same class position as White people are still experiencing racism. DiAngelo (2006) speaks to this in her personal nar-rative of growing up poor and White:

> From an early age I had the sense of being an outsider; I was acutely aware that I was poor, that I was dirty, that I was not normal and that there was something "wrong" with me. But I also knew that I was not black. We were at the lower rungs of society but there was always someone on the periphery, just below us. I knew that "colored" people existed and that they should be avoided. I can remember many occasions when I reached for candy or uneaten food laying on the street and was admonished by my grandmother not to touch it because a "colored person" may have touched it. The mes-sage was clear to me; if a colored person touched something it became dirty. The irony here is that the marks of poverty were clearly visible on me: poor hygiene, torn clothes, homelessness, hunger. Yet through comments such as my grandmother's, a racial

Other was formed in my consciousness; an Other through whom I became clean. Race was the one identity which aligned me with the middle class girls in my school. As I reflect back on the early messages I received about being poor and being white, I now realize that my grandmother and I needed people of color to cleanse and realign us with the dominant white culture that our poverty had separated us from (pp. 51–53).

Poor Whites are most often in closest proximity to people of Color because they tend to share poverty (hooks, 2000). Consider the term *white trash*. It is not without significance that this is one of the few expressions in which race is named for Whites. This may be because poor urban Whites are more likely to live in proximity to peoples of Color. Thus race is named for poor Whites because of their closeness to peoples of Color. In a racist society, this closeness both highlights—and pollutes—whiteness. Owning-class people also have peoples of Color near them because the latter are often their domestics and gardeners—in other words, their servants. But they do not interact with them socially in the same way that poor Whites do. Middle-class Whites are generally the furthest away from peoples of Color. They are the most likely to say that, "there were no people of Color in my neighborhood or school. I didn't meet a Black person until I went to college" (often adding, "so I was lucky because I didn't learn anything about racism"). Focusing attention solely on class oppression—rather than ameliorating racism—simply serves to deny the realities of racism in the lives of peoples of Color, and the privileges of whiteness for White people.

"Anyone who wants a job can get one." While it is likely true that anyone—no matter their level of ability—can get some kind of work, it is not likely that anyone can find work that pays a living wage. In fact, *the majority* of workers in the United States (59%) work for hourly wages (Bureau of Labor Statistics, 2016). Of these, 2.6 million workers earn at or below the minimum wage. As an example of classist ideology, the media most often represents the middle class as the majority and politicians speak to the concerns of the middle class. Yet the majority of the United States is better defined as working class or poor.

The U.S. federal minimum wage in 2017 is $7.25 per hour, or $15,080 per year. The federal poverty level for a two-person household is $15,930. Further, federal minimum wage standards are not guaranteed because states can set their own minimum wages. For example, Georgia's minimum wage is $5.15 per hour, while Alabama, Tennessee, South Carolina, Louisiana, and Mississippi have no minimum wage at all and employers can pay workers whatever they choose. The federal minimum wage of $7.25 per hour has not been raised since 2010 (U.S. Department of Labor, 2017). Between the years 1999 and 2009, it remained at $5.15 per hour. The minimum wage does not include health insurance or retirement benefits, nor does it guarantee full-time work. Further, under section 14(c) of the Fair Labor Standards Act (FLSA), employers are able to pay a wage below the federal minimum wage to workers whose work is affected by a mental or physical disability (the ADA does not change this provision). This means that some workers with disabilities can make significantly less than the minimum wage, in some cases even less than a dollar per hour.

Congress sets the federal minimum wage, and efforts to raise it are regularly defeated by congressional representatives. It is worthy of note that the House of Representatives is 81% male and 80% White and the Senate is 80% male and 94% White (while White men are 34% of the U.S. population). Members of Congress earn $174,000 annually in base salaries. Their salaries include access to a comprehensive health insurance and retirement package. Fifty-one percent of congressional representatives are millionaires (Manning, 2010).

Comparatively, in Canada the minimum wage is set provincially and as of 2014 ranges from 10–11 Canadian dollars (approximately $7.50 USD). Some provinces (such as Saskatchewan and Manitoba) allow persons with disabilities to be paid lower than the minimum wage (Canadian Labour Congress, 2015). In 2013, 6.7% of Canadian workers worked for minimum wage (Statistics Canada, 2014), a higher percentage of workers than in the United States, where 3.3% of hourly wage workers worked for minimum wage (Bureau of Labor Statistics, 2016). Women as a group make up 60% of minimum wage workers in Canada—mostly in retail, food, and accommodation industries (Canadian Labour Congress, 2015). Further, while the minimum wage number seems high, its buying power determines whether it is a *living* wage. The low income measure, LICO, is a common way that poverty is measured in Canada. It determines how much income a household must earn to meet its basic needs for food, clothing, and shelter, based on the size of the household and the size of the community it lives in. The LICO in 2012 for a two-person family living in a metropolitan area of about 500,000 people was $29,440 before taxes. Taking $10/hour as the average minimum wage for 2012, a worker working a 40-hour week without any sick or vacation days would have earned $20,000 for a 50-week working year—putting them below the income threshold if only one member of the family is working (Canadian Labour Congress, 2015).

"People just need to work hard and not expect handouts." Most people understand that minimum wage work is among the hardest. It tends to be physical, of lower status, and exceptionally grueling (e.g., fast food, retail, factory, and agricultural work). Further, a person working at minimum wage to support a family will likely need to work more than one job. To say that these people do not work hard is grossly unfair. Yet their hard work will not typically pay off in the sense of "making it." These workers are more likely to come from families with very little net worth to begin with, and without resources such as college degrees, they are less likely to advance. When middle-class people proclaim that they have achieved with they have because they were taught the value of hard work, we need to ask

ourselves whom we believe wasn't taught that value. Further, how are we defining hard work? Is studying for exams in college (which you will graduate from debt free because your family is paying for you) harder work than working in your college's cafeteria?

Another form of hard work that is often not acknowledged is prison labor. The linkages between the exploitation of prison labor—and the profits made by private corporations from the prison system—and the ability of corporations to influence how prisons are built, filled, and maintained in ways that benefit them is called The Prison Industrial Complex (Davis, 2008). According to a study on corporate profiteering and the U.S. prison system (Cooper, Heldman, Ackerman, & Farrar-Meyers, 2016), ALEC (The American Legislative Exchange Council, a powerful, conservative lobby group) has over the past 40 years created a highly organized and sophisticated system of lobbying state and federal policy makers on behalf of the interests of its member corporations. Its influence is organized around (1) the drafting of bills such as the "stand your ground" and voter ID laws, (2) the training of legislators, and (3) media campaign supports. In their review of leaked documents that included 800+ ALEC model bills, the study's authors found that ALEC lobbied to expand the private prison industry in the following ways: by expanding the use of private prisons and their goods and services (such as food services, telecommunications, and pharmaceuticals), by promoting the use of prison labor (which had been illegal until the ALEC-supported Prison Industries Act of 1995), and by increasing the size of the prison population by expanding definitions of crime and increasing likelihood of incarceration and recidivism.

At a time when state-level incarceration rates are somewhat decreasing, ALEC has begun to turn its attention to immigration and detention centers as a new stream of income for its corporate members (Cooper et al., 2016). It is important to note that as we write this second edition, the incoming White House administration campaigned on a law and order and anti-immigration platform that is likely to reverse decreasing incarceration rates and create the need for more prisons and detention centers.

Since policy changes in the 1970s, the U.S. prison population has exploded into the largest in the world (see Figure 10.4; Wagner & Walsh, 2016; World Prison Brief, 2017). The U.S. represents just 5% of the world's population, yet holds 25% of the world's incarcerated population (American Civil Liberties Union, 2017). The United States incarcerates 693 people for every 100,000 residents, more than any other country in the world. When the incarceration rates of individual U.S. states are considered separately, 32 states[§] (and Washington, DC) have incarceration rates higher than that of Turkmenistan, which at 583 per 100,000 residents is the nation

---

§ Alabama, Alaska, Arizona, Arkansas, California, Colorado, Delaware, Florida, Georgia, Idaho, Illinois, Indiana, Kansas, Kentucky, Louisiana, Michigan, Mississippi, Missouri, Nevada, New Mexico, North Carolina, Ohio, Oklahoma, Pennsylvania, South Carolina, South Dakota, Tennessee, Texas, Virginia, Washington, DC, West Virginia, Wisconsin, and Wyoming.

Figure 10.4. Incarcerations Rates Among Founding NATO Members

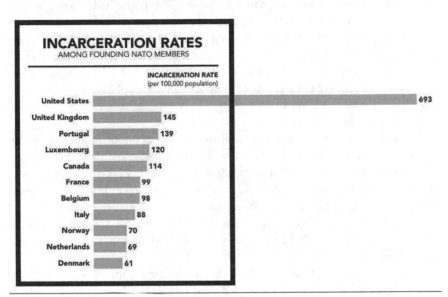

Source: https://www.prisonpolicy.org/global/2016.html

with the second-highest incarceration rate in the world (Wagner & Walsh, 2016).

Prison labor has been used in the United States since the late 18th century, with the most popular usage being agricultural labor. The labor of Black prisoners has replaced the labor of Black slaves, and in many cases to target unionized White workers and break strikes. This has resulted in violent clashes between organized labor and prison labor, and many Black prisoners (who have no protections, including no union protections) have died. Until the 20th century, the strength of trade unions was closely related to restrictions on the private use of prison labor (Kang, 2009; Thompson, 2012). Between 1970 and 2005, the U.S. prison population grew by 700%, mostly due to policy changes, such as Three-Strikes, Mandatory Minimum, and Truth in Sentencing laws (American Civil Liberties Union, 2011). Twenty to twenty-five percent of incarcerated people are locked up for nonviolent drug offenses, despite no change in drug use rates, with Blacks incarcerated for drug offenses at 10 times the rate of Whites, despite the same rates of drug use (American Civil Liberties Union, 2017); further, many hundreds of youth are behind bars for technical violations that are not adult crimes (such as truancy) (Wagner & Rabuy, 2017).

In addition to having the largest incarcerated population in the world (1.6 million people in federal and state prisons, with another 3.8 million on probation), there are close to 700,000 people held in pretrial jails—these are people who have not yet been convicted of any crime and thus are legally presumed innocent (Rabuy & Kopf, 2016). This translates to 70% of local jail population consisting of people who are unable to come up with the bail money needed (typically $10,000) to release them until their case is resolved. The Bureau of Justice Statistics data shows that in 2015 people in jail had median annual incomes of $15,109 prior to incarceration (with White men having the highest incomes and Black women having the lowest). Thus the detention of the legally innocent translates into greater housing of the poor in public jails, creating increased profits for corporations servicing jails, while simultaneously criminalizing the poor (Rabuy & Kopf, 2016).

In addition to government contracts and the use of public monies to pay for services provided to state and federal prisons, there is also corporate profiteering in the exploitation of prison laborers. Many people are unaware that the use of prisoners' labor is a huge industry. The business of detaining immigrants, refugees, and asylum seekers alone is a $2 billion industry from which private prisons stand to benefit the most from government contracts. For example, the private companies CoreCivic and the GEO Group run 90% of detention centers (American Civil Liberties Union, 2011; Gomez & Cataldo, 2016).

Corporations with huge financial stakes in profiting from mass incarceration include many of the corporations we are most familiar with, including Walmart, Hewlett-Packard, McDonald's, and many others (Thompson, 2012). The contrast between free world and prison wages is startling. Federal prisoners are paid $0.12 to $1.15 per hour while state wages range between $0.13 and $0.32 cents per hour.

These stand in stark contrast to the $7.25 minimum wage, or $13.04 an hour paid to furniture factory workers, or $10.95 per hour paid to textile workers in free world conditions (Thompson, 2012).

While not all prisoners are forced to work, most need to in order to afford very basic necessities including the ability to use a phone to speak to family members, for which they are charged (in many cases by private companies). Further, prisoners who choose not to work may lose the opportunity to reduce their sentences or be otherwise disciplined and can face prolonged isolation in their cells for up to 23 hours per day. Thus, many choose to work in conditions that can

STOP: While some people believe that prisoners should work for reasons such as health, therapy, to learn discipline, a skill, be productive, and/or repay a debt to society, when they work for private for-profit corporations who do not pay them (or who grossly underpay for their labor), their efforts are not going towards self-improvement, the good of society as a whole, their families, or even to victims/victims' families (in cases where victims exist). They are enslaved laborers for corporations earning profits for shareholders.

be toxic. For example, the BP oil corporation hired prisoners to clean up major oil spills, working the men on average 72 hours per week, and paying them little to nothing. These prisoners worked with little protection against the chemicals and crude oil, which can damage every system in the body (Thompson, 2012).

This creates important ethical questions for those among us who may be reluctant to purchase sweatshop- or prison labor–produced goods from so-called developing or third world countries (Kang, 2009), while having little knowledge about the conditions under which labor is exploited in the United States itself by American citizens.

Further, when thinking about the relationship between mass incarceration and corporate profits made from the prison industry, we are led back to the very definition of crime and whose crimes we are most likely to focus on, prosecute, and punish. For example, while Wall Street executives and bankers essentially defrauded and robbed millions of their homes and economic stability through illegal practices and caused a global economic crisis in 2008, they evaded major prosecutions (Pontell, Black, & Geis, 2014). Not only does this illustrate the social construction of crime and how we perceive, name, and prosecute crime, but it also illustrates how we define work, whose labor is visible and under what conditions, and who is seen as working hard and who isn't. We can't understand how these forces work together without considering class in relation to race and gender. This brings us back to the concept of intersectionality.

Understanding Intersectionality

Intersectionality is the idea that identity cannot be fully understood via a single lens such as gender, race, or class alone—what legal scholar Kimberlé Crenshaw (1989) called a "single axis framework" (p. 139). Rather, our identities and the social meaning attributed to them must be understood in their interdependence on one another; identity is multidimensional. For example, one is not just a woman but a *white heterosexual cisgender able-bodied* woman. All of these identities interact in complex ways that shape how this particular woman will experience gender. Prior to Crenshaw popularizing the term, scholars had been writing about the problematics of a single axis of analysis for many years. Many of these scholars were and are Black, transnational, and queer feminists who have problematized the idea that there is a singular female experience that feminism speaks to and under which all women can be gathered.

In the mid-19th century, at a time of struggle against slavery as well as patriarchy, abolitionist Sojourner Truth advocated for both the abolition of slavery and equal rights for women. In a famous speech she gave in 1851 at the Ohio Women's Rights convention, known as the "Ain't I a Woman" speech, Truth expressed concern that abolitionists were focused primarily on the issues of Black men to the exclusion of Black women and issues of women's political rights. Truth was also concerned with property rights, which most women did not have (Brah & Phoenix, 2004). In the 1970s, 1980s, and 1990s, many feminists of Color theorized about intersectionality (though not always using that term). Among them were the Combahee River Collective of Black feminist activist scholars such as Cathy Cohen and Angela Davis, and artist activists such as Audre Lorde and Alice Walker, who examined the intersections of gender, sexuality, and race (Brah & Phoenix, 2004; Collins & Bilge, 2016). Other Black feminists also continued the theorizing and interrogation of lived intersectionality in such institutions as justice, education, and the family (Collins, 2000; Crenshaw, 1991; hooks, 1994). Transnational feminists such as Chandra Mohanty and Inderpal Grewal challenged the notion that there was an essential experience of womanhood and examined the experiences of women living under colonialism. Among the issues they were concerned with was the fetishizing of non-Western bodies (Grewal & Kaplan, 1994; Mohanty, 1988; Shohat, 1998). Chicana feminists such as Gloria Anzaldúa and Norma Alarcón critiqued the nature of borders, nationhood, and belonging under multidimensional axes of difference including gender, sexuality, class, status, and language (Garcia, 1989). Asian feminists such as Grace Lee Boggs, Yuri Kochiyama, and Celine Parreñas Shimizu, Indigenous feminists such as Paula Gunn Allen and Lee Maracle, queer feminists such as Andrea Smith and Judith Butler, and crip feminists such as Kim Q. Hall and Nirmala Erevelles all contributed (and some continue to contribute) to our collective understanding of intersectional oppressions.

This is by no means an exhaustive list. Our intention is to illustrate how widely the issues related to intersectionality of race, gender, sexuality, ability, class, and other identities have been examined, and the role that women—and women of Color in particular—have played in this theoretical examination. This is important because much of class theorizing has been centered on the work of male scholars. Yet intersectional theorizing has not only informed academia but also contemporary activist movements such as Occupy, Black Lives Matter, Standing Rock, and Idle No More.

When Occupy, women's rights, or gay rights activists gather around a single issue, the tensions of intersectionality inevitably arise. For example, in the early AIDS crisis of the 1980s, the programs and outreach created in response did not take into account the barriers different communities faced. Peoples of Color with HIV were dealing with racism as well as homophobia, yet existing programs were based on White cultural norms and networks. Indeed, the sympathetic face of HIV/AIDS is a gay White man. Without an intersectional analysis, peoples of Color with HIV were left out of drug trials, educational campaigns, and support systems. In many major cities they were forced to start their own organizations or be left behind.

As activists who may be part of such movements there are some strategies you can consider, including some of the key tenets of intersectionality:

- Social inequality cannot be understood by examining categories such as gender, race, and socioeconomic status in isolation. For example, Sarah is White, cis-female, heterosexual, able-bodied, working class, and middle-aged. To understand her experience under sexism she also has to take into account her experience under racism; while she is female, she is most particularly a White female. Thus, her experience under sexism will be different than a Black female's experience. While she is disadvantaged under sexism and will face barriers rooted in patriarchy, she still benefits from racism; racism is not a form of oppression she will face. In fact, she will benefit from racism and these benefits may help her get further ahead in male-dominated environments than women of Color.
- People can experience privilege and oppression simultaneously depending on what situation or specific context they are in. So while Sarah may be paid less than a White man in her workplace, she will likely be paid more than a Black woman in that same workplace. While her clothes and toiletries cost more than a man's—even though she is likely to earn less than a man in her same occupation—she won't likely be followed around in the mall under the assumption that she will steal, as her Black coworker more likely will be.
- Intersectionality is more than a theoretical standpoint. It is intended to build coalitions among diverse groups so that their actions are more equitable and effective. Imagine what could be accomplished if Mr. Poor White from our opening parable had joined with the Black man to challenge the exploitation by Mr. Rich White.

An intersectional analysis of oppression requires that we attend to the above tenets. When we want to address a particular oppression such as classism, we often seek out statistical data alone to inform our understanding of the issue. But doing so from this single lens limits our understanding. If we add an intersectional analysis, our understanding of classism deepens and becomes multidimensional. This gives us a much more complex and nuanced view and will drive more complex and nuanced interventions.

Examples of Everyday Class Privilege[¶]

You have class privilege if the following applies to you:

- You can readily find accurate (not caricatured) representations of members of your class depicted in films, television, and other media.
- Experts appearing on mass media are from your social class.
- New consumer products are designed and marketed with your social class in mind.

[¶] In the style of Peggy McIntosh's White privilege list (1988).

- If you find yourself involved in a police situation, you can easily hire an attorney to ensure your perspective is heard justly.
- You can choose to eat healthy food if you wish, and it is readily available.
- Your eyesight, smile, and general health aren't inhibited by your income.
- If you become sick in the United States, you can seek medical care immediately and not just "hope it goes away."
- As a child, you were able to participate in organized sports, clubs, music, and other extracurricular activities.
- Your decision to go to college, and the type of college you chose, wasn't based entirely on financial determinants.
- Your parents are college graduates and could help you navigate the application process, as well as pay for college and living expenses.
- An annual raise in pay at your job is measured in dollars, not cents.
- Whenever you've moved out of your home it has been voluntary, and you had another home to move into.

Class may arguably be the foundational form of oppression as it is ultimately about the distribution of resources. This does *not* mean, however, that if we eliminate class all other forms of oppression will disappear, but that we cannot understand social inequality without understanding class. How we justify the distribution of resources is shaped and rationalized by how we socially construct various groups and our ideas about what these groups do or don't deserve. Given this, we have barely scratched the surface of the complex ways that classism works. However, our goal has been to provide a basic framework for understanding classism so that we may continue the lifelong work of personal reflection, political analysis, and ultimately, action.

Common Classist Beliefs

Our early and continual socialization into our class positions makes it challenging to break free from the hegemony of dominant narratives. We speak back to some of the most challenging of those narratives here:

"Immigrants are stealing our jobs." Immigrants do not and cannot steal jobs. Rather, immigrants tend to cluster in the very vocations and jobs that locally born people don't want to do. These immigrants are hired by companies who chose to hire them, and who benefit from their cheap (or exploited) labor. The work they do is typically the most grueling, demeaning, and dangerous work that others have refused to do (or that unionized workers have collectively bargained against doing under unsafe conditions). If immigrant workers are undocumented, they cannot complain about working conditions or unjust practices. This benefits the corporation, not the workers. The companies who exploit immigrant labor are

whom we should be concerned with, not those being exploited. The discourse of "immigrants stealing jobs" puts attention on to the actions of the vulnerable, and away from the actions of the powerful.

"Poor people should stop having so many babies." This claim rests on the assumption that women have complete control over their bodies and receive no pressure from society to be sexual, much less pressure or even force from men to engage in unprotected sex. Further, many of the forms of birth control available to women can be dangerous, faulty, expensive, and difficult to access. Perhaps the simplest, cheapest, and safest form of birth control beyond abstinence (which again assumes women are the sole decisionmakers in whether or not they have sex) is the use of condoms. But condom use depends on men being willing to use them. The claim that the poor should stop having babies is particularly interesting in the face of ever increasing curtailment of women's reproductive rights and options. These limitations go so far as to decrease funding for organizations that give birth control or family planning information. For example, in 2017 the U.S. president has reinstated and expanded the Global Gag Rule of 1984, a policy that blocks federal funding to international nongovernmental organizations that provide abortions, family planning services, or information about family planning. This expansion includes global health assistance programs across all departments and agencies. This means that the Global Gag Rule will now not only apply to organizations that receive family planning funding, but also to foreign NGOs that receive funding to work on a broad range of health programs including HIV/AIDS, the Zika virus, malaria, tuberculosis, nutrition, and maternal and child health (Starrs, 2017). It is important to note that most of the arguments for limiting women's reproductive rights are rooted in religion, despite a professed separation of church and state. It is also important to notice how class is at play in who we believe should not have too many children, who is valorized for being a stay-at-home mom, and who is vilified for staying home while raising children. Social class plays a powerful role in these judgments.

"It's easy when you get a government handout every month." It is a common stereotype that Indigenous people get "free money" from the government and that peoples of Color (and African Americans in particular) are the beneficiaries of welfare and other "handout" programs. Further, it is a common stereotype that these groups cheat these programs. When considering this belief, we need to look at several interrelated dynamics: historical oppression, what programs are actually available, and who uses them.

When we think of historical oppression toward Indigenous peoples in Canada and the United States and African Americans in the United States, we might consider the following in terms of stolen goods (Coates, 2015). It is by no means an exhaustive list:

- African Americans: kidnapping; 246 years of enslavement and brutality; the rape of Black women; torture; separation of families; selling of children; forbidden to speak their own language or practice their religion; forced Christian conversion; medical experimentation; slave codes and Black codes; mandatory segregation; lynching, murder and mob violence; imprisonment and forced labor; disempowering Black entrepreneurs; bans on marriage and imprisonment for interracial couples; redlining to profit banks and real estate brokers; documented discrimination in employment, biased laws and policing practices; White flight; cultural erasures and attacks; subprime mortgages; racist media representation; mass incarceration; and educational inequality.

- Indigenous Peoples: stolen land; intentional spreading of disease; cultural and physical genocide; death marches; rape; forced onto reservations; forced into residential schools; sexual exploitation; separation of families; forbidden to speak their language or practice their ceremonies; torture; forced conversions to Christianity; racist representations in media, literature, and textbooks; broken treaties; cultural mockery through such practices as racist sports team names and Halloween costumes; cultural appropriation; omitted history; educational inequality; mass incarceration; environmental destruction; corporate pollution and resource extraction from Indigenous lands; destruction of ancestral territories and sacred burial grounds; stolen artifacts and the display of stolen bones in museums; cultural erasure; profiting from an international tourism industry on the "cowboys and Indians" White settler colonial story.

The wealth of these two countries absolutely depended—and continues to depend—upon what was stolen from these groups. There is widespread misinformation about what government-assistance supports are actually in place and who uses them. For example, many people think that citizens who receive welfare benefits live lives of luxury and that Black people in particular abuse the welfare system. Yet, in fact, to qualify for welfare—officially know as Temporary Assistance for Needy Families (TANF)—you need to have income below half the poverty line; in some states, the income limit is much lower. Even then, states have no legal obligation to provide TANF. The amount that the federal government allocates to states for TANF has not changed since 1996 (The Center on Budget and Policy Priorities, 2015). There are three times the number of children (3.2 million) than adults (1.1 million) receiving monthly TANF benefits. The highest amount of cash assistance from TANF in any state is $400.00 per month. States can set their own time limits, and no state allows for more than 60 months (5 years) on TANF for an adult. In addition to how temporary, meager, and tenuous TANF support is, the percentage of people using TANF is roughly the same by race (U.S. Department of Health & Human Services, 2012). As this book goes to press, the Republican-controlled House of Representatives in the United States has submitted a budget that would drastically cut welfare benefits even further than they currently are.

"This is socialist propaganda (a.k.a. 'commie crap')." There are many political perspectives various people have taken on the issues of inequality addressed in this book. These perspectives can be thought of as ranging on a continuum from nature to nurture. Nature arguments claim that inequality is natural or biological and thus will always be with us (positivism). Nurture arguments claim that inequality is constructed by society and thus can be changed (constructivism). While this book takes a constructivist stance, we recognize the difficulty of ever fully separating nature from nurture. Thus the question we offer when developing your own perspective is: "Who or what does this narrative serve?" Assuming that the person raising this dismissal recognizes that people do in fact occupy different class positions but is dismissing the explanation that this is due to classism (rather than to personal merit), we would ask: "Whose interests are served by the ideology of meritocracy? The owning class? The middle class? The working class?"

"This is class warfare." The term *class warfare* is frequently raised when class inequality is questioned. Traditionally it refers to the tension and antagonism between the various classes. Today, it behooves us to notice who is in the position to disseminate widely their use of the term and to what effect. Certainly activists marching in the street have carried signs referring to class warfare. But the most common usage that circulates throughout society comes from commentators on news shows and politicians. These commentators and politicians most typically represent the upper classes and invoke the term when tax breaks, deregulation, subsidies, and other "wealth-fare" programs and loopholes are questioned. Given the negative association with the term and the lack of an understanding of how class works in society, invoking the charge of class warfare effectively silences or at least invalidates further exploration. Yet when we understand how classism works, we understand that the actual direction of class warfare has always been directed toward the poor and working classes. In fact, as discussed earlier, rather than ameliorating class inequality over time, class inequality has grown to a level never before seen in human history. Questioning a system that has allowed the concentration of wealth into fewer and fewer hands is not class warfare, but rather class education and awareness in the pursuit of greater justice.

"We need to stop putting labels on everything." When thinking about the pressure to not name a social reality, consider the various issues that were once taboo but have now become more acceptable to discuss. A key aspect of gaining acceptance has been the ability to openly explore the issue. For example, younger readers may not be aware that it was once as taboo to talk about cancer as it once was to talk about AIDS. Today it should be clear that not only must we talk

about cancer and AIDS if we are going to be able to support those who have it, but that opening the conversation has also released resources that are critical to eliminating these diseases. When the stigma was reduced, funding for research was advanced, and as a result therapies and support flourished. Today, people living with cancer or AIDS have a radically different experience than in the past; there are myriad support programs, cutting-edge medications and therapies, and less stigma. In other words, there is a relationship between talking about issues and the ability to address them; silence has never moved interventions forward. This also applies to issues such as domestic violence, eating disorders, child abuse, and sexual exploitation and assault. We live in a society in which our class positions profoundly shape our access to resources in far-reaching and inequitable ways. We cannot achieve more equity if we do not understand how it is reproduced and our role in that reproduction. Again we must ask ourselves, "Who does it serve to not name classism?"

The opening of this chapter is based on Lillian Smith's 1949 parable titled "Mr. Rich White and Mr. Poor White Strike a Bargain." Smith used satire to name and critique how White men of the owning class used White men of the poor and working class to secure their positions. In essence, the bargain was that the owning class would continue to exploit the poor and working class of all races, but reward the White people of these classes with the additional resource of Whiteness (Roediger, 2007). The African American scholar W. E. B. Du Bois posed the question as early as 1935: Why have working class Blacks and Whites not found common cause in their shared suffering at the bottom of the social ladder? Roediger argues that Whiteness is a symbolic wage that has pacified the White working class by allowing both psychological and tangible (albeit limited) rewards. This wage also draws the White working classes' resentment to those below rather than above them. Smith's parable captures this dynamic and offers us the following lessons about class and its intersections with race and gender:

- Given that class is a key axis of social inequity, we must continually ask whose interests are served by particular class narratives. Had Mr. Poor White considered how his race was used against his economic interests, he might have found more rather than less economic leverage and empowerment. Discourses that we cherish and believe to be true (rags to riches, the myth of upward class mobility, and critiques of classism as class warfare or socialist propaganda) prevent critical thinking and action, thereby holding class inequity in place.
- We each play a role in the class system. While Ms. Poor White, the Black woman, and others were not a part of the parable, we must not assume that they have no part to play. The exploitation of the poor by the rich requires that the middle class look away (for example, in our consumption of cheap goods produced via exploited labor) and that Ms. Poor White exploit the

Black woman rather than build coalitions with her around their shared interests. While Ms. Poor White has been placed below Mr. Poor White, she too is still above the Black woman in the classist order.

To challenge and ultimately dismantle classism and its intersections with other forms of oppression, we must be willing to look at these issues rather than avoid them; no one is outside of these systems.

Discussion Questions

1. In your own words, what are the differences between *wealth* and *income*? What are the differences between *capitalism* and *socialism*?
2. Many people say, "My parents worked hard for what they have." Practice speaking back to this narrative from a social justice framework.
3. Pick an institution (e.g., government, prisons, policing, healthcare, schooling, media) and practice explaining how class manifests in that institution. That is, how are the owning class, middle class, and working class represented? What kind of influence does each class have? For example, who does what work within it, who profits from that work, who makes the rules and policies, whose work is visible and whose isn't? Who creates and benefits from the discourses that are circulating about class in this institution?
4. Examine the Capitalist Pyramid political comic published in 1911 (Figure 10.3). To what extent has the class pyramid changed in the past 100+ years? Provide specific examples.

Extension Activities

1. Look at the labels on three items you used the most today (e.g., clothes, shoes, technology, or food). Track down the corporate chain between you and the producer. Where was the product made? What are the working conditions under which the product was made? How much did you pay for it? How much does the average worker who made the product earn, under what conditions? How much did the corporation make for its shareholders in profits?
2. We have named many feminist scholars whose work is foundational to understanding intersectionality. Identify two of these scholars and select a work from each to compare and contrast. What core tenets of intersectionality are illustrated in their writings?
3. This chapter argues that contemporary activist organizations such as Idle No More and Black Lives Matter draw on the foundational theorizing of scholars, artists, and activists who preceded them. Identify and research the history of other activist organizations that were established prior to the 2000s (e.g., NAACP, ACLU, Native Women's Association of Canada, Student Nonviolent

Coordinating Committee). Also find and study other nonprofit, activist organizations emerging since the 2000s that advocate and operate from an intersectional framework (for example, Showing Up for Racial Justice, CorpWatch, and End the Prison Industrial Complex). In your report explain the history of the organization, its commitments to intersectionality, and how its activism has changed over time.

Patterns to Practice Seeing

1. Consider your friends, family, and most trusted business associates. What classes are they from? Do you notice a pattern in the class positions of those in your closer social circles?
2. How do you and the people in your social circles talk about people of other classes? What class assumptions about people are evident in this talk?
3. How are race and gender embedded in the patterns identified above?

CHAPTER 11

"Yeah, But . . .":
Common Rebuttals

"So, I have to watch everything I say?"

> Based on our experiences teaching critical social justice in a variety of forums, we predict that readers will raise some common questions, objections, and critiques. This chapter addresses the most commonly raised issues and objections. Drawing on all that has been discussed in previous chapters, we briefly but explicitly speak again to these concerns.

The primary goal of this book is to explain key concepts in critical social justice education in ways that deepen our readers' understanding. Deepening understanding is not dependent on agreement; the back-and-forth arguing inherent to winning or losing debates is not useful to this goal. We expect that some ideas will be new and difficult to understand. But struggling to understand and struggling to rebut are very different choices. Raising questions because you are working through an idea is important, and we encourage you to seek out critical social justice education well beyond this book. However, rebuttals that function to block out, cut off, and negate explanations are counter to the goals of education, be it critical social justice or any other kind. We ask our readers to reflect on whether the goals of their questions are greater clarity or greater protection of their existing worldview. Once a level of fluency has been gained, one is of course free to reject the arguments, but will be able to do so from a much more informed and nuanced position.

As we have explained, our socialization is the foundation of our identity. Thus to consider that we have been socialized to participate in systems of oppression that we don't condone is to challenge our very sense of who we are. But this socialization is not something we could choose or avoid, and doesn't make us bad people. It does, however, make us responsible for reeducating ourselves and working to change oppressive systems. This is unquestionably very challenging but can also be personally rewarding as we gain insight, expand our perspectives, deepen our cross-group relationships, align what we *believe* and *say* with what we *do*, and increase our personal and political integrity.

Based on our experience teaching critical social justice to a wide range of people in a variety of forums, we can predict that certain rebuttals will be made. While we have discussed many of these issues in detail elsewhere, given their tenacity, we want to revisit the most common ones. In the examples below, when we refer to "students" we are referring primarily to our students in university and college classrooms. However, the objections, as well as our responses to them, should be familiar to people outside of these contexts and easily transferable.

Claiming That Schools Are Politically Neutral

- "Politics has no place in schools."
- "It's not a school's place to teach values."

Many people believe that schools are apolitical spaces and that the knowledge taught in them is neutral. However, schools have a very long history of political struggle. Specific debates such as whether creationism and/or evolution should be taught; legal cases such as *Brown v. Board of Education* that ended legal segregation in schools; and residential schools for Aboriginal children are all examples that demonstrate the political and value-based nature of schooling. There is no neutral space and schools are not now, nor have they ever been, politically neutral.

If we believe in a just and democratic society (as the U.S. Constitution implies and the Canadian Charter of Rights and Freedoms states), then we must recognize that politics have a central place in school. Citizens must be prepared to foster a healthy democracy, and preparing students for democratic citizenship is a key responsibility of public schools. To do so, schools have to educate students about the nation's social history; provide a multitude of perspectives; foster critical thinking and perspective taking; enhance students' stamina for engaging with challenging ideas; and improve students' ability to engage with research, raise critical questions, evaluate alternative explanations, tolerate ambiguity, and foster collaboration. Without these skills, young people are ill equipped to advance a socially just, democratic nation state.

All change for a more just society has come from great struggle. Enslaved Africans were not freed because White people overall thought it would be good to free them. Emancipation required decades of struggle, sacrifice, and activism including physical violence and a death toll in the hundreds of thousands. Residential schools weren't closed, Chinese workers weren't granted citizenship, and domestic violence against women wasn't made illegal because the dominant group thought it was a good idea; the dominant group was forced to change due to pressures that took decades to build and sustain.

We can take a basic level of acceptance for granted today because of the hard work and the activism of people before us: feminist, gay and lesbian, civil rights, Indigenous activists, and others. The capacity to recognize the need for and engage in social justice activism is part of what it means to participate in a healthy democracy, and public schools play a fundamental role in fostering this.

Dismissing Social Justice Scholarship as Merely the Radical and Personal Opinions of Individual Left Wing Professors

- "Your opinions are so strong."
- "These ideas are radical."
- "This is all so one-sided. I wish you would include the other side of the conversation."

The "radical scholars" objection reduces scholarship in critical social justice education to personal values and political correctness. But "radical" must have a referent; what knowledge is it radical *in contrast to*? When we object that social justice perspectives are radical and subjective, we are also saying that mainstream perspectives are neutral and objective.

When the scholarship that professors are drawing upon is reduced to subjective and biased personal opinions, that scholarship is transformed from a highly complex and informed body of knowledge into the personal opinions of a single professor. The effect of this is that all opinions become equally valid and therefore the scholarship, now reduced to opinion, can simply be dismissed. This strategy effectively positions social justice classrooms as places of ideology, opinion, and subjectivity, while simultaneously positioning other kinds of classrooms—those in which allegedly neutral or "transparent" frameworks are taught— as objective spaces of real and preferred knowledge.

Critical theory challenges the claim that any knowledge is neutral or objective, and outside of humanly constructed meanings and interests. Yet ironically, only forms of knowledge that name their perspective are perceived as biased and open to debate; in other words, only when someone *acknowledges* their subjectivity are they seen as having subjectivity. Accusations that professors have a liberal bias ("radical" or "Marxist" or "socialist" or "left wing") typically emerge in courses that attempt to challenge the idea of neutral knowledge.

Citing Exceptions to the Rule

- "Barack Obama was president so racism has ended in the United States."
- "I have a friend who's Latina and she's the CEO of the company."
- "My professor is openly gay and he still got tenure."

There are two types of exceptions that people commonly raise. One type is citing examples of public figures from minoritized groups who have "made it." The second type is giving personal or anecdotal examples. In both cases—one that we *all* know and one that only *you* know—the goal is to prove that anyone can make it if they try and that there are no structural barriers. We are not arguing that the system is inflexible and cannot allow for a single exception, or that people don't have agency to challenge oppressive systems. Of course there are exceptions to every rule, but the exceptions also prove the rule. Why are these examples so notable that we know them by name?

Take the commonly cited public example of the presidency of Barack Obama. This was indeed a highly symbolic milestone in U.S. history and worthy of celebration. However, racism is very complex and can't be corrected when an individual person of Color succeeds. The system can accommodate some exceptions, but these exceptions don't actually change the system overall. In many ways Obama's presidency surfaced a great deal of racism while simultaneously allowing dominant society to deny it. Obama's presidency, for example, did nothing to affect increasing racial segregation. This segregation is more powerful because it occurs at the ground level—how we *actually* live our lives.

The personal example ("There was one Asian guy at my school and no one saw him as different") is problematic in that it is very difficult to engage with; we are only hearing the dominant member's necessarily limited perception. The personal example is almost impossible to question with and thus works to cut off, rather than expand, exploration. The public example is at least familiar and we have had the opportunity to hear a range of perceptions on it. Either way, while there are always exceptions, the patterns of oppression are consistent and well documented.

Arguing That Oppression Is Just Human Nature

- "Injustice exists in every society—it's just human nature."
- "Somebody has to be on top."

Because it's virtually impossible to separate nature (biology) from nurture (culture), claims that specific human dynamics are natural are very difficult to substantiate. There is no line at which we can say that some pattern of human relations occurs before or beyond the forces of socialization. Even patterns we observe in infants can only be interpreted through our cultural lenses. The more useful question for our purposes is, *whom does it serve to say that oppressing others is natural?* In other words, who is more likely to say that oppressing is human nature: those on the top doing the oppressing, or those on the bottom being oppressed? This argument always serves to support the dominant group and not the minoritized group.

The human nature argument also demonstrates how oppression changes and adapts over time. While it would no longer be acceptable in mainstream society to justify some oppressions as natural (for example, racial), it is still acceptable to justify other oppressions this way (such as gender). A more constructive and ethical use of a human nature argument is to notice that, throughout history, humans have strived to overcome oppression and make society more just.

Appealing to a Universalized Humanity

- "Why can't we all just be humans?"
- "We all bleed red."
- "It's focusing on difference that divides us."

Biologically we are all humans, of course. But socially we are members of hierarchically organized groups. Where we are in dominant groups, we are taught to see our perspectives as neutral, objective, and representative of a universal reality; our group is the standard for what it means to be normal or "just human." Thus dominant group members have the privilege of seeing themselves as outside of any group, and thus able to represent all of human experience. However, when we are in a minoritized group, our group is almost always named. Continually limited to our group identification, we are perceived as capable of speaking only for that particular group; where a "guy" can speak for all guys, a "gay guy" can't speak for all guys, he is seen to be able to speak only for/about other gay men.

Further, because dominant group members are taught to see themselves as normal, we assume that people in the minoritized group share our reality. This assumption imposes our reality on them, prevents us from learning more about their perspectives, and invalidates the oppression they experience. Insisting that "we are all just human" in response to evidence of oppression is a way to deny that oppression exists at all and to end any further discussion.

As for insisting that addressing difference is what divides us, dominant and minoritized groups are already divided from one another by virtually every measure, both physically and in life outcomes. In a society in which group difference clearly matters, we suggest that *not* addressing our differences and pretending that they have no significance serves to hold them in place.

Insisting on Immunity from Socialization

- "I was taught to treat everybody the same."
- "My parents raised me to believe that it didn't matter that I was a girl, I could be anything I wanted."
- "That's not my experience."

In addressing the claim that one has been immune to the forces of socialization, we offer the following reminders:

- Our families are not the sole forces of our socialization.
- Our families are themselves not free from socialization.
- We consistently receive many contradictory messages from a multitude of sources.
- It is impossible not to be affected by these mixed messages.
- We cannot simply decide that these messages have no effect; it takes conscious and ongoing effort to challenge them.
- Our experiences occur within a socially stratified society and must be contextualized as such.

Hopefully by this point our readers understand that they cannot be immune from the larger forces of socialization and that they couldn't avoid having been socialized into groups that are positioned hierarchically in relation to each other.

Ignoring Intersectionality

- "I am oppressed as a lesbian, so I might be White but I have no privilege."
- "I think the true oppression is classism. If we address class, all the other oppressions will disappear."

People who raise this kind of objection have usually spent a lot of time thinking about their own oppression. This is understandable; the currents we swim against are often clear to us and it is much more difficult to identify the currents we swim with. Yet identifying all of the currents we swim in is a powerful next step in our growth.

Someone who is of Asian heritage, while experiencing racism, may simultaneously have several other forms of privilege if, for example, that person is heterosexual, able-bodied, and male. Of course racism will affect how he experiences these privileges; for example, racist stereotypes about Asian men often undercut how they experience male privilege. But while the dominant White culture may diminish Asian male masculinity, he will still experience male privilege in relation to Asian women, and he will still have the right to marry the woman of his choice.

The dynamics of intersectionality are deeply significant and it is impossible to develop critical social justice literacy without an ability to grapple with their complexities. For example, in addition to other intersecting oppressions, classism and racism affect the gay community; racism and heterosexism affect people with disabilities; heterosexism and sexism affect people who are poor or working class; heterosexism and classism affect peoples of Color. Rather than rejecting the possibility that we can have any privilege if we experience oppression somewhere in our lives, the more constructive approach is to work to unravel these intersections to see how we may be upholding someone else's oppression.

Refusing to Recognize Structural and Institutional Power

- "Women are just as sexist as men."
- "I'm the only male in my group so I am oppressed."
- "People of Color are racist too."

Given the deeply embedded patterns that develop from our group identities, simply being the only dominant member in a given setting will not be a reversal of oppression. Dominant group members bring their patterns of privilege with them. For example, men in relation to women (and White men in particular) are socialized *overall* to take up more physical and social space than others. Men will tend to talk first, last, and most often; set the tone and the agenda of meetings; have a disproportionate effect on decisions; and be perceived as (and presume themselves to be) leaders in almost every context (internalized dominance).

STOP: Remember that this book is an introduction to complex ideas. While men are socialized into norms of masculinity and women into norms of femininity, we acknowledge that gender identities are not so clear-cut. For instance, many women have interests, characteristics, and mannerisms that would be labeled "masculine," and many men have those that would be labeled "feminine." The next level of analysis would be to explore how masculinity and femininity are socially constructed through norms and expectations that shape what it means to "act like a man" or "act like a woman."

Conversely, minoritized group members also have conditioned patterns (internalized oppression) that predispose them to defer to the dominant member. Women *overall* will talk less when men are present and defer to men's presumed leadership (or risk being perceived as overbearing if they do not). These patterns and relations do not reverse or change based on the ratio of dominant to minoritized members present. Without intentionality and skills of alliance, the group members will enact the inequitable relationship. The new member will not be suddenly "oppressed" or have a "minority" experience because he is the only man in a workgroup. Of greater importance, then, are the skills and perspectives the dominant group member brings.

Another common objection is that of numbers. Statements such as "We don't have much racial diversity here because we don't have very many people of Color in our area" or conversely, "We are doing well because we have a lot of people of Color in our department" are often heard in response to questions of racial diversity in the workplace. There are a few important dynamics to notice about these statements:

- They reflect the dominant perspective; for example, a workplace that seems racially diverse to White people may not seem diverse to peoples of Color.
- They assume that all that is needed to interrupt inequality is the presence of the minoritized group.
- Both of these statements defend and rationalize the situation in question and thereby limit, rather than expand, further action.

As for the claim that peoples of Color are just as racist as White people, this is to confuse discrimination with racism. We are all just as prejudiced as the next person, and we all discriminate. But when we use the "ism" words, we are describing a dynamic of historical, institutional, cultural, and ideological oppression. Without the language to describe structural oppression, we continue to hide and deny its existence. Using the terms interchangeably obscures the reality that discrimination across race is not the same in its effects, because only the discrimination of White people is backed by historical, institutional, cultural, ideological, and social power and thus has far-reaching and collective impact on the lives of peoples of Color. A more interesting and fruitful line of inquiry might be why so many people are so invested in insisting that the minoritized group is "just as" prejudiced or oppressive as the dominant group. What does this insistence rationalize or excuse? What is served by the refusal to acknowledge institutional power?

Rejecting the Politics of Language

- "What do they want us to call them now?"
- "You mean I have to watch everything I say?"

Language is a form of knowledge construction; the language we use to name a social group shapes the way we think about that group. To think critically about language is to think critically about power and ideology. Take the example of homelessness. Just 20 or so years ago, the term *homeless* was not common. The terms we used at that time for people we would now term homeless included *bums, derelicts, tramps, transients, hobos,* and *winos.* These are clearly negative terms that conjure negative images and are all typically associated with men. Over time, advocates came to realize that many women and children were also homeless, and that women and children had different issues and needs because of their gender and age. In other words, the kinds of challenges that a single man living on the street might have are different from those that a single woman living on the street might have, and different still from those of a single woman living with children.

Advocates realized that they had to change the public perception of this population in order to increase the resources available to them; few people were interested in helping "bums" and "winos" (notice how some people are perceived as worthy of resources and others are not). There was a deliberate political effort to introduce the term *homeless* in order to change the public perceptions of this diverse population. When the language changed, so did the perception; this change enabled greater access to resources, illustrating the political power of language.

The traditional names that dominant groups use for minoritized groups have their roots in racist history and were not chosen by the minoritized group (such as "Colored People" "Oriental" or "Eskimo", which are all terms that should be avoided). Further, it really isn't that difficult to keep up with changes in language. Many of us manage to keep up with popular language of the day, whether it was slang like "groovy" and "cool" in the past or "OMG" and "LOL" more recently. It is easy for us to keep up with language when we are invested in the social context. To choose not to be aware of changes in language regarding minoritized groups indicates that we may be living in a great deal of segregation from them. It is also an indication of a lack of interest that is not accidental. On the other hand, to be aware of changes in language yet still insist that we have the right to say anything we want is willful irresponsibility. Of course we all have the right to say whatever we want, but there are consequences for what we say.

In a pluralistic society that claims to uphold the ideals of equality, speech must be chosen in ways that are cognizant of the context. We wouldn't speak to our boss the way we might to our friends. These are choices of context-appropriate speech, and we all conform to these speech considerations on a daily basis. Rather than feeling resentful (an indicator that our internalized dominance is being challenged), we might consider our ability to adapt to changes in language as an indicator that we are growing in our critical social justice literacy.

Invalidating Claims of Oppression as Oversensitivity

- "People just need to lighten up."
- "Why don't you people just get over it?"
- "I didn't mean it that way; can't you take a joke?"

This objection is a variation on the "political correctness" objection, which implies that whenever minoritized groups and their allies speak to oppression they are just being oversensitive and taking things too seriously. There are several problematic dynamics in this dismissal. First, the arrogance of someone in the dominant group feeling qualified to determine the legitimacy of a minoritized group member's reaction to oppression. Remember that for many of us in the dominant group, our socialization is invisible, and so we often assume that others will share our frames of reference and see a situation the same way that we do. If we are committed to critical social justice, then we recognize that the burden of understanding should rest with the dominant group.

Another problematic dynamic is that dominant group members often do not understand the collective weight of oppression. What is "just a comment" for us is one of a thousand daily microaggressions for the minoritized group. That someone from the minoritized group would be willing to let us know how oppression impacts them takes a lot of courage, given how freely dominant groups tend to trivialize this information. Dismissing the feedback as oversensitivity conveys that we are not open to or interested in understanding the impact of our behavior on others. A more constructive use of this feedback is to use it as an entry point to consider what understanding *we* are lacking.

Focusing on intentions is another way we often dismiss the impact of our behavior. Common dominant group reasoning is that as long as we didn't *intend* to perpetuate oppression, then our actions don't count as oppressive and we don't need to take responsibility for them. We then tend to spend a great deal of energy explaining to the minoritized group why our behavior is not oppressive at all. This invalidates minoritized experiences while enabling us to deny responsibility for the impact of our behavior in both the immediate interaction and the broader, historical context.

Finally, this dismissal allows dominant group members to project the problem outward onto minoritized groups and their allies while simultaneously minimizing it—the problem now belongs to the minoritized group and they themselves create it by taking life too seriously. According to this reasoning, it isn't really an issue at all; the minoritized group itself could easily solve oppression by simply getting over it and moving on. From a critical social justice perspective, this is the equivalent of the dominant group telling the minoritized group to accept their oppression.

The life and activism of Nora Bernard (Figure 11.1) illustrate the impact of oppression and minoritized groups' struggles for justice.

Reasoning That If Choice Is Involved It Can't Be Oppression

- "It's not oppression if people choose to participate."
- "Women in those videos could just say no; they're getting paid and choose to enact those scenes."

The discourse of choice is pervasive in dominant society. Much like individualism, *choice* claims that we are each free to participate in any opportunities made available to us. In the example of music videos, this argument claims that the women in the videos are adults, they are getting paid, and they could choose not to participate if they had a problem with the videos. Further, we can just choose not to watch the video if *we* have a problem with it.

Figure 11.1. Nora Bernard (1935–2007)

Nora Bernard was a Canadian Mi'kmaq activist, member of the Millbrook First Nation, and survivor of the residential school in Shubenacadie, Nova Scotia.

She testified before a House of Commons Committee in 2005 saying, "Sexual and physical abuse was not the only abuse that the survivors experienced in these institutions. Abuses included such things as being incarcerated through no fault of their own; the introduction of child labor; the withholding of proper food, clothing, and proper education; the loss of language and culture; and no proper medical attention."

She initiated and won the largest class action lawsuit in Canadian history, on behalf of over 80,000 survivors of the Canadian residential school system. After 12 years of tireless activism on the part of Bernard and others, the federal government settled the suit, conservatively estimated at between 3 and 5 billion dollars. She received her compensation check for $14,000 in 2007.

Nora Bernard was posthumously awarded the Order of Nova Scotia in 2008.

Source: www.danielnpaul.com/scan_image/NoraBernard.jpg

While choice is important in all social exchanges, the choice discourse shifts the focus away from a big-picture understanding of injustice and toward an individual one. Were we instead to account for the structural forces shaping what choices are available to us, we might ask questions such as: What *other* opportunities to earn a living wage in the music industry do young women have? What opportunities do young women have to participate in this industry without furthering the same sexist plots? In other words, if they choose to say no, could they still work? The discourse of choice diverts our attention away from structural oppression by placing responsibility wholly in the hands of (in this example) individual young women. And when there are rewards for conformity (such as conform and earn a salary, or don't conform and don't earn a salary), how much choice is really on the table? Further, only a very limited pool of women who are considered highly attractive have the choice to star in these videos at all.

It may be worthy of reflection to consider in which contexts we see women's choices about how to use their bodies as free, and in which contexts we see those choices as up for debate. For example, in the context of music or porn videos, many argue that a woman has the right to use her body in any way that she chooses. In this context, the politics surrounding her choice (such as limited economic opportunities for women) are made irrelevant. But in the context of other kinds of choices, such as reproductive health, it is often argued that a woman should *not* have choice. What is considered her individual choice over her body in one context is considered open for public debate in another. This indicates that there are more institutional interests surrounding how women make choices around their bodies than mere individual freedom would imply. Still, regardless of the choices of the individual women that star in them, the industry markets these videos to all of us, and we are all affected by their virtually unavoidable circulation throughout the culture.

Positioning Social Justice Education as Something "Extra"

- "We have to prepare students for the test; that's just the way it is."
- "Dealing with social justice in the classroom (or workplace) takes time away from the real work we have to do."

We often hear this rationale for inaction in school (or workplace) contexts wherein teachers (or leaders) explain that they wish they had time to deal with social justice but they have to deal with the curriculum (or the bottom line) first, and there just isn't time in the day to do everything. Because dominant institutions in society are positioned as being neutral, challenging social injustice within them seems to be an extra task in addition to our actual tasks.

Yet, as we have argued, the way we act in the world is based on how we perceive the world. Our worldviews are not neutral; they are shaped by particular ideas about how the world is or ought to be. For example, if you believe that we are all unique human beings, that our group memberships are irrelevant, and that the best remedy for injustice is to attempt to see everyone as an individual, then that perspective will be visible in everything you do and how you do it.

If, on the other hand, you believe that our group memberships are important, that different groups have different levels of access to resources, that this inequitable access is shaped by institutional forces, and that we have agency to positively influence those institutions for the betterment of everyone, then that too will be evident in everything you do.

Although it does take ongoing study and practice before a social justice framework will fundamentally shape your work, to decide not to take on this commitment does not mean you are being neutral. Indeed, to decide not to take on this commitment is to actively support and reproduce the inequitable status quo. When we have developed a critical social justice consciousness, it is evident in all that we do and no longer seen as outside our job description.

Being Paralyzed by Guilt

- "I feel so bad and I don't know what to do."
- "This is all just a guilt trip."

When we begin to realize that contrary to what we have always believed, categories of difference (such as gender, race, class, and ability), rather than merit alone, *do* matter and significantly shape our perspectives, experiences, opportunities, and outcomes, we can feel overwhelmed. These feelings are part of the process of understanding oppression and injustice, and it's normal to feel frustrated when answers don't come easily. But it's important

> 🖐 **STOP:** Remember that it isn't actually possible to see everyone as an individual and thus to treat them as one. From a critical social justice perspective we understand that we are all socialized to see people from groups other than our own in particular and often problematic ways.

that these feelings be only temporary and don't become an excuse to avoid action, because when we are in the dominant group, guilt is rooted in privilege and functions to legitimize inaction on equity. In other words, paralysis due to guilt ultimately protects our positions and holds existing oppressions in place. Consider the collective impact of wealthy people who benefit from classism claiming, "I feel so overwhelmed by my wealth, I don't know what to do," or of men who benefit from sexism claiming, "I feel so overwhelmed by men's domination of every institution, I don't know what to do," or of White people who benefit from racism claiming, "I feel so overwhelmed by my unearned privileges, I don't know what to do."

Another way that paralysis manifests is by waiting for instructions before acting. Our students often lament that they are being told about all of the problems but not given any solutions. Yet the desire to jump to the "end" or to the answers can be a way to avoid the hard work of self-reflection and reeducation that is required of us.

This lament can also work as a way to rationalize inaction: "If you can't tell me what to do, then I don't have to do anything." But the solutions are not simple formulas that can be applied by any person in any situation; they are dependent upon the specific context and social position of the person undertaking them. Knowing the privileges and limitations afforded by your group positions is the most powerful first step in evaluating how you might act. Further, it is also important that we don't focus solely on an individualistic approach; critical social justice action is already underway and we need to take the initiative to find out what is happening in our community (schools, workplaces, nonprofit organizations) and get involved.

In the concluding chapter we offer some concrete suggestions for what one can do, but we encourage our readers to remember that the best antidote to guilt is action.

Discussion Questions

1. How would the authors respond to the rebuttal, "So, I have to watch everything I say?"
2. Which of the rebuttals have you felt yourself (or perhaps still feel)? Which is the most challenging for you and why? If you could speak back to yourself with the voice of the authors, how would you counter the rebuttal?
3. Pick two rebuttals and discuss the contexts in which you have heard or used them (or variations of them). Using the concepts explained in this book, how might you respond to this rebuttal were it to be raised again in your presence? What challenges might there be in responding in a public context (such as a meeting at school or in the workplace), and how will you meet these challenges?

Extension Activities

1. a. The following are common suggestions people make for achieving an equitable climate:

    » Respect people
    » Treat everyone equally
    » Don't take things personally
    » Don't judge anyone
    » Don't see color

    In small groups, see if you can come to consensus on describing what each of these would look like in action. Be sure that your description includes indicators that would allow anyone to know it when they saw it in action.

   b. What were the challenges of this activity? How might we understand these challenges from a critical social justice lens?
2. a. Working with a partner with whom you share a dominant group identity, identify a local organization that works from a critical social justice framework, such as Black Lives Matter, Idle No More; Showing Up for Racial Justice; Occupy. Attend a meeting or event.
   b. Write talking notes to explain the position that we cannot ignore the past if we want to move forward in the present (in other words, it's not as simple as "just getting over it"). Come up with at least three strong reasons for this position, using information from the organization that you chose above.

CHAPTER 12

Putting It All Together

"What Now?"

Understanding social justice means that we must be able to recognize that relations of unequal social power are constantly being negotiated at both the micro (individual) and macro (structural) levels. We must understand our own positions within these relations of unequal power. We must be able to think critically about knowledge. And most importantly, we must be able to act from this understanding, in service of a more just society. This final chapter reviews key principles of critical social justice and offers some concrete suggestions for action.

What does it mean, then, to put critical social justice into action? In this chapter we return to the four key elements of understanding from the preface and offer practical suggestions to guide the next phase of the journey.

To review, understanding critical social justice means that an individual must be able to do the following:

- Recognize how relations of unequal social power are constantly being negotiated at both the micro (individual) and macro (structural) levels
- Understand our own positions within these relations of unequal power
- Think critically about knowledge
- Act on the above in service of a more just society

Below, we illustrate these elements through vignettes and organize them into two general areas: critical social justice *perspectives* (how we understand the issues) and *skills* (how we act on that understanding). We offer some questions and suggestions (*critical justice considerations*) to guide your next steps in developing your critical social justice literacy. Keep in mind that these are only examples intended to illustrate key elements; we are not suggesting that oppression is limited to these situations, nor are our suggestions meant to be foolproof formulas. Expect to make mistakes, and consider them learning opportunities.

Recognize How Relations of Unequal Social Power Are Constantly Being Negotiated

Imagine . . . a classroom of 20 teacher education students. In this class, there are 17 female students and 3 male. The female students are early childhood or elementary education majors and the male students are all secondary education majors. Seventeen of the students come from a middle-class suburban background, two from a working-class rural background, and one from a working-class urban background. The students' ages range from 19 to 25. All of them are White. Two of the students have learning disabilities; none of them have visible disabilities. English is their first language. The professor, a White woman, points out that much like the demographic of teachers and teacher educators, the class is not very diverse. Many of the students, feeling defensive, argue that there is a great deal of diversity among them.

Critical social justice considerations: What do you see? One of the dynamics at play in this scenario is in the difference between how a person using a critical social justice lens sees diversity and how people who are using a mainstream lens see diversity. The students, looking through the lens of individualism, see diversity in terms of personality. From this lens, everyone is first and foremost a unique individual and social group memberships are unimportant. The instructor, who is looking through a critical social justice lens, sees the room in terms of key social groups. From this perspective, many major minoritized groups are absent, including: peoples of Color, people with visible disabilities, people from a range of socioeconomic classes, people in non-traditional gender career tracks, and people with different linguistic and cultural capital.

STOP: There are a few schools specifically for minoritized groups, such as the African American Academy, women's colleges, and The Triangle Program alternative schools for LGBTQ youth. While these schools are segregated, their intent via the curriculum, pedagogy, staff, and faculty, is to *counter* the oppressive forces in mainstream education. Mainstream schools are not created to counter these forces. Therefore, the reasons and effects of the segregation in these schools versus mainstream schools are not the same.

The absence of these key groups is not an accident nor is it irrelevant; it is the result of long-term structural oppression. The homogeneity of the class in these terms is never neutral or benign, and the forces that have led to it are always in play. Because we are socialized to think of ourselves as individuals, especially in our dominant groups, it is often difficult to understand why it is useful to think about people in terms of their social groups. However, when we think in terms of groups, we can begin to see patterns of structural injustice, recognize that key perspectives are missing, and know to pursue those missing perspectives.

When we don't see our social surroundings in terms of groups, we don't notice how segregated we often are from minoritized people; segregation becomes normal and unremarkable. Thus we are not compelled to change this segregation. This is another reason why colorblindness is so pernicious. If the students in this scenario insist that they don't see color, they can deny seeing segregation and its impact on schools, neighborhoods, and children's educational opportunities. They can also deny their own racial socialization and how it shapes their worldview. But not seeing how structural power circulates through segregation does not mean that power is absent and no oppression is occurring. Indeed, power is reinforced in the very fact that we can look around and not see anything of value missing. Expanding your capacity to see at the group level—where groups are and where they aren't—is critical for seeing how power is reproduced in institutions.

From a critical social justice perspective, the more social group diversity there is in any social context, the more we increase our collective ability to consider multiple perspectives. Of course the presence of multiple perspectives (or social group diversity) is only the first step. The second is to foster an environment wherein people from minoritized groups (and their allies) can voice their perspectives and have them listened to and taken seriously; environments that are numerically diverse around key social group memberships are not necessarily prepared to support and engage with those perspectives.

✋ **STOP:** This does not mean that an all-White, or all-male, or all-able-bodied group cannot engage with critical social justice principles. The key factors are the awareness and skills that those dominant group members bring to the table and how they apply those skills to address challenges such as the absence of minoritized perspectives.

Critical social justice considerations: Defensiveness. Another dynamic in this scenario is the defensiveness the students feel when the instructor points out the lack of diversity. This defensiveness signals that the ideology of individualism has been challenged. In our dominant groups, we are not socialized to see ourselves as *group* members and it is common to take umbrage at the suggestion that this aspect of our identity matters, for example, to feel defensive at the suggestion that our race, or class, or gender is relevant to our life experiences. To point out the relevance of our group memberships is to challenge a privilege to which we often feel entitled: the privilege to see ourselves and be seen by others as individuals, outside of social groups.

The students' defensiveness also indicates that they are coming from a good/ bad binary; the teacher has raised the issue of race, among other things, and implied that something is racially problematic about the demographics of the class. Unfortunately, their defensiveness indicates that they might not be as open to the discussion as they could be and this makes it harder for the instructor to broach it. Their defensiveness also sends an unwelcoming message to anyone else in the room who may want to engage constructively with the issue. Of course we do not mean to imply that the defensiveness is not normal or temporary, or that the students are not open to the discussion at all. But defensiveness in this context is an indication of a dominant worldview, and it functions to protect that worldview rather than expand it. From a critical social justice perspective, defensiveness should be an indicator to us that we are falling into the good/bad binary or that some aspect of our dominant group position is being threatened. In this way, we can use our defensiveness as an entry point into deeper self-awareness.

Critical social justice considerations: Additional layers of complexity. Now let's imagine that the person who points out the lack of diversity is a person of Color (or a member of any other minoritized group who is not represented in any significant way in that setting). In this case, there are at least two key dynamics to consider. The first dynamic is the risk it takes to bring up an issue of critical social justice to dominant group members, and particularly dominant group members who are the numerical majority in the setting. Remember, key patterns of dominant group members include: they are usually not aware of injustice and/or deny its existence; they are defensive about the suggestion that it exists; they don't like to be reminded of forms of injustice that benefit them; and they tend to lack the humility to listen to minoritized groups. These patterns make it very difficult for minoritized people to speak out. Based on well-grounded past experience, they are likely to be acutely aware of the risks and know that they are outnumbered and unable to count on anyone else in the room to support them. Even if there is a dominant group member in the room who understands the point being made and the importance of engaging with it, if they play it safe and don't use their position to support the person who raised the issue, they are de facto supporting the unwelcoming climate in the setting.

> ✋ **STOP:** Although the instructor does have a temporary position of authority in that setting, this position is of status, not of rank (see Chapter 5), and they will still be dealing with racism or other relevant forms of oppressions.

A second key dynamic to consider is that dominant group members tend to dismiss the voices of minoritized group members as: representing "special" or biased interests; angry and disruptive; emotional and illogical; and therefore, as unworthy of consideration. When the minoritized person is the instructor of the class, the chair of a meeting, or the facilitator of a session, their status of temporary authority will be overridden by their rank as a minoritized group member, and any expertise they bring to the discussion may quickly be dismissed.

In order to constructively interrupt the dynamics of oppression in this scenario the following perspectives and skills are necessary:

Critical social justice perspectives

- See at the group level and understand the saliency of your group memberships.
- Recognize that colorblindness hides, rather than addresses, social injustice.
- Recognize what is lost in homogeneity.
- Move beyond good/bad binaries.
- Work from the knowledge that the societal default is oppression; there are no spaces free of it. Thus, the question becomes, "How is it manifesting here?" rather than "Is it manifesting here?"

Critical social justice skills

- Lower any defensiveness you may be feeling.
- Educate yourself about groups you have been separated from.
- Build authentic cross-group relationships. (Authentic means committed, ongoing, and mutual relationships, and does not mean seeking out a lone member of the minoritized group to educate you.)

Understand Our Own Positions Within Relations of Unequal Power

Imagine . . . a workplace meeting with 14 people sitting around the table. Only 3 in the meeting are men, and all of these men are White. Of the rest of the group of women, 3 are women of Color. A White woman is chairing the meeting and opens the discussion by asking for suggestions for addressing a problem the group is working on. One of the men makes the first suggestion. Without waiting for other suggestions to be brought to the table, a second man rebuts the first man's suggestion. They begin a back and forth exchange that goes on at length. Every now and then one of the women asks a question for clarification. One of the men occasionally prefaces his comments with, "I know I've been talking a lot, but . . ." and then continues to talk. Eventually, they wrap up their debate and a woman of Color makes the next suggestion. As soon as she begins speaking, one of the men checks his email and another gets up to refill his coffee.

Let's look at the dynamics of the meeting through a critical social justice lens. The first task is to identify the most salient group memberships at play in this part of the meeting. Once we've identified them, we can begin to notice what patterns these groups bring and how they might be manifesting in ways that reinforce, rather than interrupt, inequitable outcomes. Then we can decide what actions would be most constructive for each player to take.

Critical social justice considerations: Salient group memberships. The most salient social group memberships in this scenario are *gender* and *race*.

Critical social justice considerations: What are the patterns at play? The first pattern manifesting in the meeting is that of male domination of the discussion. Men, and White men in particular, tend to take up an inordinate amount of talk time. They are apt to speak first, speak next, and afford very little if any "wait time" during a discussion (Ridgeway & Correll, 2004). They may believe that the space is open and free and that the solution is simply for other people to just speak up, that is, to act like them; the presumption is that anyone can speak if they want to. In reality, however, airtime is a limited resource; due to typical time constraints, not everyone can speak even if they want to, and certainly not for as long as they want to. Further, wait time is subjective—what seems to dominant group members as a very long pause may not feel long to others. And certainly, women overall have not been socialized to "just speak up."

Another pattern in this scenario is that of the men shifting their attention away when a woman begins to speak. The men's behavior reinforces the dominant messages that men's voices are more important than women's, that men are entitled to speak first and most, and that what a woman has to say is not as valuable to men. These messages are reinforced for all of the women in the meeting, but are further problematic because the woman who begins to speak is a woman of Color. In addition to what this communicates to women overall, this also communicates to the women of Color that their voices are less valuable and reinforces not only

> 🖐 **STOP:** It is highly unlikely that any of these patterns are conscious or intentional. Remember, from a critical social justice perspective, intentions are not as relevant as impact. Patterns, although enacted by individuals, accrue collectively at the group level and are the result of socialization; they are not our fault, but we *are* responsible for becoming aware of and interrupting them.

male privilege, but White privilege. While this may seem to be an isolated incident in which the men just happened to get up or check their email at the moment a woman of Color began to speak, it is only one example of the kinds of microaggressions the women of Color endure every day; to the women of Color this is likely

> **STOP:** Remember, injustice is not about numbers, it is about *power*. Although women were the numerical majority in this scenario, the men were still able to dominate.

not an isolated exception. The enactment of White privilege is also reinforced for the White women; while the White women are disadvantaged by the male dominance, they still benefit from the White privilege manifesting in the room.

Critical social justice considerations: Why these patterns matter. Those who speak first set the agenda, guide the discussion, disproportionately influence decisions, are seen as leaders, and gain more social capital. Social patterns in groups are well documented; dominant groups lead *overall*. While an *individual* member of a dominant group might not be dominating (in this case, the third White man who was at the meeting but silent), in proportion to the ratio of men in the meeting, White men *collectively* are still dominating. In fact, the third man sitting silently and not interrupting the dominance of the other White men supports their ability to dominate (e.g., he could say, "I'm curious what other people think; could we hear from some others?"). These patterns are independent of individual members' intentions; they are not personal but they are always at play. To challenge social injustice we have to challenge our group's patterns (whether we personally see ourselves participating in them or not).

This scenario also demonstrates a point made earlier in the classroom scenario: Although there were members of minoritized groups present in the meeting (in this case women and peoples of Color), because of the lack of critical social justice skills and perspectives of the men and the White people, the environment did not support the inclusion of their perspectives.

> **STOP:** Remember that we are simultaneously members of multiple social groups. While in one domain we may be oppressed (e.g., as women), in another domain we may enact dominance (e.g., as *White* women). These identities don't cancel each other out.

Critical social justice considerations: Additional layers of complexity. Now let us add an additional layer of complexity: intersectionality. Imagine that the meeting is absent of the men and consists instead of 14 women: 11 White women and 3 women of Color. In this context, the dynamics of race will rise to salience and the White women will tend to dominate. Although the White women have been socialized to defer to the voices of the White men (internalized gender oppression), they have also been socialized to dominate over the peoples of Color (internalized racial dominance).

In order to constructively interrupt the dynamics of oppression in this scenario the following perspectives and skills are necessary:

Critical social justice perspectives

- Recognize the range of social group memberships in the context.
- Think from the group rather than individual level.
- Remember that patterns are not personal.
- Understand that these patterns are deeply rooted and will not interrupt themselves.
- Understand that although you are in the same room, you are not having the same experience as others due to dynamics of inequitable power. When a member of the minoritized group speaks, be cognizant of your body language and of when you decide to take a break, either mental or physical.

> STOP: It is *always* the primary responsibility of the dominant group members to use their positions to interrupt oppression.

Critical social justice skills

For the dominant group:

- In general, don't speak first (this guideline may be bypassed if the speaker is making a strategic move to use his or her voice in order to interrupt broader group dynamics, but this is an advanced strategy that is best taken up in consultation with minoritized group members and other allies).
- Self-monitor your participation.
- Build your tolerance for listening.
- Push your wait time beyond your comfort zone (try counting to 10 before speaking).
- Invite different voices into the discussion ("Could we go around the table and hear from each person?").
- Stating awareness of your pattern ("I know I'm talking a lot, but . . .") without stopping the pattern is disingenuous, allowing one to appear sensitive while still not letting go of control. If you are aware that you are dominating, stop dominating.

Intersectionality (in this case, the White women):

- Understand that because of racism and White privilege, you and the women of Color do not experience the White men's sexism in the same way.
- While there are always other dynamics at play, use your White privilege when you can to support peoples of Color.
- A powerful step in challenging inequity is to recognize how your own internalized (gender) oppression may be silencing you and thus inadvertently contributing to the oppression of the women of Color.
- Your role is not to protect or save peoples of Color; if you choose to act as an ally, do so for your own growth and interest in fostering a just society, and not because you expect gratitude or believe yourself to be the most qualified.

Intersectionality (in this case, the women of Color):

- Practice seeing how your group's socialized racial patterns may contribute to upholding racism for people from minoritized racial groups other than your own. Challenge these patterns where they uphold internalized racial oppression for you and other peoples of Color.
- Utilize the privilege you may have in other aspects of your life (e.g., language, religion, class, sexuality, status in the workplace). Use your positions to leverage power and be heard. ("As the director of this program, I agree that we must address the fact that our students are not prepared to teach in urban schools" or "As a native-English-language speaker, I can see the value of actively recruiting more multilingual people into our department.")

Think Critically About Knowledge

Imagine... You have been practicing your critical social justice literacy by working to identify ideology in a range of texts (books in school, news coverage, advertisements, and movies). Over coffee, a friend tells you about an "amazingly inspirational" movie she saw called *Saving Miguel*. The plot of the film revolves around a White family who saves a poor Puerto Rican child from the "drug-infested ghetto" of a large urban city. Midway in the story, Miguel returns to the barrio seeking a reunion with his drug-addicted birth mother. As he walks down the street of his old neighborhood, he is surrounded by a gang who try to intimidate him into joining them. He is considering his limited options when the White mother arrives and confronts the gang leader, who backs down and retreats. The mother whisks Miguel out of the ghetto and back to her safe suburban home. The story highlights the White family's challenges as they adjust to having a Puerto Rican child in their lives. The movie has a happy ending when Miguel wins a spot at a prestigious arts school where he will specialize in dance.

You feel a little uncomfortable with the stereotypes the film reinforces. You raise this concern by cautioning your friend to remember that this film was written, produced, and directed by White people, and told from the White perspective. Therefore, you tell her, some of the characters and representations of life in the ghetto might be a bit stereotypical.

"But," your friend protests, "it's a true story!" She seems genuinely confused by your suggestion that this story, which she found so inspirational, could be problematic. After all, she says, it isn't just about the White family, it is about a Puerto Rican kid "making it."

The following considerations can be useful for thinking about how to respond to your friend.

Critical social justice considerations: Key aspects of the exchange. A central element in this exchange is your friend's belief that the story is true. The idea that stories told in media are true is common (be they historical accounts of a battle described in a textbook or a movie that was "based on a true story"). As we described in detail in Chapter 2, one of the key skills in adopting a critical social justice perspective is asking questions about the meaning given to any event. In this example we would ask: From whose perspective is the story true? Whose perspectives are missing? Are all of the elements true, or were some of those elements (such as the neighborhood being ruled by a gang or Miguel's mother being an addict) added to make the story more exciting or "real" (appealing to a mainstream audience who has come to expect these tropes)? How much was rearranged, added, or subtracted in order to create the dramatic pacing a movie requires, and who made these decisions? Do these decisions reinforce stereotypes, or challenge them? Asking questions such as these is an important first step in unpacking the social construction of knowledge.

Frank Chin's work (Figure 12.1) illustrates the struggle of peoples of Color to tell their own stories in ways that don't reproduce racist stereotypes in mainstream culture.

If we consider other kinds of texts (e.g., school history textbooks) we can see the effects of omitted or obscured truths which give us an incomplete picture of our histories. In order to gain a more complex understanding, we must be able to tolerate alternative accounts that challenge the familiar stories that have shaped our national identities. This process unsettles what we think we know, and also the rituals that may have deep meaning and importance for us, such as how we celebrate Columbus Day or Thanksgiving.

Critical social justice considerations: Ideologies and discourses in the text. The plot of *Saving Miguel* may sound familiar to you because many of us have seen some variation of this story many times. The story is a classic narrative of White

Figure 12.1. Frank Chin (b. 1940)

Author, playwright, and educator Frank Chin is the first Asian American to have had his plays performed on major New York stages with 1972's *The Chickencoop Chinaman* and 1974's *The Year of the Dragon*. Chin is an important figure in American theater, helping establish the Asian American Theatre Company in 1973. His works of fiction often examine the theme of stereotypes about Chinese and Asian Americans in mainstream society. His work brings attention to the importance of thinking critically about any text; all stories are constructed and audiences must ask questions about what is being reproduced. Chin recognizes that there is a complicated relationship between being presented with the stories and experiences of "others" and actually "knowing" or understanding these experiences.

Source: cemaweb.library.ucsb.edu/images/chinfrank.jpg

supremacy. The following are some of the key narratives of White supremacy repeated and reinforced in the story:

- The story is told from the perspective of White people.
- White people act as saviors of peoples of Color.
- Children of Color are innocent, but adults of Color are morally and criminally corrupt.
- Whites who are willing to save/help peoples of Color, at seemingly great personal cost, are noble and courageous.
- Individual peoples of Color can overcome their circumstances but usually only with the help of White people.
- Urban spaces and the peoples of Color living in them are inherently threatening, dangerous, and criminal.
- All peoples of Color are poor, belong to gangs, are addicted to drugs, and are bad parents.
- The most dependable route for escaping the "inner city" is to assimilate into White society and become "civilized."
- White people are willing to deal with individual "deserving" peoples of Color, but Whites do not become a part of their community in any meaningful way.
- White people who are willing to "deal with" individual peoples of Color are morally superior to other White people.

Stories with characters of Color as protagonists who make it in White society and return to their former community in order to help civilize the others also reinforce White supremacy.

Critical social justice considerations: Economic and social interests in the production of the text. There are social and economic interests in the telling of any story, be it in popular film or school textbooks. In addition to understanding the concept of perspective, it is also important to ask whose interests are best served by a particular story.

- Who wrote and produced the text?
- Who is the primary audience for this text?
- Why will this story appeal to its intended audience? (In the case of a movie, in order to appeal to the masses, it must reinscribe familiar plots and characters. In the case of a textbook, a governing body that represents specific interests must approve it.)
- Who will profit from this text?

Critical social justice considerations: Additional layers of complexity. Now let us add an additional layer of complexity to this vignette by considering the element of the audiences' reading and interpretation of the text. From a critical social justice perspective, it is always important to question narratives that are inspirational to a mass audience. Generally, racial narratives will be inspirational to a mass audience only when they reinforce familiar ideologies of White supremacy. For example, while the movie *Crash* was widely loved by mainstream audiences and received the 2006 Academy Award for Best Picture, its ultimate racial message was "Everybody is racist." This of course reinforces the dominant understanding of racism (which conflates prejudice and racism) and hides structural racial inequality and White power (Howard & Dei, 2008).

While a text's ideologies and the economics of its production may be fixed, the way that text is interpreted and valued by audiences is not. Herein lies the audience's agency: The more layers of complexity we can see in the knowledge constructed by a text, the more critically we can read that text and resist the ideologies embedded in it.

Critical social justice perspectives

- There is no neutral text; all texts represent a particular perspective.
- All texts are embedded with ideology; the ideology embedded in most mainstream texts functions to reproduce historical relations of unequal power.
- Texts that appeal to a wide audience usually do so because they reinforce dominant narratives and serve dominant interests.

- Expect there to be social consequences for challenging dominant ideology.

Critical social justice skills

- Identify the ideology and what or whom it serves.
- Build your tolerance for the social resistance you will likely get when you challenge dominant ideologies.
- Develop the skills to lower defensiveness and diplomatically provide an alternative perspective. For example, regarding your friend in the opening vignette, you might say, "I was talking to a friend who is Puerto Rican about this film and he gave me a perspective on it I hadn't considered before. May I share it with you?"

Act in Service of a More Just Society

Although all of the previous principles are necessary for critical social justice literacy, they are meaningless without action. From a critical social justice framework, the term *ally* refers to a member of the dominant group who acts to end oppression in all aspects of social life by consistently seeking to advocate alongside of the group who is oppressed in relation to them. The following are examples of allies: men who work to identify and challenge their internalized superiority, work with other men to do the same, and speak out alongside of women; White people who work to identify and challenge their internalized superiority, and work with other White people to do the same; heterosexuals who don't assume everyone else is heterosexual and who break silence and lobby alongside of gay, lesbian, bisexual, and transgender people to have equal rights for all.

In general, being an ally means:

- Validating and supporting people who are socially or institutionally minoritized in relation to you, regardless of whether you completely agree with or understand where they are coming from
- Engaging in continual self-reflection to uncover your socialized privilege and internalized superiority
- Working with other members of the dominant group and not positioning yourself as better or more advanced than they are
- Advocating when the oppressed group is absent by challenging misconceptions
- Letting go of control and sharing power when possible
- Taking risks to build relationships with minoritized group members
- Taking responsibility for mistakes

- Having humility and willingness to admit not knowing
- Earning trust through action

In institutional spaces, such as meetings, allies can take these actions:

- Support members of minoritized groups in whatever ways you can.
- Recognize minoritized people in relation to you, both in terms of rank (race, class, gender) and in terms of status (the job title they have and its relative power).
- Generate a working definition of critical social justice and a way to assess it. There are many tools available from various critical social justice organizations, as well as many excellent examples of organizations that have implemented definitions and assessments (such as the United Steelworkers union, described below).
- Pay attention to the dynamics in meetings and facilitate to interrupt inequitable patterns.
- Recognize that it matters who is in our environment and the roles they play (such as in the workplace, schools, and neighborhoods); work not only to increase representation along multiple fronts—gender, race, ethnicity, class, sexuality, ability, first language—but also to create a supportive climate.
- Recognize and affirm the importance of discussing critical social justice issues.
- Be honest about your lack of experience while demonstrating your willingness to try.
- Change the process, for example, move away from depending solely on voluntary participation in large-group discussions (sometimes called "popcorn style"), try calling for a go-around, or working in small groups, or working in pairs.
- Facilitate by inviting other voices in; for example ask, "Does anyone have a different perspective?" "Who hasn't spoken yet?" and "Whose perspective is missing?" and then wait.
- Facilitate dialogue rather than debate, using a both/and rather than either/or framework.
- Work in solidarity with others and not in isolation; don't distance yourself from others in your dominant group.
- Be humble about your skills; members of the dominant group are the least qualified to judge their ally effectiveness.
- Be accountable to minoritized group members—check in and build relationships.
- The "isms" are always operating and thus feedback about something

problematic you've done is not an accusation. Appreciate the courage it takes to give feedback on critical social justice issues, learn from it, and keep trying.

While the above are examples of actions an individual can take, the following is an example of action that an organization can take: The United Steelworkers of Canada's diversity statement on gay, lesbian, bisexual, and transgendered issues incorporates critical social justice into its mission. In the opening, they state (much like many organizations do) that they value diversity:

> Proud to represent lesbian, gay, bisexual and transgender workers, Steelworkers are actively working for equality in the workplace, at the bargaining table and in our communities. Steelworkers are helping to raise understanding and respect for the diversity and differences that make us strong, proud and, indeed, Everybody's Union. . . . The Steelworkers union must continue to take steps to help create "positive space" for gay, lesbian, bisexual and transgendered workers. (United Steelworkers of Canada, n.d.)

But what distinguishes this diversity statement from most (and makes it exceptional) is that the authors do not stop there. They operationalize (i.e., make concrete) the critical social justice work that is necessary in order to create a "positive space." For example, they identify concrete objectives, where and how they will act, and explicitly name their goals, which include:

At the bargaining table:

- Negotiate anti-harassment workplace training, policies and procedures. The United Steelworkers' Anti-Harassment Workplace Training Program has reached over 45,000 front line workers, supervisors and managers.
- Bargain for anti-discrimination language to be included into [the] collective agreement.
- Make sure your definition of spouse includes same sex partners. In Canada, it is illegal to deny same-sex spousal benefits.

In the union:

- Start a Steelworker Pride Committee. . . . Pride Committees are opportunities for gay, lesbian, bisexual, transgendered workers and their supporters to talk about issues, and plan how to raise awareness in our workplaces and in the union of gay, lesbian, bisexual and transgendered rights. Steelworker Pride Committees join with other labor and community groups to hold events and parades to both celebrate and educate.

Take action:

- Help fight HIV/AIDS. HIV/AIDS is a union issue. We work with people who have HIV/AIDS and care for people who have HIV/AIDS. We must make sure our workplaces are safe, healthy and harassment free for all workers. That means preventing harassment and discrimination of people with HIV/AIDS.
- The Steelworkers Humanity Fund is helping to support the work of Stephen Lewis and the United Nations to build a global fund to fight AIDS, tuberculosis and malaria. Canadian workers can demonstrate leadership in raising the resources, and pressuring other countries to do the same, to stop this epidemic.
- The Federal Government is appealing a court decision which granted Canada Pension Plan survivor spousal pensions to persons who lost their same sex partners between 1985-1998. LGBT persons paid into the CPP just like everyone else and are entitled to equal benefits. Let your Member of Parliament know that you disapprove of their wasting tax money to promote inequality (United Steelworkers of Canada, n.d.)

The Steelworkers offer a powerful example of collective action and accountability, and the critical social justice vision that guides them. While these will not be easy goals to achieve given the embedded nature of oppression, their articulation is a fundamental step. Without a framework to keep the organization accountable, it is unlikely that there would be much institutional change.

At the beginning of this chapter we asked the question, "What does it mean, then, to put critical social justice into action?" We offered vignettes to illustrate different elements of critical social justice literacy and discussed them in some depth. Now we ask our readers to use the example of racism (or any other form of oppression), to reflect upon the following and jot down some examples for each:

- Active racism
- Passive racism
- Active antiracism
- Passive antiracism

Perhaps your list looks something like the following:

For ***active racism,*** your examples might include telling or encouraging racist jokes, excluding or discriminating against peoples of Color in the workplace, racial profiling, and accusing peoples of Color of "playing the race card" when they try to bring up racism.

For **passive racism,** your examples might include silence, ignoring incidents and dynamics that you notice, the inequitable funding of schools, lack of interest in learning more about racism, having few if any cross-racial relationships, apathy toward, and lack of awareness about, movements for racial justice, and not getting involved in antiracist efforts or in continuing education.

For **active antiracism,** examples might include working to identify internalized racial dominance if you are White, working to identify internalized racial oppression if you are a person of Color, making sure there are multiple racial perspectives on an issue in the workplace, joining organizations working for racial justice, and seeking out continuing education.

But now we come to **passive antiracism**. If you were able to come up with any examples, reconsider them from the lens of *action* and you will likely find that they don't hold up; antiracism requires action—by definition it cannot be passive. There really are no examples of passive antiracism. Antiracism, or any other endeavor to challenge injustice, is by definition not passive.

To illustrate the complexity of action, consider this analogy. Most of us know the basic rules of basketball. There are two teams, and each team is trying to get the ball into the opposing team's basket while simultaneously preventing the other team from doing the same. Each player has a position on the team, and novice players focus on their assigned role. However, skilled players are able to see beyond their own position and synthesize all of the dynamics in play. This enables them to think strategically about every move, consider the positions of every other player in relation to their own, and base their next moves on multiple, shifting, and contextual factors. Although these players must know how the game is played and have a familiar style of playing, they do not follow a set plan and likely do not make the exact same decision twice. Instead, they are always taking into account the bigger picture based on their knowledge of the other players, the rules of the game, and which other players are nearby to support them, as well as their own developing skill level. All of these factors inform the decision they will make about their next move (DiAngelo & Sensoy, 2010).

Developing critical social justice literacy requires a lifelong commitment to an ongoing process. This process challenges our worldview and our relationships to others. It asks us to connect ourselves to uncomfortable concepts such as prejudice, privilege, and oppression. It challenges simplistic dos-and-don'ts approaches such as "*do* treat everyone equally" and "*don't* see Color." Of course it's so much easier when we believe that attaining social justice is as simple as a list of dos and don'ts. We wouldn't have to take account of the history of oppression in our nation states or trace that history into our present lives. We wouldn't have to think deeply, engage in uncomfortable self-reflection, admit to our prejudices and investments in inequality, strive for humility in the face of the unknown, and build relationships with people that we haven't been taught are valuable. We *would* have to acknowledge that our achievements are not simply or solely the result of merit and hard work, for within a society that is socially stratified, most of us benefit in some aspects of our lives from the disadvantages of others. And finally, we would have to take risks, make mistakes, and *act*.

Discussion Questions

1. Now what? What are your next steps (tomorrow, next week, next year) to continue the work of developing critical social justice literacy? What might be the easiest of these steps to accomplish? What will take longer? Identify what might be your key challenges. How will you meet these challenges?
2. The authors state that it is always the responsibility of the dominant group to interrupt oppression. Why? Discuss the dynamics involved in this statement.
3. Revisit the scenario of the meeting, when the two men who have been dominating the discussion choose to get up or open their laptop when a woman of Color begins to speak. Imagine now that these men claim that their timing had nothing to do with the woman speaking. Using the concept of "intention versus impact," explain why their behavior was problematic, regardless of their intentions. Discuss all of the various dynamics at play in the meeting. Imagine you are at the meeting and develop a response from your position.

Extension Activities

1. Identify two people, one with whom you share a dominant group identity and one with whom you share a minoritized group identity. Make a plan to check in with one another in a month. Decide what you will commit to doing in that month's time in working toward the goals of critical social justice.
2. Produce an essay examining your life through a critical social justice lens. This activity is meant to integrate your personal experiences with the theoretical framework of the book (the activity is *not* meant to be an unanalyzed narrative of your life story or your opinions about the various groups you do or do not belong to). Please draw upon the chapter themes (socialization, oppression, racism, privilege) to provide an analysis of what shapes your perspectives, values, expectations, and beliefs as a member of the various social groups you belong to.

   In your essay, explain how your group memberships shape and affect your life. Describe how key influences (such as family, friends, schools, communities, ideas, values, your culture(s), and/or the wider society) have been formative in your thinking about your memberships in the different groups.

   It may be helpful to focus your analysis on one or two key group memberships (for example, race and gender), or to select one identity in which you experience privilege and one in which you experience oppression (for example, as a White woman).

Some guidelines for working on your essay and questions to stimulate your thinking:

> » You must be a member of the groups you are writing about.
> » Consider the historical, institutional, ideological, and cultural dimensions of your group's position in U.S. or Canadian society that also influence your understanding of each group (societal level).
> » Name a minoritized group that you are a member of. What is the dominant group in relation to your group? What kind of feelings do you experience as a member of this group? In what ways is your group made visible or invisible? In what circumstances? How has oppression manifested in your life as a member of this group? In what ways does this group membership affect your daily lifestyle? How does membership in this group affect your understanding of and attitudes toward the dominant group?
> » Name a dominant group that you are a member of. What groups are minoritized in relation to yours? What feelings do you experience as a member of this dominant group? Do you notice a difference in your ability to identify feelings when thinking about dominant group membership compared with minoritized group membership? In other words, is this question harder to answer than the questions relating to your minoritized group identity? If so, what are the implications of that difficulty? How is your group powerful? What forms of power does your group hold? Who are some agents of this power? What institutions are used to exert this power? In what ways? What privileges do you have as a member of the dominant group? How does membership in this group affect your daily lifestyle? How does membership in this group affect your understanding of and attitudes toward the minoritized group? (This is a widely used activity called Multicultural Mapping. This version is adapted from Dr. Biren Ratnesh Nagda).

3. Research the work of Frank Chin (see Figure 12.1). Watch the film *The Slanted Screen: Asian Men in Film and Television* (J. Adachi & A. Yeung, Producers; J. Adachi, Director: San Francisco, CA: Asian American Media Mafia Productions, 2006. Retrieved from www.slantedscreen.com/).

Choose one of the films featured in *The Slanted Screen* and write an analysis of the film and Chin's work. What does Chin show us about the social construction of knowledge in film?

Glossary

Because language is infused with ideology, it is a significant area of attention for critical social justice scholars. Definitions, interpretations, and terms vary between lay and academic usage, as well as among social groups. The terms we do or do not use at any given moment in history play a fundamental role in dynamics of visibility and invisibility, legitimacy and illegitimacy, normalcy and deviancy. For these reasons, it is important to be thoughtful about the political and evolving nature of language.

For example, in 1970 the U.S. Census offered nine racial categories. In 2010 the Census offered 15 racial categories, in addition to offering places to write in one's racial identity. In Canada, the term *visible minority* is a classification created by the Canadian state to reflect and include people who are not White or Aboriginal, but could be of biracial or multiracial heritage and be either native or nonnative born. These changes and adaptations illustrate the role language plays in constructing the reality of social group identities. They also demonstrate the political nature of language and the role that institutions play in formalizing our understanding and recognition of social others.

Given that race, class, gender, sexuality, and ability are socially constructed, the boundaries between groups are both rigid (in terms of their consequences for our lives) and fluid (because they can change). For example, while we have worked to show that racial categories are not "real" in the sense that there are no true biological racial groups among humans, racial categories play a profound role in social dynamics such as segregation and quality of life. Yet at what point does someone *become* "Black" or "Brown" or "White"? Why is former U.S. President Barack Obama generally considered Black but not White, when he has one parent from each racial group? His case illustrates how *perceptions* of race can be as powerful as a person's actual heritage. This is why academics have developed concepts such as *racialization* and *minoritized*, and *identity* versus *identification* (Gupta, James, Maaka, Galabuzi, & Anderson, 2007; Miles, 1989; Mukherjee, Mukherjee, & Godard, 2006; Omi & Winant, 1986). These concepts are intended to capture the fluid and constructed nature of race. In some cases scholars are calling for a move away from using categories of race altogether, in favor of categories of ethnicity (Miles & Torres, 2007). This is intended to avoid reproducing the problematic and false notions of scientifically determined races. It has been argued that by using these terms, the scholarship may play a part in upholding these false notions. However, this should not be confused with the recognition that race has real consequences for our lives.

There is another layer of language complexity: how the language we have available to us limits our options and makes it nearly impossible to escape being pressed into rigid social categories. For example, while gender identity and sexual orientation are often conflated, they are not the same. A person's gender identity and sexual orientation may also not line up in simple binary terms, further illustrating the limitations of language regarding gender in this cultural and historical context.

Racial categories, like gender categories, are also in a constant state of flux. For example, many European ethnic groups only "became" White over time and with effort, motivated by the increased social status and access to resources of the state that came with the legal classification of "White" (Backhouse, 1999; Brodkin, 1998; Haney-López, 2006). One of the ways that legal and governmental policies structure our ideas about race is through the census. In the U.S. Census 2000, "White" referred to those who have origins in any of the original peoples of Europe, the Middle East, or North Africa. In Canada, the 2006 census category White referred to people who were not a visible minority. However, while governments may organize ethnic and racial identifications in these ways, how a given person experiences race at the social level can be different. In everyday life our race is a complex interaction between our internal identity and how others see us.

For example, a person who identifies as Portuguese American but looks White as commonly understood, will still receive White privilege (because others perceive him as White). Society's perception of him as White will deeply impact his experience as he moves through the world, and this will in turn impact his internal identity, expectations, assumptions, and behavioral patterns. Thus his ethnicity may be Portuguese but his race and racial experience is White. On the other hand, someone who is of Arab heritage might be identified as White in the U.S. Census, but his experience in the social world will be mediated by factors including his skin color, how he is dressed, his fluency with English, and religious markers. These factors will impact whether he is *perceived* as White and result in either access to or denial of White privilege. In these ways, social categories such as gender and race are in a constant state of negotiation.

Our goal with this glossary of terms is to provide guidance that is responsive to all of these complexities and avoids essentializing these categories (making it appear that they are real and natural). Regarding race, class, and gender terms defined in this glossary, not all people who identify with a specific group will agree to terms we define here. It is best to continually educate yourself about the politics of language in general, and how specific individuals identify in particular.

Ableism or Disableism: The systematic oppression of people with (perceived) disabilities. Ableism is based on the assumption that there is a physical, intellectual, and emotional standard for human beings and that this standard is the only one accepted as normal. All other variations of the human body are considered abnormal, deviant, and inherently inferior. This norm is institutionalized in architectural structures, school policies, and practices, and legal segregation of persons with disabilities. Some activists prefer the term disableism because it centers the reason for the oppression—one's disability status.

Aboriginal: People who are indigenous to (native or the original habitants of) a specific continent or geographic region. See also *Indigenous peoples.*

African American, African Canadian, African Heritage, Caribbean, or Black: The range of terms used to indicate someone who identifies and is identified as having origins in the Black populations of Africa. A person of Black or Black African heritage.

American Indian: Native or indigenous people of the United States. This term is used interchangeably with Native American. In Canada, the preferred term is Aboriginal or Indigenous. Please note: it is best to refer first to the person by their tribal nation, such as Cherokee, Sioux, etc. See also *Indigenous peoples.*

Androcentrism: The term used to describe a male-centered society and institutions, in which men are positioned as superior to women. Androcentrism is not simply the idea that men are superior to women, but a deeper premise that supports this idea—the definition of males and male experience as the norm or standard for human, and females and female experience as a deviation from that norm.

Anecdotal Evidence: Evidence that is based on personal stories and single, isolated or nonrepresentative examples—"I know a guy that . . . and that proves that . . . ."

Antiracism: A framework for ending racism that goes beyond tolerating or celebrating racial diversity and addresses racism as a system of unequal institutional power between Whites and peoples of Color.

Asian or Asian Heritage: Refers to people of Asian ancestry. This broad category includes South Asian (including Indian, Sri Lankan, Pakistani, Nepalese), East Asian (including Chinese, Japanese, Korean), and Southeast Asian (including Filipino, Thai, Vietnamese, Cambodian, Burmese, Laotian). The term Asian or Asian Heritage is preferred when speaking of macrolevel dynamics. However, the multitude of groups under the broad category of Asian have very different histories, languages, and experiences. Thus Asian can be a problematic term because it collapses this wide range of Asian groups into a unified collective.

Binary: An either/or construct. Presenting only two options, which are seen as polar opposites, e.g., male/female, young/old, gay/straight.

Biracial: A person with parentage or grandparentage from two distinct racial groups.

Capitalism: A profit-driven political and economic system in which a nation's resources and means of production and profits are privately held (e.g., by corporations and shareholders).

Caucasian: This term originally refers to people from the Caucasus mountain range although today it is primarily used to refer to people of White European ethnic heritage. These people were thought to be the perfect race of humans by early race scientists. Because the term is from outdated race science classifications that included Negroid, Mongoloid, and Caucasoid, it is a problematic term and *should be avoided*. White is the preferred term.

Cisgender: The term for people whose gender assignment at birth and subsequent socialization are the same as their identity. See also *Gender*.

Classism: The systematic oppression of poor and working people by those who control resources (including jobs, wages, education, housing, food, services, medicine, and cultural definitions). There are economic, political, and cultural dimensions to class oppression.

Class vernacular: The terms commonly used to identify the various class positions—e.g., working class and middle class.

Colonialism: The name given to European nations' political and economic exploration, settlement, occupation, and exploitation of large areas of the world beginning in the 15th century (sometimes called the "Age of Discovery"). Colonialism resulted in the spread of White European institutional and culture via domination over non-White and Indigenous peoples globally.

Colored or Colored People: This term is connected to legal racial segregation and is considered extremely outdated and derogatory. *People or Peoples of Color* is the preferred term when referring to non-White people broadly. Please note: we have included these terms in the glossary only as an opportunity to inform those with limited racial awareness that the terms *should not be used*.

Commodification: The action of treating a person, place, or culture as an object that can be bought, sold, privately owned, and consumed.

Critical theory: A body of scholarship that examines how society works. This scholarship offers an examination and critique of society engaging with questions of social justice and change.

Culture: The norms, values, practices, patterns of communication, language, laws, customs, and meanings shared by a group of people in a given time and place.

Discourse: The academic term for meaning that is communicated through language in all of its forms. Discourses include myths, narratives, explanations, words, concepts, and ideology. Discourses are not universal; they represent a particular cultural worldview and are shared among members of a given culture. Discourse is different from ideology because it refers to all of the ways in which we communicate ideology, including verbal and nonverbal aspects of communication, symbols, and representations.

Discrimination: Action based on prejudice. When we act on our prejudices, we are discriminating.

Dominant Group: The group at the top of the social hierarchy. In any relationship between groups that define each other (men/women, able-bodied/person with disability), the dominant group is the group that is valued more highly (avoid referring to the minoritized group as "non" dominant group, e.g., "non-White"). Dominant groups set the norms by which the minoritized group is judged. Dominant groups have greater access to the resources of society and benefit from the existence of the inequality.

Enlightenment: An intellectual movement that emerged in Europe in the 17th century and that elevated science and rationality over superstition and religion. Also referred to as the Age of Reason.

Feminism: The belief that women are equal to men. The advocacy for the social, economic, and political equality of all sexes.

First Nations: First Nations (or sometimes First Peoples) refers to the various groups of Indigenous peoples first present during the colonization of the North American continent. Examples of First Nation communities include the Blackfoot Nation (primarily in parts of Montana and Alberta), the Cherokee Nation (primarily in the southern United States), and Ojibwe Nation (north and south of the Great Lakes region). The term First Nations refers to these groups collectively.

Framework: A fundamental theory, paradigm, or thought pattern through which we make meaning of a given phenomenon; a particular way of seeing and knowing.

Gender: The socially prescribed and enforced roles, behaviors, and expectations that are assigned to us at birth. These roles determine how you are "supposed" to feel and act based on your body.

Gender Identity: The development of one's self as a male or female in relation to others.

Genderqueer (or Genderfluid, non-Binary): People who do not identify in binary terms and /or whose gender identity and expression is fluid and dynamic. See also *Sex* and *Gender*.

Globalization: The process by which corporations and other large enterprises exert international influence. In exerting this influence, they channel resources away from local communities and usually erode local industry, culture, environment, and identity.

Hegemony: The imposition of dominant group ideology onto everyone in society. Hegemony makes it difficult to escape or to resist believing in this dominant ideology, thus social control is achieved through conditioning rather than physical force or intimidation.

Heterosexism: The values, attitudes, beliefs, and behaviors that support the primacy of male-female intimate relationships. Heterosexism is enforced by institutions and the creation of laws, social policies, and everyday practices that maintain heterosexuality as the innate norm for human intimacy. Heterosexism rests on the assumption that male-female bonding is superior to any other form of intimacy, and anything other than heterosexuality is deviant or nonexistent.

Hispanic: There is great diversity and complexity within the category that dominant culture terms Hispanic. For example, according to the U.S. Census, a person who is Hispanic can be of any race, therefore the Census asks for race identification as well as identification as Hispanic or Latino.

Generally this group includes peoples of Cuban, Mexican, Puerto Rican, Central American, and South American heritage, and/or of other Spanish culture. *Hispanic is not a preferred term* for critical scholars because its roots are colonialist ("of Spain") and thereby merge diverse communities of people through the language of the colonizers. Latino/a can be problematic because it also merges many diverse countries together. Chicano/a is a self-applied political term for Mexican Americans who want to acknowledge that they live on lands stolen from Mexico by the United States.

Homophobia: The prejudice, fear, contempt, and hatred of gay, lesbian, bisexual, and transgender people and associations. Homophobia includes misinformation about and prejudice against people who do not perform the expected gender roles assigned to them at birth. Homophobia affects all people in that it is a powerful tool for enforcing gender roles. Homophobia is rooted in sexism. See also *sexism* and *heterosexism*.

Ideology: The big, shared ideas of a society that are reinforced throughout all of the institutions and thus are very hard to avoid believing. These ideas include the stories, myths, representations, explanations, definitions, and rationalizations that are used to justify inequality in society. Individualism and Meritocracy are examples of ideology.

Indigenous or Indigenous Peoples: The United Nations defines Indigenous peoples as precolonial inhabitants of any settler society, such as Canada and the United States. There are differences in the terms used to refer to them, which are related to the colonial context of Indigenous relations in Canada and the United States. In Canada, it is acceptable to use the terms Indigenous and Aboriginal. Indigenous Peoples are defined under three prominent subgroups: First Nations (various distinct tribal communities), Inuit (the distinct group of the Northern continent), and Métis (referring to Indigenous people of mixed ancestry). In the United States, it is acceptable to use the terms Indigenous and Native American. Indigenous Peoples are defined under the two prominent subgroups: American Indian (various distinct tribal communities) and Alaska Native (various distinct tribal communities in the Northern part of the continent). *We use Peoples here in plural to acknowledge that myriad distinct and diverse groups are included under this broad umbrella term.*

Native and Native American are terms that are sometimes used in the United States. However, Indigenous serves as the most universal term. While the term "Indian" in the context of "American Indian" is in use in the United States, in Canada "Indian" was used predominantly in the past, and has very important legal connotations. To be a status or nonstatus Indian (as defined by government) gave/denied certain rights. Today, the term Indian should be avoided (especially by outsiders). It is best to refer to Indigenous communities by their specific tribal affiliation. In either country, *avoid using the term Eskimo*, as it is not what people of the north called themselves and it is considered derogatory.

Institutions: Large-scale organization within a society. Examples of institutions are media, criminal justice, economics, marriage and family, education, medicine, government and military.

Institutional/ized: Embedded into the policies, practices, norms, traditions, and outcomes of institutions. When a form of social bias is institutionalized, it is reproduced automatically and no longer depends on the intentions or awareness of individuals; it is the default or status quo outcome of that institution's work.

Internalized Dominance: Internalizing and acting out (often unawarely) the constant messages circulating in the culture that you and your group are superior to whichever group is minoritized in relation to yours and that you are entitled to your higher position.

Internalized Oppression: Believing in and acting out (often unawarely) the constant messages circulating in the culture that you and your group are inferior to whichever group is dominant in relation to yours and that you are deserving of your lower position.

Intersectional/ality: The understanding that we simultaneously occupy multiple social positions and that these positions do not cancel each other out; they interact in complex ways that must be explored and understood.

Mainstream Society: The dominant framework for making sense of society that is circulated across all institutions and that all members of society are exposed to. This framework is circulated via mechanisms such as films, TV shows, advertisements, public school curriculum, holidays, and the stories, myths, representations, explanations, definitions, theories, and historical perspectives that are used to rationalize and hide inequality.

Meritocracy: The ideology that everyone succeeds on their own effort or merit. In a meritocracy, each individual earns what they have through their own talent and skills and no one has more advantage than anyone else.

Métis or Mètis Nation: A group of people who are of mixed European and Indigenous ancestry. See also *Indigenous peoples.*

Microaggressions: The everyday slights and insults that minoritized people endure and that most people of the dominant group don't notice or take seriously.

Minoritized Group: A social group that is devalued in society. This devaluing encompasses how the group is represented, what degree of access to resources it is granted, and how the unequal access is rationalized. Traditionally, a group in this position has been referred to as the minority group. However, this language has been replaced with the term *minoritized* in order to capture the active dynamics that create the lower status in society and also to signal that a group's status is not necessarily related to how many or few of them there are in the population at large.

Misogyny: The contempt for and hatred of women and characteristics that are associated with women or femaleness.

Multiracial or Mixed Race: A person of mixed (or multiple) racial heritage. This term refers to people with parentage or grandparentage from two or more racial (rather than ethnic) groups.

Native Hawaiian and Pacific Islander: According to the U.S. Census, this term refers to people with origins in any of the original peoples of Guam, Hawaii, Samoa, or other Pacific Islands.

Net worth: What you have when you subtract what you owe from what you own free and clear. What is left is your net worth.

Normalized (norm, normative): Taken for granted and seen as normal, natural, unremarkable, and universal.

Objective: The perception that some things are factual and not informed by social or cultural interpretations; a universal truth outside of any particular framework. A person or position that is seen as objective is seen as having the ability to transcend social or cultural frameworks and engage without bias or self-interest.

Oppression: The discrimination of one social group against another, backed by institutional power. Oppression occurs when one group is able to enforce its prejudice throughout society because it controls the institutions. Oppression occurs at the group or macro level, and goes well beyond individuals. Sexism, racism, classism, ableism, and heterosexism are forms of oppression.

Oriental: In a general sense this term means "of the East," with the referent being Europe; that which is east in relation to Europe. It is a term that was used to refer to people of Asian ancestry and of the Asian continent and Near, Middle, or Far East. Please note: the term Oriental is considered derogatory. We have included this term in the glossary only as an opportunity to inform those with limited racial awareness that the term *should not be used*.

Orientalism: The term "Orientalism" is not derogatory, as it refers to the specific study of how racism was institutionalized by Western European colonial powers toward people of "the Orient." Scholars who study Orientalism study the representations of the history, culture, language, and literature of the Near, Middle, or Far East by Western European nations and how those representations have impacted historical and current relations.

Patriarchy: The belief in the inherent superiority of men and male norms and the organization of society based on this belief.

Peoples of Color (People of Color; Person of Color): The term used to describe people who are racialized (seen by dominant society as having race) based on phenotypical features (such as hair texture, bone structure, and skin color). The term is useful in that it acknowledges the racial binary that organizes society under White supremacy (Whites/Peoples of Color), and the overall shared experiences of racism and internalized racial oppression for people who are racialized. However, the term is also problematic in that it conflates the wide range of very diverse groups of people into one group and thus obscures their specific histories, experiences, and challenges under White supremacy. As with all racial terms, the interplay between self-identity and identification within the social political context must be taken into account. *We use it here in plural to acknowledge that myrid distinct and diverse groups are included under this broad term.*

Peer Review: The evaluation of scholarly work—often done anonymously to ensure fairness—by peers with expertise in the same field in order to maintain or enhance the excellence of the work in that field and to advance knowledge.

Platitude: a trite, simplistic, and meaningless statement, often presented as if it were significant and original, e.g., "People just need to take personal responsibility" or "Anyone can make it if they have a good attitude."

Populism: A political movement based in concern for the common person. Usually centered around an authoritarian and charismatic leader.

Positionality: The recognition that where you stand in relation to others in society shapes what you can see and understand about the world.

Positivism: A perspective or philosophy of the scientific method as objective, neutral, and the ideal approach to understanding the world.

Postfeminism: The belief that we have achieved equality between men and women and no longer need to advocate for women's equality.

Prejudice: Learned prejudgment about members of social groups to which we don't belong. Prejudice is based on limited knowledge or experience with the group. Simplistic judgments and assumptions are made and projected onto everyone from that group.

Racialized: Perceived in racial terms; seen as having race.

Racism: In the United States and Canada, racism refers to White racial and cultural prejudice and discrimination, supported by institutional power and authority, used to the advantage of Whites and the disadvantage of peoples of Color. Racism encompasses economic, political, social, and institutional actions and beliefs that perpetuate an unequal distribution of privileges, resources, and power between White people and peoples of Color.

Sex: The biological, genetic, or phenotypical markers that distinguish male and female bodies. Sex refers to one's genitals, body structure, and hormones. See also *Gender*.

Sexism: The systematic oppression of women by men. Sexism is based on the belief that men are inherently superior to women. Sexism encompasses economic, political, social, and institutional actions and beliefs that perpetuate an unequal distribution of privileges, resources, and power between men and women.

Signifier: A sign or symbol that conveys specific cultural meaning. Signifiers connect to larger discourses that work together to construct that meaning.

Social capital: Social resources other than money that are valuable and grant status.

Socially Constructed: Meaning that is not inherently true, but agreed upon by society. Once society agrees to this meaning, it becomes real in its consequences for people's lives.

Social Stratification: The concept that social groups are relationally positioned in a hierarchy of unequal value (e.g., people without disabilities are seen as more valuable than people with disabilities). This ranking is used to justify the unequal distribution of resources among social groups.

Structural: Built into the foundation of society; norms, traditions, culture, institutions, ideologies, economics, politics, attitudes, etc.

Subjective: An individual's personal perspective, feelings, beliefs, interests, or experience, as opposed to those made from a source considered independent, unbiased, universal, and objective. A person or position that is considered subjective is assumed to be biased and/or self-interested, while a person considered to be objective is seen as unbiased and outside of any cultural influences.

Transgender: A person who feels that their gender does not match the sex category given at birth (male or female); they may feel themselves to be neither like a woman or a man, that they are a combination of both genders, or that their gender is opposite to their sex. A transgender person can appear to others to partially, occasionally, or entirely perform their gender in a way that does not conform to traditional gender roles. See also *Gender*.

Two Spirit: An Indigenous concept that recognizes that someone has both (or multiple variations of) feminine and masculine spirits. While many world-views acknowledge that everyone has both feminine and masculine qualities, this term is specifically used to indicate someone who does not have a primarily heterosexual, or male or female, identity. The English term, as a translation, is incomplete in that in using the word "two," the idea that gender and sexuality are binaries is reinforced. Two spirit is a cultural term, used by some within Indigenous communities. The term should not be used by outsiders to those communities.

White: People whose ancestry is or is perceived to be from Europe. While there are no true biological races, being perceived as White has very real privileges within the system of White supremacy. As with all identity terms, the interplay between self and group identity within the social political context must be taken into account.

Whiteness: The academic term used to capture the all-encompassing dimensions of White privilege, dominance, and assumed superiority in society. These dimensions include: ideological, institutional, social, cultural, historical, political, and interpersonal. Whiteness grants material and psychological advantages (white privilege) that are often invisible and taken for granted by Whites.

White supremacy: The academic term used to capture the all-encompassing dimensions of White privilege, dominance, and assumed superiority in mainstream society. These dimensions include: ideological, institutional, social, cultural, historical, political, and interpersonal.

References

Adair, M., & Howell, S. (2007). Common behavioral patterns that perpetuate power and relations of domination. *Tools for Change*. Retrieved from www.toolsforchange.org/resources/org-handouts/patterns%20.pdf

Adams, M., Bell, L., Goodman, D.J., & Joshi, K.Y. (2016). *Teaching for diversity and social justice* (3rd ed.). New York, NY: Routledge.

Adelman, L. (Executive Director & Producer). (2003). *Race: The power of an illusion*. San Francisco, CA: California Newsreel.

Adjei, P. B. (2016). The (em) bodiment of blackness in a visceral anti-black racism and ableism context. *Race Ethnicity and Education*, 1–13.

AFL-CIO. (2013). *CEO to worker pay ratios around the world* [report]. Retrieved from: www.aflcio.org/Corporate-Watch/Paywatch-Archive/CEO-Pay-and-You/CEO-to-Worker-Pay-Gap-in-the-United-States/Pay-Gaps-in-the-World

Alexa. (2017). Top 500 websites. Retrieved from www.alexa.com/topsites

Alexander, M. (2010). *The new Jim Crow: Mass incarceration in the age of colorblindness*. New York, NY: New Press.

Allen, B. (1996). *Rape warfare: The hidden genocide in Bosnia-Herzegovina and Croatia*. Minneapolis, MN: University of Minnesota Press.

American Civil Liberties Union (ACLU). (2011). *Banking on bondage: Private prisons and mass incarceration*. New York, NY: ACLU. Retrieved from www.aclu.org/banking-bondage-private-prisons-and-mass-incarceration

American Civil Liberties Union (ACLU). (2017). *Mass incarceration: What's at stake*. New York, NY: ACLU. Retrieved from: www.aclu.org/issues/mass-incarceration

Anyon, J. (1981). Social class and school knowledge. *Curriculum Inquiry, 11*(1), 3–42.

Anyon, J. (2011). *Marx and education*. New York, NY: Routledge.

Anzaldúa, G. (2009). La conciencia de la mestiza. In R. Warhol-Down & D. Price Herndl (Eds). *Feminisms redux: An anthology of literary theory and criticism* (pp. 303–313). New Brunswick, NJ: Rutgers University Press.

Apple, M. W. (1993). *Ideology and curriculum*. New York, NY: Routledge.

Arias, E., Heron, M., & Xu, J. (2016). United States life tables, 2012. *National Vital Statistic Reports, 65*(8). Retrieved from www.cdc.gov/nchs/data/nvsr/nvsr65/nvsr65_08.pdf

Assembly of First Nations (AFN). (n.d.). History of residential schools. Retrieved from www.afn.ca/residentialschools/history.html

Backhouse, C. (1999). *Colour-coded: A legal history of racism in Canada: 1900–1950*. Toronto, Ontario: University of Toronto Press.

Baker, H. A. Jr. (1990). Handling "crisis": Great books, rap music, and the end of Western homogeneity (reflections on the humanities in America). *Callaloo, 13*(2), 173–194.

Ballantine, J. H., & Spade, J. Z. (2008). *Schools and society: A sociological approach to education* (3rd ed.). Los Angeles, CA: Sage.

Banks, J. A. (1996). The canon debate, knowledge construction, and multicultural education. In J. A. Banks (Ed.), *Multicultural education, transformative knowledge, and action: Historical and contemporary perspectives* (pp. 3–39). New York, NY: Teachers College Press.

Banks, J. A., & Banks, C. A. M. (Eds.). (1995). *Handbook of research on multicultural education*. San Francisco, CA: Jossey Bass.

BC Society of Transition Houses. (2016). *Violence against women in Canada: Facts and stats.* Retrieved from bcsth.ca/wp-content/uploads/2016/11/POVAWW2016.jpeg

Bem, S. L. (2004). Transforming the debate on sexual inequality: From biological difference to institutionalized androcentrism. In J. C. Chrisler, C. Golden, & P. Rozee (Eds.), *Lectures on the psychology of women* (pp. 3–15). Boston, MA: McGraw-Hill.

Bergvall, V. L., Bing, J. M., & Freed, A. F. (Eds.). (1996). *Rethinking language and gender research: Theory and practice.* London, UK: Longman.

Bertrand, M., & Mullainathan, S. (2004). Are Emily and Greg more employable than Lakisha and Jamal? A field experiment on labor market discrimination. *The American Economic Review, 94*(4), 991–1013.

Bishu, S. G., & Alkadry, M. G. (2016). A systematic review of the gender pay gap and factors that predict it. *Administration & Society, 49*(1), 65–104.

Block, S., & Galabuzi, G.-E. (2011). *Canada's colour-coded labour market: The gap for racialized workers* Toronto, Canada: Wellesley Institute and Canadian Centre for Policy

Bloomberg. (2017). Bloomberg billionaires index. Retrieved from www.bloomberg.com/billionaires/

Bonilla-Silva, E. (2006). *Racism without racists: Color-blind racism and the persistence of racial inequality in the United States* (2nd ed.). New York, NY: Rowman & Littlefield.

Box Office Mojo. (2017). All time box office worldwide grosses. Retrieved from www.boxofficemojo.com/alltime/world/

Brah, A., & Phoenix, A. (2004). Ain't I a woman? Revisiting intersectionality. *Journal of International Women's Studies, 5*(3), 75–86.

Brodkin, K. (1998). *How Jews became White folks and what that says about race in America.* New Brunswick, NJ: Rutgers University Press.

Brown v. Board of Education of Topeka. 347 U.S. 483 (1954).

Brzuzy, S. (1997). Deconstructing disability: The impact of definition. *Journal of Poverty 1,* 81–91.

Budig, M. J. (2002). Male advantage and the gender composition of jobs: Who rides the glass escalator? *Social Problems, 49*(2), 258–277.

Bureau of Labor Statistics (2016). *Characteristics of minimum wage workers, 2015.* BLS Reports. Retrieved from https://www.bls.gov/opub/reports/minimum-wage/2015/home.htm

Butler, J. (1999). *Gender trouble: Feminism and the subversion of identity.* New York, NY: Routledge. (Original work published 1990)

Calliste, A. (1996). Antiracism organizing and resistance in nursing: African Canadian women. *Canadian Review of Sociology, 33*(3), 361–390.

Campaign for a Commercial-Free Childhood. (n.d.). Marketing to children overview. Retrieved from www.commercialfreechildhood.org/factsheets/overview.pdf

Campbell, F. K. (2012). Stalking ableism: Using disability to expose "abled" narcissism. In D. Goodley, B. Hughes, & L. Davis (Eds.), *Disability and social theory* (pp. 212–230). London, UK: Palgrave Macmillan.

Canadian Labour Congress (2015). *The minimum wage in Canada: Research paper #54.* Retrieved from canadianlabour.ca/issues-research/minimum-wage-canada

Canadian Press. (2010, August 9). Canadian Women's hockey league to have first draft. *CBC News.* Retrieved from www.cbc.ca/sports/hockey/story/2010/08/09/sp-cwhl-draft.html

Canadian Women's Foundation (2016). Sexual assault and harassment: Fact sheet. Retrieved from www.canadianwomen.org/sites/canadianwomen.org/files//Fact%20sheet_SexualAssaultHarassmentFormatted_18_08_2016.pdf

Cavalli-Sforza, L. L., Menozzi, P., & Piazza, A. (1994). *The history and geography of human genes.* Princeton, NJ: Princeton University Press.

Center for Disease Control (2017). *The national intimate partner and sexual violence survey (NISVS): 2010–2012 state report.* Atlanta, GA. Retrieved on June 24, 2017 from www.cdc.gov/violenceprevention/pdf/NISVS-infographic-2016.pdf

Center on Budget and Policy Priorities (June 15, 2015). *Policy basics: An introduction to TANF.* Retrieved from: www.cbpp.org/research/policy-basics-an-introduction-to-tanf

Chronicle of Higher Education. (2009). Number of full-time faculty members by sex, rank, and racial and ethnic group, fall 2007. Retrieved from chronicle.com/article/Number-of-Full-Time-Faculty/47992/

Clark, K. B., & Clark, M. P. (1950). Emotional factors in racial identification and preference in Negro children. *The Journal of Negro Education, 19*(3), 341–350.

Coates, T. (2015). *Between the world and me.* New York: Random House.

Collins, P. H. (2000). It's all in the family: Intersections of gender, race, and nation. In U. Narayan & S. Harding (Eds.), *Decentering the center: Philosophy for a multicultural, post-colonial, and feminist world* (pp. 156–176). Bloomington, IN: Indiana University Press.

Collins, P. H., & Bilge, S. (2016). *intersectionality.* Cambridge, United Kingdom: Polity Press.

Combahee River Collective. (1983). The Combahee River Collective statement. In B. Smith (Ed.), *Home Girls: A Black feminist anthology* (pp. 264–274). New Brunswick, NJ: Rutgers University Press.

Conley, D. (1999). *Being Black, living in the red: Race, wealth, and social policy in America.* Berkeley, CA: University of California Press.

Connor, D. J., Ferri, B. A., & Annamma, S. A. (2016). *DisCrit: Disability studies and critical race theory in education.* New York, NY: Teachers College Press.

Cooley, C. H. (1922). *Human nature and the social order.* New York, NY: Scribner Books.

Cooper, R., Heldman, C., Ackerman, A.R., & Farrar-Meyers, V.A. (2016). Hidden corporate profits in the U.S. prison system: The unorthodox policy-making of the American Legislative Exchange Council. *Contemporary Justice Review, 19*(3), 380–400.

Cooper, R. S., Kaufman, J. S., & Ward, R. (2003). Race and genomics. *New England Journal of Medicine, 348*(12), 1166–1170.

Copley-Woods, H. (2010, February 15). Disability bingo. Retrieved from copleywoods.com/disabilitybingo2.pdf

Crane, A., & Kazmi, B. A. (2010). Business and children: Mapping impacts, managing responsibilities. *Journal of Business Ethics, 91*(4), 567–586.

Crenshaw, K. (1989). Demarginalizing the intersection of race and sex: A Black feminist critique of antidiscrimination doctrine, feminist theory, and antiracist politics. *University of Chicago Legal Forum, 1,* 139–167.

Crenshaw, K. (1991). Mapping the margins: Identity politics, intersectionality, and violence against women. *Stanford Law Review, 43*(6), 1241–1299.

Crenshaw, K. (1995). Mapping the margins: Intersectionality, identity politics, and violence against women of color. In K. Crenshaw, N. Gotanda, G. Peller, & K. Thomas (Eds.),

Critical race theory: The key writings that formed the movement (pp. 357–383). New York, NY: New Press.

Davis, A. Y. (1981). *Women, race & class.* New York, NY: Random House.

Davis, A.Y. (2008). The prison industrial complex. In A. Bailey & C. Cuomo Eds., *The feminist philosophy reader* (pp. 412–420). New York, NY: McGraw-Hill.

Davis, K. (Director). (2005). *A girl like me* [Documentary]. Brooklyn, NY: Reel Works Teen Filmmaking. Retreived from www.mediathatmattersfest.org/watch/6/a_girl_like_me

Dechief, D., & Oreopoulos, P. (2012). Why do some employers prefer to interview Matthew but not Samir? New evidence from Toronto, Montreal, and Vancouver (Canadian Labour Market and Skills Researcher Network; Working Paper No. 95). Retrieved from ssrn.com/abstract=2018047.

Dei, G. J., Karumanchery, L. L., & Karumanchery-Luik, N. (2004). *Playing the race card: Exposing white power and privilege.* New York, NY: Lang.

DeKeseredy, W. S. (2015). Critical criminological understandings of adult pornography and woman abuse: New progressive directions in research and theory. *International Journal for Crime, Justice and Social Democracy, 4*(4), 4–21.

DeKeseredy, W.S. & Schwartz, M.D. (2013). *Male peer support and violence against women: The history and verification of a theory.* Boston, MA: Northeastern University Press.

DeNavas-Walt, C. & Proctor, B. D. (2015). Income and poverty in the United States: 2014. U.S. Government Printing Office, Washington, DC. Retrieved from www.census.gov/content/dam/Census/library/publications/2015/demo/p60-252.pdf

Devereux, C. (2005). *Growing a race: Nellie L. McClung and the fiction of eugenic feminism.* Montreal, Canada: McGill-Queen's University Press.

DiAngelo, R. J. (2006). My class didn't trump my race: Using oppression to face privilege. *Multicultural Perspectives, 8*(1), 51–56.

DiAngelo, R. (2016). *What does it mean to be White? Developing White racial literacy* (2nd ed.). New York: Peter Lang.

DiAngelo, R., & Sensoy, Ö. (2010). "OK, I get it! Now tell me how to do it!": Why we can't just tell you how to do critical multicultural education. *Multicultural Perspectives, 12*(2), 97–102.

Dickason, O. P. (2002). *Canada's first nations: A history of founding peoples from earliest times* (3rd ed.). Don Mills, Canada: Oxford University Press.

Dines, G. (2010). *Pornland: How porn has hijacked our sexuality.* Boston, MA: Beacon.

Dovidio, J., Glick, S., & Rudman, L. (2005). *On the nature of prejudice: Fifty years after Allport.* Malden, MA: Blackwell.

Doyle, A. B., & Aboud, F. E. (1995). A longitudinal study of White children's racial prejudice as a social-cognitive development. *Merrill-Palmer Quarterly, 41*(2), 209–228.

Du Bois, W. E. B. (1989). *The souls of Black folk.* New York, NY: Bantam Books. (Original work published 1903)

Duncan, P. (2014). Hot commodities, cheap labor: Women of color in the academy. *Frontiers: A Journal of Women Studies, 35*(3), 39–63.

Dyer, R. (1997).*White.* New York, NY: Routledge.

Elsass, P. M., & Graves, L. M. (1997). Demographic diversity in decision-making groups: The experiences of women and people of color. *The Academy of Management Review, 22*(4), 946–973.

Equal Voice (2014). *Fundamental facts: Elected women in Canada by the numbers.* Retrieved

from   www.equalvoice.ca/assets/file/Fundamental%20Facts%20-%20Elected%20
Women%20in%20Canada%20by%20the%20Numbers(1).pdf

Fausto-Sterling, A. (1992). *Myths of gender: Biological theories about women and men* (2nd
ed.). New York, NY: Basic Books.

Fausto-Sterling, A. (2000). *Sexing the body: Gender politics and the construction of sexuality.*
New York, NY: Basic Books.

Federal Reserve Board. (2007). *Survey of consumer finances.* Retrieved from www.federalre-
serve.gov/PUBS/oss/oss2/scfindex.html

Federal Trade Commission, Bureau of Economics. (2007, June 1). *Children's exposure to TV
advertising in 1977 and 2004.* Retrieved from www.ftc.gov/os/2007/06/cabecolor.pdf

Federation of Canadian Municipalities. (2015). *2015 Municipal statistics: Elected officials gender statistics.* Retrieved from www.fcm.ca/Documents/reports/
Women/2015-05-01_FCM_gender_stats_EN.pdf

Fine, M. (1997). Witnessing Whiteness. In M. Fine, L. Weis, C. Powell, & L. Wong (Eds.),
Off White: Readings on race, power, and society (pp. 57–65). New York, NY: Routledge.

Flax, J. (1998). *American dream in Black and White: The Clarence Thomas hearings.* New
York, NY: Cornell University.

Forbes (2016). *Forbes 400: The full list of the richest people in America 2016.* Retrieved from
www.forbes.com/sites/chasewithorn/2016/10/04/forbes-400-the-full-list-of-the-rich-
est-people-in-america-2016/#3903a6922f4b

Foucault, M. (1995). *Discipline and punish: The birth of the prison* (2nd ed.). New York:
Vintage Books. (Original work published 1977)

Fournier, E. P. (Director), Fournier, E. P., Keehn, D., & Nakao, S. (Producers). (2000). *Of
civil wrongs and rights: The Fred Korematsu Story* [Motion Picture]. Available via ko-
rematsuinstitute.org

Frankenberg, E., Lee, C., & Orfield, G. (2003). *A multiracial society with segregated schools:
Are we losing the dream?* Cambridge, MA: Civil Rights Project.

Frankenberg, R. (1993). *The social construction of Whiteness: White women, race matters.*
Minneapolis, MN: University of Minnesota Press.

Freire, P. (1970). *Pedagogy of the oppressed.* New York, NY: Continuum.

Frye, M. (1983). *The politics of reality: Essays in feminist theory.* Trumansburg, NY: The
Crossing Press.

Gaddis, M. S. (2015). Discrimination in the credential society: An audit study of race and
college selectivity in the labor market. *Social Forces, 93,* 1451–1479.

Gallavan, N.P. (2000). Multicultural education at the academy: Teacher educators' challenges, conflicts, and coping skills. *Equity & Excellence in Education, 33*(3), 5–11.

Garcia, A. M. (1989). The development of Chicana feminist discourse, 1970–1980. *Gender
and Society, 3*(2), 217–238.

Gatto, J. T. (2002). The seven-lesson schoolteacher. In *Dumbing us down: The hidden curriculum of compulsory schooling* (2nd ed., pp. 1–19). Gabriola Island, CA: New Society
Publishers.

Gomez, J. & Cataldo, P. (2016). *Private prisons and political contributions: How big money shackles immigration policy.* Retrieved from freespeechforpeople.org/wp-content/
uploads/2016/12/Immigration-and-Money-in-Politics-Issue-Report-EN.pdf

Gomez, R. A. (2007, Fall). Protecting minors from online pornography without violating
the first amendment: Mandating an affirmative choice. *SMU Science & Technology Law
Review.* Retrieved from litigation-essentials.lexisnexis.com

Gossett, T. E. (1997). *Race: The history of an idea in America*. New York, NY: Oxford University Press.

Gould, S. J. (1996). *The mismeasure of man*. New York, NY: Norton. (Original work published 1981)

Government of Canada. (2010). *Departments and agencies*. Retrieved from canada.gc.ca/depts/major/depind-eng.html

Government of Canada (2013). *Poverty profile: A snapshot of racialized poverty in Canada*. Retrieved from https://www.canada.ca/content/dam/esdc-edsc/migration/documents/eng/communities/reports/poverty_profile/snapshot.pdf

Green, E. C. (1997). *Southern strategies: Southern women and the woman suffrage question*. Chapel Hill, NC: University of North Carolina Press.

Greenwald, A. G., & Krieger, L. (2006). Implicit bias: Scientific foundations. *California Law Review, 94*(4), 945–967.

Gregory, A., Skiba, R. J., & Noguera, P. A. (2010). The achievement gap and the discipline gap: Two sides of the same coin? *Educational Researcher, 39*(1), 59–68.

Grekul, J., Krahn, A., & Odynak, D. (2004). Sterilizing the "feeble-minded": Eugenics in Alberta, Canada, 1929–1972. *Journal of Historical Sociology, 17*(4), 358–384.

Grewal, I., & Kaplan, C. (Eds.). (1994). *Scattered hegemonies: Postmodernity and transnational feminist practices*. Minneapolis, MN: University of Minnesota Press.

Grogan, S. (2016). *Body image: Understanding body dissatisfaction in men, women and children, third edition*. New York, NY: Routledge.

Gupta, T. D., James, C. E., Maaka, R. C. A., Galabuzi, G. E., & Anderson, C. (Eds.). (2007). *Race and racialization: Essential readings*. Toronto, Canada: Canadian Scholars Press.

Haig-Brown, C. (1998). *Resistance and renewal: Surviving the Indian residential school*. Vancouver, Canada: Arsenal Pulp Press.

Hamermesh, D. S., & Parker, A. M. (2005). Beauty in the classroom: Professors' pulchritude and putative pedagogical productivity. *Economics of Education Review, 24*(4), 369–376.

Haney-López, I. (2006). *White by law: The legal construction of race* (rev. ed.). New York, NY: New York University Press.

Harding, S. (1991). *Whose knowledge, whose science? Thinking from women's lives*. New York, NY: Cornell University Press.

Hare, J. (2007). First Nations education policy in Canada: Building capacity for change and control. In R. Joshee & L. Johnson (Eds.), *Multicultural education policies in Canada and the United States* (pp. 51–68). Vancouver, Canada: University of British Columbia Press.

Harris, C. I. (1993). Whiteness as property. *Harvard Law Review, 106*(8),1707.

Harry, B. (2007). The disproportionate placement of ethnic minorities in special education. In L. Florian (Ed.), *The Sage handbook of special education* (pp. 67–84). London, UK: Sage.

Harry, B., & Klinger, J. (2006). *Why are so many minority students in special education?* New York, NY: Teachers College Press.

Haskell, L., & Randall, M. (2009). Disrupted attachments: A social context complex trauma framework and the lives of Aboriginal peoples in Canada. *Journal of Aboriginal Health, 5*(3), 48–99.

Henry, F., & Tator, C. (2006). *The colour of democracy: Racism in Canadian society*. Toronto, Canada: Thomson Nelson.

Herrnstein, R. J., & Murray, C. (1994). *The bell curve: Intelligence and class structure in American life*. New York, NY: Free Press.

Hilliard, A. (1992, January). *Racism: Its origins and how it works*. Paper presented at the meeting of the Mid-West Association for the Education of Young Children, Madison, WI.

hooks, b. (1994). *Teaching to transgress: Education as the practice of freedom.* New York, NY: Routledge.

hooks, b. (2000). *Where we stand: Class matters.* New York, NY: Routledge.

HOPE: Domestic Violence Homicide Help (n.d.) Domestic violence statistics. Retrieved on June 24, 2017 from: domesticviolencehomicidehelp.com/statistics/

Howard, P. S. S., & Dei, G. J. S. (Eds.). (2008). *Crash politics and antiracism: Interrogations of liberal race discourse.* New York, NY: Peter Lang.

Hughes, M., & Thomas, M. E. (1998). The continuing significance of race revisited: A study of race, class, and quality of life in America, 1972–1996. *American Sociological Review, 63*(6), 785–795.

Hulchanski, J. D., & Murdie, R. A. (2013). Canada's Income Polarization Trend: An International and a Four Metropolitan Area Comparison. A brief submitted to the House of Commons Standing Committee on Finance for its study on income inequality in Canada, 5 April 2013. Retrieved from www.ourcommons.ca/content/Committee/411/FINA/WebDoc/WD6079428/411_FINA_IIC_Briefs/MurdieRobertAE.pdf

Ignatiev, N. (1995). *How the Irish became White.* New York, NY: Routledge.

Inter-Parliamentary Union (IPU). (2010, October 31). *Women in national parliaments.* Retrieved from www.ipu.org/wmn-e/classif.htm

Isaacs, J. B. (2007, November). Economic mobility of families across generations. *Economic Mobility Project,* Pew Charitable Trusts. [Online]. Retrieved from www.brookings.edu/wp-content/uploads/2016/06/11_generations_isaacs.pdf

Jacobson, M. F. (1998). *Whiteness of a different color: European immigrants and the alchemy of race.* Cambridge, MA: Harvard University Press.

James, C. E. (2007). "Reverse racism?" Students' responses to equity programs. In T. D. Gupta, C. E. James, R. C. A. Maaka, G. E. Galabuzi, & C. Andersen (Eds.), *Race and racialization: Essential readings* (pp. 356–362). Toronto, Canada: Canadian Scholars' Press.

Jankowski, G. S. (2016). Who stops the sweatshops? Our neglect of the injustice of maldistribution. *Social and Personality Psychology Compass, 10*(11), 581–590.

Jefferson, T. (2002). *Notes on the state of Virginia: With related documents.* (D. Waldstreicher, Ed.). New York, NY: Bedford/St. Martins. (Original work published 1787)

Jensen, R. (2007). *Getting off: Pornography and the end of masculinity.* Boston, MA: South End Press.

Jhally, S. (Producer & Director). (2007). *Dreamworlds 3: Desire, sex, and power in music video* [Motion Picture]. Northhampton, MA: Media Education Foundation.

Jhally, S. (2009). Advertising, gender, and sex: What's wrong with a little objectification? In R. Hammer & D. Kellner (Eds.), *Media/cultural studies* (pp. 313–323). New York, NY: Peter Lang.

Johnson, A. G. (2006). *Power, privilege, and difference* (2nd ed.). Boston, MA: McGraw-Hill.

Johnson, H. B., & Shapiro, T. M. (2003). Good neighborhoods, good schools: Race and the "good choices" of White families. In A. W. Doane & E. Bonilla-Silva (Eds.), *White out: The continuing significance of racism* (pp. 173–187). New York, NY: Routledge.

Joshee, R. (1995). An historical approach to understanding Canadian multicultural policy. In T. Wotherspoon & P. Jungbluth (Eds.), *Multicultural education in a changing global economy: Canada and the Netherlands* (pp. 23–40). New York, NY: Waxmann.

Joshee, R. (2004). Citizenship and multicultural education in Canada: From assimilation to social cohesion. In J. A. Banks (Ed.), *Diversity and citizenship education: Global perspectives* (pp. 127–156). San Francisco, CA: Jossey-Bass.

Kang, S. (2009). Forcing prison labor: International labor standards, human rights and the privatization of prison labor in the contemporary United States. *New Political Science, 31*(2), 137–161.

Kang, S. K., DeCelles, K. A., Tilcsik, A., & Jun, S. (2016). Whitened resumes: Race and self-presentation in the labor market. *Administrative Science Quarterly, 61*(3), 469–502.

Kimmel, M. S., & Ferber, A. L. (Eds.). (2016). *Privilege: A reader* (4th ed.). New York, NY: Westview Press.

Kincheloe, J. L. (2008). *Knowledge and critical pedagogy*. Dordrecht, Netherlands: Springer Press.

Kirmayer, L. J., & Valaskakis, G. G. (Eds.). (2009). *Healing traditions: The mental health of Aboriginal peoples in Canada*. Vancouver, Canada: University of British Columbia Press.

Kline, W. (2005). *Building a better race: Gender, sexuality, and eugenics from the turn of the century to the baby boom*. Berkeley, CA: University of California Press.

Kozol, J. (1991). *Savage inequalities: Children in America's schools*. New York, NY: Crown.

Kraus, M.W., & Tan, J.X. (2015). Americans overestimate social class mobility. *Journal of Experimental Social Psychology, 58,* 101–111.

Kunjufu, J. (2005). *Keeping Black boys out of special education*. Chicago, IL: African American Images.

Leistyna, P. (2009, Fall). Exposing the ruling class in the United States using television and documentary film. *Radical Teacher, 85,* 12–15.

Leonardo, Z. (2004). The color of supremacy: Beyond the discourse of "White privilege." *Educational Philosophy and Theory, 36*(2), 137–152.

Leonardo, Z. (2009). *Race, whiteness, and education*. New York, NY: Routledge.

Levin, D. E., & Kilbourne, J. (2008). *So sexy so soon: The new sexualized childhood and what parents can do to protect their kids*. New York, NY: Ballantine Books.

Li, E. P. H., Min, H. J., Belk, R. W., Kimura, J., & Bahl, S. (2008). Skin lightening and beauty in four Asian cultures. *Advances in Consumer Research, 35,* 444–449. Retrieved from www.acrwebsite.org/volumes/v35/naacr_vol35_273.pdf

Li, P. S. (1988). *The Chinese in Canada*. Toronto, Canada: Oxford University Press.

Linn, S. (2004). *Consuming kids: The hostile takeover of childhood*. New York, NY: New Press.

Little, W. (2016). *Introduction to sociology: 2nd Canadian edition*. Vancouver, Canada: BC Campus Open Source Textbook.

López, I. F. H. (2000). The social construction of race. In R. Delgado & J. Stefancic (Eds.), *Critical race theory: The cutting edge* (2nd ed., pp. 163–175). Philadelphia, PA: Temple University Press.

Lorde, A. (1984). The master's tools will not dismantle the master's house. In *Sister Outsider: Essays and Speeches by Audre Lorde*. Trumansburg, NY: Crossing Press.

Lund, D. E. (2006). Social justice activism in the heartland of hate: Countering extremism in Alberta. *The Alberta Journal of Educational Research, 52*(2), 181–194.

Manning, J. E. (2010). *Membership of the 111th Congress: A profile*. Washington, DC: Congressional Research Service.

Mar, L. R. (2010). *Brokering belonging: Chinese in Canada's exclusion era, 1885–1945*. New York, NY: Oxford University Press.

Marable, M., Ness, I., & Wilson, J. (2006). *Race and labor matters in the new U.S. economy*. Lanham, MD: Rowman & Littlefield.

Marshall, E. & Sensoy, Ö. (2016). *Rethinking popular culture and media,* (2nd ed.). Milwaukee, WI: Rethinking Schools.

Mauer, M., & King, R. S. (2007). *Uneven justice: State rates of incarceration by race and ethnicity.* Washington, DC: The Sentencing Project. Retrieved from advancabag.com/documents/rd_stateratesofincbyraceandethnicity.pdf

McIntosh, P. (1989, July/August). White privilege: Unpacking the invisible knapsack. *Peace and Freedom,* 10–12.

McIntosh, P. (1988). *White privilege and male privilege: A personal account of coming to see correspondences through work in women's studies.* Wellesley, MA: Center for Research on Women. Working paper 189. Retrieved from http://www.collegeart.org/pdf/diversity/white-privilege-and-male-privilege.pdf

McMurry, T. B. (2011). The image of male nurses and nursing leadership mobility. In *Nursing Forum, 46*(1), 22–28.

Metzgar, J. (2003). Politics and the American class vernacular. *WorkingUSA, 6*(5). Retrieved from http://classmatters.org/materials/metzgar.pdf

Metzgar, J. (2010). Are "the poor" part of the working class or in a class by themselves? *Labor Studies Journal, 35*(3), 398–416.

Mikkonen, J., & Raphael, D. (2010). *Social determinants of health: The Canadian facts.* Retrieved from www.thecanadianfacts.org

Miles, R. (1989). *Racism.* New York, NY: Routledge.

Miles, R., & Torres, R. (2007). Does "race" matter? Transatlantic perspectives on racism after "race relations." In T. D. Gupta, C. E. James, R. C. A. Maaka, G. E. Galabuzi, & C. Anderson (Eds.), *Race and racialization: Essential readings* (pp. 65–73). Toronto, Canada: Canadian Scholars Press.

Milloy, J. S. (1999). *A national crime: The Canadian government and the residential school system, 1879–1986.* Winnipeg, Canada: University of Manitoba Press.

Milloy, J. S. (2000). The early Indian Acts: Developmental strategy and constitutional change. In I. A. L. Getty & A. S. Lussier (Eds.), *As long as the sun shines and water flows: A reader in Canadian native studies* (pp. 56–64).Vancouver, Canada: University of British Columbia Press.

Mohanty, C. T. (1988). Under Western eyes: Feminist scholarship and colonial discourses. *Feminist Review, 30*(1), 61–88. doi:10.1057/fr.1988.42

Moraga, C., & Anzaldúa, G. (Eds.). (1981). *This bridge called my back: Writings by radical women of color.* Watertown, MA: Persephone Press.

Morrison, T. G., & Halton, M. (2009, Winter). Buff, tough, and rough: Representations of muscularity in action motion pictures. *The Journal of Men's Studies, 17*(1), 57–74.

Motaparthi, K. (2010). Blepharoplasty in Asian patients—Ethnic and ethical implications. *Virtual Mentor: American Medical Association Journal of Ethics, 12*(12), 946–949.

Mukherjee, A., Mukherjee, A., & Godard, B. (2006). Translating minoritized cultures: Issues of caste, class and gender. *Postcolonial Text, 2*(3), 1–23.

Mullaly, R. (2002). *Challenging oppression: A critical social work approach.* Toronto, Canada: Oxford University Press.

Myers, K. (2003). White fright: Reproducing White supremacy through casual discourse. In W. Doane & E. Bonilla-Silva (Eds.), *White out: The continuing significance of racism* (pp. 129–144). New York, NY: Routledge.

National Network to End Domestic Violence (2012). *Each day, 3 women die because of domestic violence.* Retrieved from: nnedv.org/getinvolved/dvam/1307-dvam-blog-series-1.html

National Coalition Against Domestic Violence (NCADV). (2015). Domestic violence national statistics. Retrieved from www.ncadv.org/files/National%20Statistics%20 Domestic%20Violence%20NCADV.pdf

Newman, L. M. (1999). *White women's rights: The racial origins of feminism in the United States*. New York, NY: Oxford University Press.

The New York Times (Feb 26, 2016). *The faces of American power, nearly as White as the Oscar nominees*. Retrieved from nyti.ms/2jR0NEs

Nieto, L., Boyer, M., Goodwin, L., Johnson, G., Collier Smith, L., & Hopkins, J. P. (2010). *Beyond inclusion, beyond empowerment: A developmental strategy to liberate everyone.* Olympia, WA: Cuetzpalin.

Nisbett, R. E. (1998). Race, genetics, and IQ. In C. Jencks & M. Phillips (Eds.), *The Black-White test score gap* (pp. 86–102). Washington, DC: Brookings Institution Press.

Oakes, J. (1985). *Keeping track: How schools structure inequality*. New Haven, CT: Yale University Press.

OECD (2015). *Better life index*. Retrieved from www.oecdbetterlifeindex.org/topics/health/

Omi, M., & Winant, H. (1986). *Racial formation in the United States: From the 1960s to the 1980s*. New York, NY: Routledge.

Oreopoulos, P. (2011). Why do skilled immigrants struggle in the labor market? A field experiment with thirteen thousand resumes. *American Economic Journal: Public Policy, 3*, 148–171.

OXFAM (2017). *An economy for the 99%*. Retrieved from https://www.oxfam.org/en/ research/economy-99

Pager, D. (2007). *Marked: Race, crime, and finding work in an era of mass incarceration.* Chicago, IL: University of Chicago Press.

Parliament of Canada (2017a). *Indemnities, salaries, and allowances: Members of the House of Commons*. Retrieved from www.lop.parl.gc.ca/ParlInfo/Lists/Salaries.aspx-?Menu=HOC-Politic&Section=03d93c58-f843-49b3-9653-84275c23f3fb

Parliament of Canada (2017b). *List of Committees: 42nd Parliament, 1st Session (Dec 3, 2015–present)*. Retrieved from www.parl.gc.ca/Committees/en/List

Payne, R. K. (2005). *A framework for understanding poverty*. Highlands, TX: Aha! Process.

Pew Research Center. (2015). *Teens, social media, and technology overview 2015*. Retrieved from www.pewinternet.org/files/2015/04/PI_TeensandTech_Update2015_0409151. pdf

Picca, L., & Feagin, J. (2007). *Two-faced racism: Whites in the backstage and frontstage.* New York, NY: Routledge.

Picower, B. (2009). The unexamined Whiteness of teaching: How White teachers maintain and enact dominant racial ideologies. *Race Ethnicity and Education, 12*(2), 197–215.

Pontell, H. N., Black, W. K. & Geis, G. (2014) Too big to fail, too powerful to jail? On the absence of criminal prosecutions after the 2008 financial meltdown. *Crime, Law, and Social Change, 61*(1), 1–13.

Rabuy, B., & Kopf, D. (2016). Detaining the poor: How money bail perpetuates an endless cycle of poverty and jail time. *Prison Policy Initiative.* Retrieved from www.prisonpolicy.org/global/2016.html

Rajotte, J. (2013). Income inequality in Canada: An overview. Report of the Standing Committee on Finance, December. Retrieved from www.parl.gc.ca/content/hoc/ Committee/412/FINA/Reports/RP6380060/finarp03/fina rp03-e.pdf

Rhode, D. L. (2010). *The beauty bias: The injustice of appearance in life and law.* New York, NY: Oxford University Press.

Rideout, V., Foehr, U., & Roberts, D. (2010). *Generation M2: Media in the lives of 8- 18-year-olds*. Menlo Park, CA: Henry J. Kaiser Family Foundation. Available at www.kff.org/entmedia/mh012010pkg.cfm

Ridgeway, C. L., & Correll, S. J. (2004). Unpacking the gender system: A theoretical perspective on gender beliefs and social relations. *Gender and Society, 18*(4), 510–531.

Roediger, D. R. (1999). *The wages of Whiteness: Race and the making of the American working class*. London, United Kingdom: Verso.

Roediger, D. (2007). *The wages of Whiteness: Race and the making of the White working class*. New York, NY: Verso.

Rudman, L. A., & Kiliansky, S. E. (2000). Implicit and explicit attitudes toward female authority. *Personality and Social Psychology Bulletin, 26*(11), 1315–1328.

Rueschemeyer, D. (1986). *Power and the Division of Labour*. Redwood City, CA: Stanford University Press.

Sakala, L. (2014). Breaking down mass incarceration in the 2010 census: State-by-state incarceration rates by race/ethnicity [Brief]. Prison Policy Initiative. Retrieved from https://www.prisonpolicy.org/reports/rates.html

Schick, C. (2000). White women teachers accessing dominance. *Discourse: Studies in the Cultural Politics of Education, 21*(3), 299–309.

Schisgall, D., & Alvarez, N. (Directors). (2007). *Very young girls* [Documentary]. New York, NY: Swinging T Productions.

Schoenfish-Keita, J., & Johnson, G. S. (2010). Environmental justice and health: An analysis of persons of color injured at the work place. *Race, Gender, and Class*, 270–304.

Sensoy, Ö., & DiAngelo, R. (2006). "I wouldn't want to be a woman in the Middle East": White female student teachers and the narrative of the oppressed Muslim woman. *Radical Pedagogy, 8*(1). Retrieved from radicalpedagogy.icaap.org/content/issue8_1/sensoy.html

Sensoy, Ö. & DiAngelo, R. (2014). "Respect differences"?: Challenging the common guidelines in social justice education [Online]. *Democracy & Education, 22*(2), (Feature Article, Article 1).

Sexual Assault Centre of Hamilton Ontario (SACHA). (n.d.). *Sexual assault statistics*. Retrieved from www.sacha.ca/home.php?sec=17&sub=43

Sharma, N. (2002). Immigrant and migrant workers in Canada: Labour movements, racism and the expansion of globalization. *Canadian Woman Studies, 21/22*(4/1), 18–25.

Shohat, E. (Ed.). (1998). *Talking visions: Multicultural feminism in a transnational age*. New York, NY: MIT Press.

Skuterud, M., Frenette, M., Poon, P. (2004). *Describing the distribution of income: Guidelines for effective analysis*. Ottawa, Canada: Statistics Canada. Catalogue no. 75F0002MIE2004010. Retrieved from statcan.ca/cgi-bin/downpub/research.cgi

Smith, L. (1949). *Killers of the dream*. New York, NY: Reynal & Hitchcock.

Starrs, A. M. (2017). The Trump global gag rule: An attack on U.S. family planning and global health aid. *The Lancet, 389*(10068), 485–486.

Statistics Canada. (2006a). *Aboriginal identity population, 2006 counts*. Retrieved from www12.statcan.ca/census-recensement/2006/dp-pd/hlt/97-558/pages/page.cfm?Lang=E&Geo=PR&Code=01&Table=3&Data=Count&Sex=1&StartRec=1&Sort=2&Display=Page

Statistics Canada. (2006b). *Measuring violence against women: Statistical trends*. Ottawa, Canada: Author.

Statistics Canada. (2010, June). *Average earning by sex and work pattern*. Retrieved from www40.statcan.gc.ca/l01/cst01/labor01a-eng.htm

Statistics Canada (2014) The ups and downs of minimum wage, 1975 to 2013. www.statcan.
    gc.ca/daily-quotidien/140716/dq140716b-eng.htm
Statistics Canada (2015a). *Adult correctional statistics in Canada, 2013/2014.* Retrieved
    from www.statcan.gc.ca/pub/85-002-x/2015001/article/14163-eng.htm
Statistics Canada (2015b). *Youth correctional statistics in Canada, 2013/2014.* Retrieved
    from www.statcan.gc.ca/pub/85-002-x/2015001/article/14164-eng.htm#a6
Steele, C. M. (1997). A threat in the air: How stereotypes shape intellectual identity and
    performance. *American Psychologist, 52*(6), 613–629.
Stepan, N. (1982). *The idea of race in science.* London, England: Macmillan.
Strasburger, V. C., Hogan, M. J., Mulligan, D. A., Ameenuddin, N., Christakis, D. A., Cross,
    C., . . . Moreno, M. A. (2013). Children, adolescents, and the media. *Pediatrics, 132*(5),
    958–961.
Sue, D. W. (2010). *Microaggressions in everyday life: Race, gender, and sexual orientation.*
    Hoboken, NJ: Wiley.
Sun, C., & Picker, M. (Director and Producer). (2008). *The price of pleasure: Pornography,
    sexuality, and relationships* [Motion picture]. Northampton, MA: Media Education
    Foundation.
Surf Survivors Fund. (n.d.). Statistics on Rwanda. Retrieved fromwww.survivors-fund.org.
    uk/resources/history/statistics.php
Taber, J. (2016, March 8). Canada has more women in cabinet, but fewer sit on Com-
    mon committees. *The Globe and Mail.* Retrieved from www.theglobeandmail.com/
    news/national/canada-has-more-women-in-cabinet-but-fewer-sit-on-commons-
    committees/article29093027/
Tappan, M. B. (2006). Reframing internalized oppression and internalized domination:
    From the psychological to the sociocultural. *Teachers College Record, 108*(10), 2115.
Tarr-Whelan, L. (2009). *Women lead the way.* San Francisco, CA: Berrett-Koehler.
Tatum, B. (1997). *"Why are all the Black kids sitting together in the cafeteria?" And other
    conversations about race.* New York, NY: Basic Books.
Tehranian, J. (2000). Performing Whiteness: Naturalization litigation and the construction
    of racial identity in America. *Yale Law Journal, 109*(4), 817–848.
Thobani, S. (2007). *Exalted subjects: Studies in the making of race and nation in Canada.*
    Toronto, Canada: University of Toronto Press.
Thompson, H.A. (2012). The prison industrial complex: A growth industry in a shrinking
    economy. *New Labor Forum, 21*(3), 38–47.
Trepagnier, B. (2010). *Silent racism: How well-meaning White people perpetuate the racial
    divide* (2nd ed.). New York, NY: Paradigm.
Tuana, N. (Ed.). (1989). *Feminism and science.* Bloomington, IN: Indiana University
    Press.
Tuana, N. (1993). *The less noble sex: Scientific, religious, and philosophical conceptions of
    woman's nature.* Bloomington, IL: Indiana University Press.
Tyack, D. (1976) Ways of seeing: An essay on the history of compulsory schooling. *Harvard
    Educational Review, 46*(3), 355–389.
United for a Fair Economy (2003). *Trickle down economics: Four reasons why it just doesn't
    work.* Retrieved from www.faireconomy.org/trickle_down_economics_four_reasons
United Nations. (2017). Infographic: Violence against women. *UN Women.* Retrieved
    from   www.unwomen.org/en/digital-library/multimedia/2015/11/infographic-vio-
    lence-against-women

United Steelworkers of Canada. (n.d.). Statement on gay, lesbian, bisexual and transgendered issues. Retrieved from www.usw.ca/admin/union/pride/files/Pride_jan08-1.pdf

U.S. Bureau of Labor Statistics. (2010, June). Highlights of women's earnings in 2009. Retrieved from www.bls.gov/cps/cpswom2009.pdf

U.S. Census Bureau. (n.d.). *Current population survey, 2008 and 2009 annual social and economic supplements.* Retrieved from www.census.gov/hhes/www/poverty/data/incpovhlth/2008/table4.pdf

U.S. Department of Health and Human Services (2012). *Characteristics and financial circumstances of TANF recipients, fiscal year 2010.* Retrieved from www.acf.hhs.gov/ofa/resource/character/fy2010/fy2010-chap10-ys-final

U. S. Department of Labor (2017). *Wage and hour division.* Retrieved from www.dol.gov/whd/minwage/america.htm

U.S. Department of State. (2007, June). *Trafficking in persons report.* Washington, DC: Author. Retrieved fromwww.state.gov/documents/organization/82902.pdf

U.S. Department of State. (2010, June). *Trafficking in persons report* (10th ed.). Washington, DC: Author. Retrieved from www.state.gov/documents/organization/142979.pdf

U.S. House of Representatives (2017) Salaries. Retrieved from pressgallery.house.gov/member-data/salaries

Van Ausdale, D., & Feagin, J. (2001). *The first R: How children learn race and racism.* Lanham, MD: Rowman & Littlefield.

Van Esler, M. (2016). Not Yet the Post-TV Era: Network and MVPD Adaptation to Emergent Distribution Technologies. *Media and Communication, 4*(3), 131–141.

Wagner, P. & Rabuy, B. (2017). *Following the money of mass incarceration.* Prison Policy Initiative. Retrieved from www.prisonpolicy.org/global/2016.html

Wagner, P. & Walsh, A. (2016). *States of incarceration: The global context.* Prison Policy Initiative. Retrieved from www.prisonpolicy.org/global/2016.html

Watson, D. (2011). "Urban, but not too urban": Unpacking teachers' desires to teach urban students. *Journal of Teacher Education, 62*(1), 23–34.

Watts, C., & Zimmerman, C. (2002). Violence against women: Global scope and magnitude. *The Lancet, 359*(9313), 1232–1237.

Weber, L. (2010). *Understanding race, class, gender, and sexuality: A conceptual framework* (2nd ed.). New York, NY: Oxford University Press.

Williams, D. R. (1999, December). Race, socioeconomic status, and health: The added effects of racism and discrimination. *Annals of the New York Academy of Sciences, 896,* 173–188.

Winks, R. W. (1997). *The Blacks in Canada: A history* (2nd ed.). Montreal, Canada: McGill-Queen's University Press. (Original work published in 1971)

Wise, T. (2005). *Affirmative action: Racial preference in Black and White.* New York, NY: Routledge.

Woodson, C. G. (1933). *The mis-education of the Negro.* New York, NY: Tribeca Books.

The World Bank (2017). *Annual GDP rankings.* Retrieved from data.worldbank.org/data-catalog/GDP-ranking-table

World Health Organization. (2009). Violence against women: Factsheet no. 239. Retrieved from www.who.int/mediacentre/factsheets/fs239/en/index.html

World Health Organization (2016). World health statistics 2016: Monitoring health for sustainable development goals. Switzerland: WHO. Retrieved from www.who.int/gho/publications/world_health_statistics/2016/en/

World Prison Brief. (2017). Institute for Criminal Policy Research. www.prisonstudies.org

Wyatt-Nichol, H. (2016). The enduring myth of the American dream: Mobility, marginalization, and hope. *International Journal of Organization Theory and Behavior, 14*(2), 258–279.

Zinn, H. (2010). *A people's history of the United States* (rev. ed.). New York, NY: HarperCollins. (Original work published 1980)

Zweig, M. (2000). *The working class majority: America's best kept secret.* Ithaca, NY: Cornell University Press.

Index

About the Authors

Özlem Sensoy is an associate professor in the Faculty of Education at Simon Fraser University in Vancouver, Canada. She teaches and conducts research in social justice, critical media literacy, and cultural studies. Her research articles have appeared in journals including *Gender & Education, Discourse: Studies in the Cultural Politics of Education*, and *Democracy & Education*. She is the co-editor (with C. Stonebanks) of *Muslim Voices in School: Narratives of Identity and Pluralism*, and co-editor (with E. Marshall) of *Rethinking Popular Culture and Media*.

Robin DiAngelo is a former associate professor of education. Her work is centered in Whiteness studies and discourse analysis. She has written extensively on White racial identity and her articles have appeared in journals including *Race Ethnicity Education, International Journal of Critical Pedagogy*, and *Equity & Excellence in Education*. She is the author of *What Does it Mean to Be White? Developing White Racial Literacy* and *White Fragility*. She provides racial justice training for a wide range of public and private organizations.